W9-AYI-902

The Way to Peace

Liberation Through the Bible

L. John Topel, S.J.

ORBIS BOOKS

Maryknoll, New York 10545

Third Printing, April 1982

Library of Congress Cataloging in Publication Data

Topel, L. John
  The way to peace.

  Includes bibliographical references and index.
  1.   Freedom (Theology)—Biblical teaching.
2. Liberation theology. I.   Title.
BS680.F7T66   261.8   78-9148
ISBN 0-88344-704-5

The Catholic Foreign Mission Society of America (Maryknoll) recruits and trains people for overseas missionary service. Through Orbis Books Maryknoll aims to foster the international dialogue essential to mission. The books published, however, reflect the opinions of their authors and are not meant to represent the official position of the Society.

As he drew near and came in sight of the city he shed tears over it and said, "If you especially had known, in this time, the way to peace—but now it is hidden from your eyes."

—Luke 19:41–42

Contents

Preface

This book is essentially the middle section of an undergraduate course on liberation theology elaborated over the years 1974–1977 at Seattle University. The course opens with an inductive survey of the structured dynamics of oppression in our world. Then for three weeks we study the biblical foundations of the Judeo-Christian response to oppression. Since I found no succinct yet comprehensive published book I could use for a text, I wrote my own to illustrate the theme that the Bible reveals God and humankind cooperating in bringing a reign of justice and peace in our world. The final section of the course studies the actions and doctrines of the Christian church in history and in our contemporary world that implement this vision of peace on earth.

The book need not be restricted to use as a text in liberation theology. It can serve as an introductory study of the Bible in adult religious education, for example. Since I believe liberation is the central motif of the Bible, I should think this book could be the place where any biblical study might begin. However, neither in the college course nor in adult religious education can this book substitute for the reading of the Bible itself. It is merely an aid showing how the biblical materials add up to a theology of liberation of men and women from the socio-economic oppression in which selfishness enmeshes them. Neither can a book designed as a text prescind from a teacher who can explain some of the deeper aspects of biblical history and doctrine, which necessarily have been stated very concisely in such a book.

I wish here to express my gratitude for all who assisted in the preparation of this book. First, to my students for bearing with me, and for the suggestions they offered. Second, to the typists who labored with the text, Mrs. Felicidad Oberholzer and Mrs. Betty Smith. Third, to the Jesuit Council on Theological Reflection, whose grant initiated the work and partially financed its production in a first edition called *The Liberators*. And finally to the man to whom I dedicate this work, Pope Paul VI. Preoccupations with questions of discipline within the church have often focused attention away from his real achievements as a prophetic voice discerning structural evils in our world. In his address to the General Assembly of the United Nations, the encyclical *Populorum progressio*, and his letter *Octogesima adveniens* to Cardinal Roy, he has led the church and our world to an understanding of the relationship between faith and the promotion of justice. He has been an inspiration in my own thought and life, and so this small book is the tiny tribute of a loving son.

I. Exodus as Genesis

A. REVELATION

Most of the great religions have sacred books. In these are recorded the way to God and knowledge of reality that was given to the great seer who founded the religion or at least serves as its chief model.

It is peculiar to the Hebrews that God first revealed himself to them by a great act of deliverance in history. They remembered that deliverance and passed down recollections of it by word of mouth from generation to generation; these were written down and came to form the Hebrews' national charter and the rule of their life.

Most of us in the Judeo-Christian tradition remember a time when we thought God dictated to Moses the words of the law, which he transcribed directly as our Bible. Perhaps we have seen Cecil B. De Mille's *The Ten Commandments,* where the fiery finger of God carves the commandments onto stone tablets hewed from the mountain.

Modern scholarship on the Bible has discovered that the Word of God came to be formed in quite a different way.[1] When God determined to reveal himself to humankind, he did so in a way congruent with human nature and activity. As we come to learn everything slowly by trial and error, so the Hebrews would come slowly to understand God's way with them. Different authors would perceive, according to their own different temperaments and the historical circumstances in which the nation found itself, different aspects of a divine revelation rich beyond anyone's effort to comprehend it all. These authors then began to write down, long after the events, their accounts of God's revelation in word and deed to Israel. Thus our oldest parts of the Bible were written no earlier than 950 B.C., although they give us an understanding of events that went way back to the patriarchal period of 1900 to 1700 B.C. and even describe the prehistory of the human race back to creation.[2]

The fact that people laboriously put together and even composed, under God's inspiration, accounts of historical events long since passed makes this material no less inspired than if God had dictated the very words.[3] This is revelation for us. But it does raise a problem about where we are going to

1

begin reading the texts. On the one hand, the natural way would be to begin with Genesis, the beginning of human history, and so of God's dealings with humankind. After all, that is the way the Jews have arranged the Bible, so that we would begin at the beginning and read chronologically through Israel's history to the time just before Christ. On the other hand, the materials of Genesis are not historical writing. No one, obviously, was around as a historical recorder when God called the first humans into being, nor did anyone witness the fall. In fact, it is possible that Abraham, Isaac, and Jacob were really not historical men, but rather eponymous heroes or personifications of seminomadic tribes.

It seems that Israel's first historical awareness of God's dealings with it as a nation in history is in the act of deliverance in Exodus. Then Israel reinterpreted its previous life on the pattern of that historical deliverance. The Hebrews' infidelities to God's creative love led them to conceive of the infidelities of their ancestors and even of primitive human beings, as well as of previous acts of God's deliverance.[4] It is now generally agreed that the Hebrews really became one nation when God delivered them from bondage as a large slave class in Egypt.[5] God settled them in Canaan as a league of tribes who had little more in common than their worship of Yahweh, the God of Exodus. It is in the Exodus, then, that we will begin, for the Exodus is genesis.

B. LIBERATION FROM EGYPT

Our story opens with the Hebrews as part of an enslaved class in Egypt, where they had gone from Palestine to find food in famine (Gen 12:10; 42:1–47:31) or in search of work. Originally they found favor with the Egyptian rulers,[6] got land, and prospered (Ex 1:7). However, when a new dynasty came to power and found how the Hebrews had multiplied to become an internal threat to Egyptian socio-economic order (1:8–10), it determined to strengthen their bonds of slavery.

The means chosen strike us as remarkably familiar:[7] First, they set slave drivers over the Hebrews who increased the amount of work to be done at the new cities (Ex 1:11, 13–14) on the theory that the long hours would deprive them of time to organize or plan.[8] Second, they set a policy of genocide by exterminating the male children (Ex 1:15–16). The Hebrews feared the possibility of capital punishment (2:14).

In ancient Near Eastern empires the death of the king was often the occasion for the revolt of his subjugated people. The Hebrews were not a nation, but at the death of the Pharaoh (Ex. 2:23a) they too groaned under their bondage and cried out for liberation. Seeing the oppression and their desire for deliverance, Yahweh determined to free them:

God heard their groaning and he called to mind his covenant with Abraham, Isaac and Jacob. God looked down upon the sons of Israel, and he knew [their condition] . . . (Ex 2:24f.).*

This is a first identification of God as the one who hears humans in oppression and determines to do something for them.

The scene that follows is the great explicit revelation to the Hebrews of the identity and nature of their God. Before this, God had been their tribal God, probably one among many (Josh 24:2), but powerful enough to protect them even among other people (Gen 12:17; 20:6–7).[9] Now God reveals himself to Moses as transcendently holy (3:5), faithful to his promises (3:6) to "his" people (3:7), who acts in history to deliver them and bring them to a good land:

I mean to deliver them out of the hands of the Egyptians and bring them up out of that land to a land rich and broad, a land where milk and honey flow, the home of the Canaanites, the Hittites, the Amorites, the Perizzites, the Hivites and the Jebusites. And now the cry of the sons of Israel has come to me, and I have witnessed the way in which the Egyptians oppress them, so come, I send you to Pharaoh to bring the sons of Israel, my people, out of Egypt (Ex 3:8–10).

He chose a man of the oppressed people to be the agent of their liberation. (That is to say, the liberation will be a human one, accomplished according to the human mode of liberation.) When Moses objects to being selected, the only reassurance he gets is "I will be with you" (Ex 3:10–12). This phrase, "I will be with you," will be a leitmotif throughout God's redemptive action in history: to national leaders such as Joshua (Josh 1:9) and the judges (Gideon, Judg 6:16), to kings (Solomon and David, 1 Kings 1:37), to the prophets (Jeremiah, Jer 1:8), to Jesus (Acts 10:38), and finally to the church (Mt 28:20).

In fact, it is this characteristic of faithfully "being with" that identifies Yahweh; it is his name. When Moses asks the identity of this God who is going to be with him, he gets a very mysterious response: "I am who I will be" (Ex 3:14). Scholarship has discovered various possible explanations of this *'ehyeh 'ªsher 'ehyeh:* (1) To know another person's name among early Semites was to have power over him. By responding with this mysterious pun, "I am who I am (or, will be)," Yahweh effectively says, "You cannot know my name because you can have no power over me." (2) The term affirms God as the source of being, the Creator: "I am the one who brings into being." (3) It affirms God as the very power of being, the act of existence, as God is understood by the medieval philosopher/theologians:

*f. means "and the following verse"; ff. means "and the following verses."

"I am who am," or, following the Greek translation of the Old Testament, "I am being." (4) "I am the one who will be (there) with you" means the one leading you out, the one you will discover in the liberating events of your history. For various reasons, most scholars have decided that the last interpretation best fits the context here.[10] By this name, transcribed for us as "Yahweh," God resumes precisely the previous assurance he had given to Moses: I will be with you, and in whatever way you find me faithfully delivering you in history, that is what I am.

Further, this name, interpreted as "I will be who I will be," is at the root of biblical eschatological theology or a theology of hope. It says that truth and justice lie in the future and that we grow toward their perfect unfolding. It says that God is the future of human beings, that God grows in human history: God's immense potentiality will be actualized insofar as people are liberated and liberating in their relations with one another. "All his intervention in history is directed toward forming a mankind in which he is finally able *to be*."[11] Indeed Yahweh later describes his name (in the P tradition) as the one who delivers: "Say this to the sons of Israel, I am Yahweh, and *therefore* I will free you from the Egyptian burdens . . ." (Ex 6:6).[12]

Believing, then, that Yahweh will be with him to deliver his people, and charged with the mission to deliver them into the promised land (Ex 3:16f.), Moses approaches the pharaoh. At first the pharaoh refuses to recognize Yahweh's representative and follows a sure plan to suppress the liberation movement: separate the people from their leaders. And so he requires more work from the Hebrews, thus leaving them less time to organize and making them angry at Moses for bringing this extra work on them (Ex 5:5–21). However, Yahweh hears Moses' prayer and faithfully intervenes with the miracle of the rod (Ex 7:10–13) and finally with the ten plagues (7:14—12:30),[13] forcing the pharaoh to release his people:

> And it was night when Pharaoh summoned Moses and Aaron. "Get up," he said "you and the sons of Israel, and get away from my people. Go and offer worship to Yahweh as you have asked and, as you have asked, take your flocks and herds, and go. And also ask a blessing on me" (Ex 12:31f.).

Once they go out, the strategy of the flight is ascribed to Yahweh himself:[14]

> God did not let them take the road to the land of the Philistines. . . .
> God thought that the prospect of fighting would make the people lose heart and turn back to Egypt (Ex 13:17).

And when the pharaoh decided to recapture those fleeing and pursued them with six hundred chariots (an extraordinary number, if not an exaggeration of the oral tradition), the Israelites saw the magnitude of the army, lost heart, and wanted to return to their slavery (14:11f.). But Yahweh brought on them a cloud that hid them while Moses stretched his hand over the Reed Sea, which parted so that the Hebrews could walk across dry-shod, with walls of water to the right and left of them (Ex 14:19–22). When the Egyptian army finally rushed in after the Hebrews, Yahweh inundated them so that they were destroyed (14:24–28).[15] This final act of deliverance from Egypt is celebrated in the oldest Old Testament writing, the song of Miriam and the poem built on it (Ex 15:1–21):

> Yahweh I sing: he has covered himself in glory,
> horse and rider he has thrown into the sea.
> Yah is my strength, my song,
> he is my salvation (Ex 15:1–2).

The theme of this oldest writing is that Yahweh is savior (v. 2) and redeemer (v. 13).

However, once Israel had passed through the birth canal of the Reed Sea, it still had to pass through its childhood.[16] The Hebrews still had to face the perils of the desert, hunger and thirst, and the attacks of the inhabitants through whose lands they wandered. Yahweh gives them sweet water from the bitter water to slake their three-day thirst at Marah (Ex 15:22,25). However, the Hebrews continue to complain (Ex 15:24; 16:2–3; 17:2–3), and in each case Yahweh patiently hears their complaints and remedies them, for example, by manna (Ex 16:4–36) and quail (16:12f.). Finally, however, their disobedience and childish petulancy require punishment, and Yahweh decrees that the disobedient generation (Num 14:1–9; Deut 1:26–32) will not enter the promised land (Num 14:20–38; Deut 1:34–40); in fact the whole community is chastised for its disobedience (Num 14:39–45; Deut 1:41–45). In all of these events Yahweh treated his young people like the children they were and so delivered them. Finally, when the Israelites asked for safe passage through the Transjordanian lands of two Amorite kings, Sihon in Heshbon (Num 21:21–24; Deut 2:26–37) and Og of Bashan (Num 21:33–35; Deut 3:1–11), and this was denied them, Yahweh delivered those kings into the hands of the Israelites and the time of the conquest of the promised land had come (Deut 3:12–17).

C. THE WARRIOR GOD OF THE CONQUEST

Not only did Yahweh deliver his people *from* bondage, but he led them *to* a land that was their own, where they would not be oppressed. Just before his death (Deut 31) Moses passed on to Joshua the task of leading the Israelites into the land, and Yahweh commissioned Joshua with the same words with which he had sent Moses: ". . . I myself will be with you" (31:32). Indeed, Yahweh confirms Joshua as Moses' successor with these words, "I will be with you as I was with Moses" (Josh 1:5; cf. 1:9). Thus the conquest is simply the second stage of one act of deliverance, and on this supposition the people will follow Joshua (1:17). Even the prostitute of Jericho, Rahab, knows that Yahweh is going to give the city to Israel, for has he not delivered Israel already in the Exodus?

> I know that Yahweh has given you this land, that we ourselves are afraid of you and that all who live in this territory have been seized with terror at your approach; for we have heard how Yahweh dried up the Sea of Reeds before you when you came out of Egypt and what you did with the two Amorite kings across the Jordan, Sihon and Og, whom you put under the ban. When we heard this, our hearts failed us, and no courage is left in any of us to stand up to you, because Yahweh your God is God both in heaven above and on earth beneath (Josh 2:9–11).

This belief in the inevitability of Yahweh's giving the land to Israel provokes fear and is interpreted by Joshua's spies as deliverance: "Yahweh has delivered the whole country into our hands, and its inhabitants tremble at the thought of us" (Josh 2:24).

The next day Yahweh miraculously divides the waters of the Jordan and leads Israel into Canaan, just as he had led Israel out of Egypt.[17] The parallelism is deliberate: Yahweh halts the Jordan just as he dried up the Reed Sea (Josh 3:7–4:18; Ex 14:5–31); here the Ark of the Covenant is the instrument of passage, there the rod of Moses. The ark leads the people like the pillar of cloud or fire (3:6–17; Ex 13:21f.; 14:19f.).[18]

Yahweh's conquest of Canaan begins with Jericho. It appears from archeological study to have already been destroyed before the Hebrews arrived and remained uninhabited throughout the time of the settlement (see Israel's explanation of its continuance in ruins: Josh 6:26). Later generations of Hebrews ascribed this to a mighty victory of Yahweh's forces under Joshua, described as more of a ritual act than an armed struggle:

> Then Yahweh said to Joshua, "Now I am delivering Jericho and its king into your hands. All you fighters, valiant warriors, will march round the town and make the circuit once, and for six days you will do the same thing. (But seven priests will carry seven trumpets in front of

the ark.) On the seventh day you will go seven times round the town (and the priests will blow the trumpet). When the ram's horn rings out (when you hear the sound of the trumpet), the whole people must utter a mighty war cry and the town wall will collapse then and there; then the people can storm the town, each man going straight ahead'' (Josh 6:2–5).

Joshua reminds the soldiers that Jericho is under a ban and they are not to touch anything in it.[19]

To Yahweh is ascribed the taking of Ai (Josh 8:1, 7, 18); the defeat of the five Ammonite kings at Gibeon (10:8–15), where he made the sun stand still,[20] and in the cave of Makkedah (10:16–19); the conquest of the southern towns of Canaan (10:28–43) and then those of the north (11:1–23).

And finally, Yahweh is the one who ultimately apportions to the twelve tribes their individual territories (Josh 13–21, especially 13:6f.; 21:43ff.). Yahweh had truly been "there" with his people.

If we expect to find in all of this a pattern of Yahweh always on the side of the oppressed to deliver them (cf. Ps 103:6), we encounter a difficulty. Clearly the oppressed people in the case of the conquest are not the Israelites, but the Canaanites, Gibeonites, etc., who inhabit their land. Why does God not fight for them?

At the earliest stage of their awareness, the question probably would not have occurred to the Hebrews. War between Middle Eastern kingdoms was an annual phenomenon (see 2 Sam 11:1) and considered part of the divinities' struggles. Thus it was presumed that Yahweh would fight for his own people, just as the other gods fought for theirs. Fortunately Yahweh was stronger.

However, at a later stage of development, when the prophets had identified Yahweh's nature with justice and equated salvation with justice (especially Deutero-Isaiah and Jeremiah), Israel finds it necessary to ask how Yahweh could have fought these people. The answer given was that these people were idol worshipers, and to associate with them was to tolerate contamination and apostasy to their enticing fertility rituals. Therefore they must be exterminated (Deut 7:1–6). Yahweh, then, was protecting his own from idolatrous practices and also blotting out the practices of injustice (see Ex 23:32f.; 34:13–16; Deut 7:5).[21] Even later, Leviticus 18:24–25 says that the inhabitants of the land were vomited out by the land itself, which had been defiled by the Canaanites' immorality (vv. 19–23), including adultery, homosexuality, bestiality, and child sacrifice.

The final answer of the Hebrew mind comes when it is seen that Yahweh's justice is so great that even the Hebrews, God's own people, must be punished when *they* become oppressive.[22] Yahweh is not a particularist; he chastises all oppressors.[23]

Perhaps, in concluding this section, we can give an interpretation that goes beyond the Hebrew data but may underlie it. Israel was oppressed, and simply needed land to exercise its own free destiny. Yahweh gave them the land and freedom; there was nothing else to do. It often appears that those who have "rights" find them taken away by those escaping from injustice, who therefore have prior "rights." The final solution to the problem is possible only when a total view of the earth as the possession of all people is attained, as Aquinas saw in his doctrine of common use of property *(Sum. Theol.,* II-II, q. 66, a. 2).

D. THE EXODUS AS CENTRAL EVENT OF ISRAEL'S LIFE

The Exodus, then, was the birth of Israel as a nation, comparable in religious terms to the crucifixion and resurrection of Christ for a Christian. It established Israel's identity in its relationship with Yahweh. And so throughout the conquest and its subsequent life, Israel used the Exodus event as model and imagery to signify who Yahweh was and who Israel was. Details of the Exodus were recounted in cultic songs (see Ps 107:35–38), in Wisdom literature (Wis 19), and by the prophets (see Is 63): Yahweh is the one who delivered the oppressed from oppression. In the eighth century Hosea put it thus: "I am Yahweh, your God, since the days in the land of Egypt; you know no God but me, there is no other savior" (13:4; *cf.* Is 45:21).

Yahweh begets Israel as a father not in creation, but in the act of historical deliverance, which was Israel's creation: When Yahweh found Israel in the desert, he enfolded the Israelites and cared for them and bore them on pinions and led them into a fruitful land, according to Deuteronomy 32:6, 10–14 (cf. Ezek 16:2–6 for another image of birth in the desert). Hosea again echoes this: "When Israel was a child I loved him and out of Egypt I called my son" (11:1; cf. Jer 31:9; Is 63:7–9).[24]

Further, if Yahweh had become their father by delivering them, then he would deliver them from future oppressions. And so Isaiah proclaimed to Judah when the Assyrians under Sennacherib threatened Jerusalem in 701:

> My people who live in Zion,
> do not be afraid of Assyria who strikes you with the club
> and lifts up the rod against you [as the *Egyptians* did].
> A little longer, a very little,
> and fury will come to an end,

my anger will destroy them.
Yahweh Sabaoth will whirl the whip against him,
like the time he struck *Midian at the Rock of Oreb,*
like the time he stretched out his *rod against the sea,*
and raised it over the *road from Egypt.*
That day, his burden will fall from your shoulder,
his yoke will cease to weigh on your neck

> (Is 10:24–27; italics added
> to refer to Exodus imagery).

Yahweh "will be there," just as much in Israel's present and future bondage as he was in Egypt, for that is his revealed nature. This means that the Israelites are not to entrust themselves to other deliverers, such as an alliance with Egypt (Is 31:1–4; 30:1–5), for it is adherence to Yahweh that will cast out the Assyrians (Is 14:24–27; 30:27–33; 31:4–9; 37:22–29).

One hundred years later Jeremiah predicted that an invasion by foreigners and an exile would be Yahweh's punishment for Judah's immorality (Jer 4:5–31; 1:13ff.; 6:1–30; etc.). Yet even here, Jeremiah trusted that Yahweh would eventually deliver his (reformed) people:

> See, then, that the days are coming—it is Yahweh who speaks—when people will no longer say, "As Yahweh lives who brought the sons of Israel out of the land of the North and back from all the countries to which he had dispersed them" (Jer 16:14f.; 23:7f.; 30:8–11; 31:1, etc.).[25]

When Yahweh did later redeem his people, this was itself conceived after the model of the Exodus deliverance. Isaiah 35 is a glorious hymn celebrating the return of Israel from the Babylonian exile,[26] in terms reminiscent of the Exodus: "for water gushes in the desert, streams in the wasteland" (35:6). Exodus imagery describes the deliverance from Babylonian captivity: "Prepare in the wilderness a way for Yahweh. Make a straight highway for our God across the desert" (40:3). Perhaps Isaiah 11:15–16 is the most explicit:

> And Yahweh will dry up the gulf of the Sea of Egypt . . . and stretch out his hand over the River . . . to make a pathway for the remnant of his people . . . as there was for Israel when it came up out of Egypt.[27]

Throughout Israel's history after the Exodus, Yahweh is its *gō'ēl,* the near relative on whom falls the duty of defending the interests of an incapacitated or murdered member of the family.[28] Thus Yahweh is addressed as the *gô'ēl* of Israel in Isaiah 43:14:

> Thus says Yahweh,
> your redeemer, the Holy One of Israel:
> For your sake I send an army against Babylon;
> I will knock down the prison bars
> and the Chaldeans will break into laments.
> I am Yahweh, your Holy One,
> the Creator of Israel, your King.[29]

Finally, in the time after the exile, when Israel labored to rebuild Temple and city against the odds of poverty and later political repression, Israel hoped for a definitive deliverance by Yahweh. The idea can be as simple as "Redeem Israel, God, from all her troubles" (Ps 25:19), though Israel's hopes largely rested on the anointed king of David's line[30] who would lead the nation (and world) to peace. Even this future and unspecified deliverance, however, frequently had resonances of the Exodus deliverance (cf. Esther 4:17 [LXX],* and 1 Macc 4:8–11).

The examples above all speak of Israel as a whole conceiving of Yahweh as its national deliverer. However, it was also the individual Israelite who cried out to God for deliverance from personal woes and conceived of this liberation after the manner of Exodus. This is true of King David (2 Sam 4:9, "As Yahweh lives, who has delivered me from all adversity"), since the king was always specially protected because of a special identification with God and people. However, it was true also of the average pious Israelite who came to wail a prayer of lament or sing a song of thanksgiving in the Temple (see Ps 25; 26; 69; 103; and throughout the Psalter).

E. SUMMARY

Not only does God reveal himself in history, but he reveals who he is. He is the deliverer from whatever oppression afflicts his people. He brought Israel to birth by delivering the people from slavery in Egypt. Whatever Israel as a child needed—food and drink, safe passage, a land in which to live a distinctive life—Yahweh was faithfully "there" to deliver. His very faithfulness in the past was a guarantee that he would be there in whatever future need Israel had. Yahweh is Israel's deliverer from oppression throughout time.

*LXX is an abbreviation for the Septuagint, the Greek translation of the Hebrew Bible.

II. Liberation Through Government

A. HUMAN RESPONSIBILITY IN LIBERATION

In the first chapter we saw that Yahweh delivered his people from Egypt, led them through the desert, settled them in the promised land, and promised to be present faithfully to them in future oppressions. He is the liberator.

Yet in that same chapter we said that when God deals with humans, he does so in human terms, respecting the human way of doing things. Mere physical liberation might be appropriate to brute animals, who can be freed only by someone outside themselves and never really attain interior freedom. But human persons are masters of their own fate, and if they do not act to free themselves they have less than human liberation. Removal of walls does not give inward freedom: we must responsibly act to effect our own freedom or we are not free at all. And so we must inquire of the Old Testament whether the people thus freed were merely passive recipients of a deliverance bestowed by God, or participants of a freedom won by a subtle and mysterious interaction of God and people in human society.

The problem is not confined to the Old Testament. Modern psychology also looks at the healing dynamics of the psychotherapeutic encounter and asks: "What is the proportion between the concern and love of the therapist and the patient's own determination to do something about changing his or her own life?"[1]

The theory of this relationship advanced by Erich Fromm in *The Art of Loving* seems to be an excellent solution not only to the psychotherapeutic problem, but also to the theological problem of liberation. Fromm distinguishes two types of love: mother love and father love.

> Motherly love by its very nature is unconditional. Mother loves the newborn infant because it is her child, not because the child has fulfilled any specific condition, or lived up to any specific expectation. . . . Unconditional love corresponds to one of the deepest human longings, not only of the child, but of every human being; on the other hand, to be loved because of one's merit, because

11

one deserves it, always leaves doubt; maybe I did not please the person whom I want to love me, maybe this, or that—there is always a fear that love could disappear. Furthermore "deserved" love easily leaves a bitter feeling that one is not loved for oneself, that one is loved only because one pleases, that one is, in the last analysis, not loved at all but used.[2]

On the other hand, father love is no less necessary:

The relationship to father is quite different. Mother is the home we come from, she is nature, soil, the ocean; father does not represent any such natural home. He . . . represents the other pole of human existence; the world of thought, of man-made things, of law and order, of discipline, of travel and adventure. Father is the one who teaches the child, who shows him the road into the world. . . . Fatherly love is conditional love. Its principle is "I love you *because* you fulfill my expectations, because you do your duty, because you are like me." In conditional fatherly love we find, as with unconditional motherly love, a negative and positive aspect. The negative aspect is . . . that it can be lost if one does not do what is expected. . . . Obedience becomes the main virtue. . . . Disobedience is the main sin—and its punishment is the withdrawal of fatherly love. The positive side is equally important. Since this love is conditioned, I can do something to acquire it; his love is not outside of my control as motherly love is.[3]

It is important that we see both mother love and father love as related to each other and each as indispensable. Clearly mother love is prior (Fromm speaks of a child passing into the domain of fatherly love as late as six to eight years of age). It establishes the person as a person of worth, intrinsically lovable. From this sense of worth springs, then, a desire to communicate one's worth to others and to one's society and world. Then father love leads the maturing child to a knowledge of how one can make that communication in a given society. Father teaches the child the methods of judging means to ends and insists that the child responsibly do that in action. Mother gives the child personal being; father teaches the child to grow in being through responsible self-direction and achievement. If one receives only mother love, says Fromm, that person will be dependent, passive, helpless; if only father love, one will be rigidly legalistic, obsessed with achievement, authoritarian.

Now we have already seen that Yahweh has loved Israel in liberating it. The classic statement of this was written in the seventh century B.C.:

If Yahweh set his heart on you and chose you, it was not because you outnumbered other peoples; you were the least of all peoples. It was for love of you and to keep the oath he swore to your fathers that Yahweh brought you out with his mighty hand and redeemed you from the house of slavery, from the power of Pharaoh, king of Egypt (Deut 7:7–8).

One could hardly find a better example of the unconditional love that Fromm calls motherly love.

That is not what is now at stake, however.What we really want to investigate in this chapter is whether Yahweh's love and redemptive work leaves scope for, or even encourages, human striving and responsibility, so that the child Israel can grow into adulthood and achieve the self-reliance and inner freedom which marks the truly liberated being.

B. THE GOVERNMENT OF ISRAEL

1. The Judges

We have already seen (p. 3) that when Yahweh planned to redeem Israel he chose a Hebrew to be the people's leader in that liberation. Moses clearly felt the burden of the responsibility and was wary of accepting it without guarantees of God's support. Further, we observed that when Moses died, Yahweh saw that the succession passed on to another man of the people, Joshua; leadership in liberation comes from within the people—with Yahweh's present help. Indeed, this practice of Yahweh's raising up leadership from among the people to be freed will turn out to be a pattern of Yahweh's dealings with people, a facet of his liberation.

This is seen first in the book of Judges.[4] The book of Joshua had ended without Joshua's appointing a successor to himself. Judges, then, opens with the house of Judah assuming leadership among the people.[5] This is ascribed to Yahweh (Judg 1:1f.), but it is clear that the people themselves have taken the initiative. Although they could not subdue the people of the plains who had iron chariots, they subdued the highlands, because Yahweh was with them (Judg 1:19). According to Judges, however, each of the tribes, under its own leadership, subdued the land that had been apportioned to it, and in each case Yahweh was with them (1:19,22). Here for the first time it is mentioned that the Hebrews subjected the Canaanites to forced labor (1:28,30), a part of the conquest.

After the Israelites turned from their covenanted worship of Yahweh and worshiped Baal and Astarte (Judg 2:11–13), however,[6] Yahweh punished them by allowing them to fall under the control of the other inhabitants of the land. When Israel was again reduced to the position of recognizing the oppression it had brought on itself, Yahweh appointed a judge to rule the people and deliver them. The schematic statement in Judges 2:11–19 is the theme of the whole Deuteronomic history (Joshua–2 Kings): defection from Yahweh and his covenant law→oppression by foreigners→ *metanoia,* conversion to Yahweh→deliverance under Yahweh's chosen leaders.[7] Judges 2:19 tells us that once the charismatic leader (judge)[8] died, the people would lapse into idolatry (and the process would begin anew). Thus the charismatic (religious) Yahwistic leader was a necessary part of the Hebrews' liberation. At this stage of consciousness the presence of foreign nations not exterminated under the ban (see p. 5) is explained by the necessity of their being a constant test for the Hebrews—another culture and religion challenging the Hebrews to discover and live the purity of their own revealed religion and social ethic.

Thus, repeatedly Judges recounts the succession of sin (=what displeases Yahweh), conversion (=they cried out to Yahweh; cf. Ex 2:23ff.), appointment of a judge, and deliverance, under Othniel (3:7–11), Ehud (3:12–30), Shamgar (3:31), Deborah[9] and Barak (4:1–5:31), Gideon (6: 1–8:35), Jephthah and lesser judges (11:1–12:15), and Samson (13:1– 16:31).

The book of Judges records the origin of the distinctive attitudes toward kingship in Israel. When Gideon was asked to be king, he refused, saying, "Yahweh must be your Lord" (8:23). When his son Abimelech does make himself king in a shocking way by slaughtering his sixty-nine half-brothers (9:1–6), Abimelech is opposed by the remaining son, Jotham, in a prophetic/didactic fable, and eventually killed by the Schechemites for his slaughter of the sixty-nine. Thus the northern traditions begin their polemic against having a king in Israel (see below). On the other hand, in discussing the shrine at Dan, the author says, ". . . there was no king in Israel, and every man did as he pleased" (17:6). In this view of the kingship, Israel, finding itself in a new situation, needed another form of government from Yahweh to provide a stable society faithful to his name as justice.

The judges may have been an adequate form of government at the time of the conquest, or indeed the only possible one. According to the accepted scholarly consensus today it is probable that not all the tribes descended from Canaan to Egypt in the patriarchal period. Probably it was the Rachel tribes who went to Egypt, while the Leah tribes, with the same common nomadic background (as opposed to the Canaanite) and other religious affinities (worship of a nomad's god, probably under the name El Shaddai), remained in Canaan. The Rachel tribes from Egypt, with the worship of Yahweh and observance of the Decalogue, gradually united with their cousins who had remained and had been oppressed by the Canaanite inhabitants of the land. They formed a tribal league with a common religion and a common need to fight for the land (a holy war?). Yet the tribes were still too disparate and disorganized to have a central administration or a central shrine for cult worship of Yahweh.[10] As they neared completion of the conquest and were in turn invaded or pressed by foreign influences from without (the Philistines) and from within (the Canaanites), they began to develop the unity that engendered both the capability and the need for a central administration (namely, a monarchy, after the model of their adversaries) and a centralized cult (the Temple). This development is chronicled in the rest of the Deuteronomic history (1 Samuel–2 Kings).

2. The Monarchy

The first book of Samuel opens with an account of the capture of the Ark of the Covenant by the Philistines (4:1–7:17),[11] indicating the external pressure that would create a desire for a king who could muster the armed might of Israel. The government was still in the hands of a judge, Samuel, who found the people in idolatry and led them to conversion (7:2–6), and so deliverance (vv. 7–17). The elders of Israel came to Samuel, now far advanced in years, to ask, "Give us a king to rule over us, like the other nations"(8:5). There follows the polemical account of the antimonarchical tradition (8:6–22; 10:17–24; 12), which did not want a king in Israel for the following reasons: (1) such a desire for a king is a (sinful) rejection of Yahweh as ruler of Israel (8:6–9; 10:17–19; 12:6–19; cf. Judg 8:23);[12] (2) the monarch will oppress the people.[13] However, even this polemic has Yahweh advise Samuel to follow the will of the people: the time has come for their self-determination to issue in kingly rule. They are ready to be a nation (cf. 8:5, 20).

The other, royalist tradition (1 Sam 9:1–10:16; 11) sees the naming of a king as simply part of Yahweh's providence for Israel. It is Yahweh who reveals to Samuel that he is to anoint Saul leader over Israel,[14] "and he will save my people from the power of the Philistines; for I have seen the distress of my people and their crying has come to me" (9:16). With these words, reminiscent of Exodus 2:23ff., Yahweh indicates that the anointing of a king is no less his deliverance of Israel than was the Exodus. Yahweh even makes the precise identification of Saul for Samuel (9:17).[15] And so Saul is anointed and, even though he remains more a tribal chief than a king, kingship is instituted as Yahweh's method of delivering a nation.

However, Saul's reign, as a transition to the high kingship of David, was short-lived. The sources of our biblical narrative, reflecting on Yahweh's manifest choosing of David, would like to assign a reason for Samuel's rejecting Saul in 1 Samuel 13, but do not find any. They depict Saul as violating the holy-war ban in 15:9, but even this does not seem to be the kind of apostasy needed to account for Saul's rejection and David's election. The actual fact is that David was a smooth politician who supplanted Saul by politics. Yahweh's providence over Israel extends so deeply into this human process that there is a mysterious dialectic between human process and divine election (a mystery more to be pondered than explained).

At any rate, Yahweh then chose David, the youngest of Jesse's sons, to be king (1 Sam 16). Samuel anointed him and immediately "the Spirit of Yahweh seized David and stayed with him from that day on" (16:13). Saul became ever more melancholic. David entered his service and there was a growing conflict between Saul and David (1 Sam 16–2 Sam 2), in which the Lord was continuously with David to deliver Israel (see 17:1–58, against Goliath; 18:26ff., against the Philistines), and to deliver David himself from Saul's jealous plans against him—through flight (19:8–21:16) and life as an outlaw (chaps. 22–31), until the day when Saul was killed in battle and David anointed king.

How had David risen to power? The Bible says he was chosen by Yahweh, whose Spirit guided him to the kingship. It is also true that the Spirit made him an astute politician, able to attract men and women to himself, to survive as a fugitive and an outlaw,[16] capable in war, able to be generous in gleaning political support (see 1 Sam 30:26–31). At first he was made king by his own tribe, Judah, at Hebron (2 Sam 2:1–4).The supporters of Saul, the northern tribes, followed Saul's general, Abner, in making Saul's son Ishbaal king of Israel.[17] After armed conflict between the two armies, David again prevailed, by military might (2 Sam 3:1), by political negotiations (3:12–21), by personal political astuteness (3:36f.), and especially because he alone had the power to redeem Israel from the Philistines (3:18). Thus the tribes of Israel came to Hebron to anoint him king of a united kingdom (5:1–5).

Finally, as his last stroke of genius, David took Jerusalem (2 Sam 5:6–10), the ancient Jebusite city, which was neutral to both Israel and Judah and centrally located between them, as the capital of his united kingdom. And so the tribes were united, King Hiram of Tyre established international relations (5:11), and the Philistines were routed (5:17–25). By bringing the ark into Jerusalem (6:1–19), David made Jerusalem not only the political capital, but also the religious center, the Holy City of Israel. And once all of this had come together—Yahweh's anointed, a political and religious center—the time had come for Yahweh to make a further covenant with his people, for the promise of the land had now come to completion.

David reflects on the fact that he himself has been established by Yahweh in a palace, while Yahweh still lives in a desert tent. He decides that Yahweh should be established ("institutionalized"?) as he and Israel now are. David offers Yahweh a house; surprisingly, Yahweh refuses and instead establishes a house for David, namely, the royal line that will rule forever:

I have never stayed in a house from the day I brought the Israelites out of Egypt until today, but have always led a wanderer's life in a tent. In all my journeying with the whole people of Israel, did I say to anyone of the judges of Israel, . . . Why have you not built me a house of cedar? . . . Yahweh will make you great; Yahweh will make you a House. And when your days are ended and you are laid to rest with your ancestors, I will preserve the offspring of your body after you and make his sovereignty secure. (It is he who shall build a house for my name, and I will make his royal throne secure for ever.)[18] I will be a father to him and he a son to me; if he does evil, I will punish him with a rod such as men use, with strokes such as mankind gives. Yet I will not withdraw my favour from him, as I withdrew it from your predecessor. Your House and your sovereignty will always stand secure before me and your throne be established for ever (2 Sam 7:6f., 11c–16).

The passage says two things: (1) Somehow religion cannot be tied down, institutionalized.[19] Yahweh is always moving, as he was in the desert, always out there ahead of us and drawing us out. (2) Human government is an institution, and it is necessary. While Yahweh does settle on a royal line (such as the other nations had), this is his sanction of a human line of development as providential, not the foundation of a divine right of kings.[20]

It was inevitable that an Israel with a growing consciousness of itself as a nation would develop a centralized government. Since the only models of government known to Israel in 1000 B.C. were monarchies where the king had a special relation to the nation/city god, Yahweh's providence for Israel was the graceful motion from within the people for a king.

C. MESSIAH

David had been able to support his modest administration from his own personal wealth and from subjugation of slaves and taxation of conquered territories. Under him, Israel remained mostly a land of farmers and shepherds who lived in largely self-governing villages. The expansion of the royal administration under Solomon was not balanced by increased revenues from foreign conquests, however, and costs began to exceed income. Solomon engaged in trade of copper from Etzion Geber for gold and other wealth of Arabia, but Israel was too small to produce the amount of exports needed to balance the imports that made the Solomonic monarchy a cultural center. The bureaucracy of the kingship was enormous: the royal household contained wives and concubines (a harem), the great lady, royal attendants, the royal guard. The government employed bureaucrats who drew a profit from their post and for the favors they could obtain from the king. The army was expanded by the addition of a chariot force, and fortress cities were built on the main roads and passes near the frontiers. Royal works included building the Temple and the large palace-complex alongside it. Most of this was not productive of income and so was financed in two ways: heavy taxation and forced labor.

Solomon divided the country into twelve districts, whose taxes were to support the cost of the court for a month each. Some of the smaller districts must have been at an enormous disadvantage in raising the money, and undoubtedly some farms were appropriated by the royal estate in default of the taxes.[21]

It is probable that work on the palace, work in the mines, etc., was done by state slaves, men captured in war and Canaanites subjugated by Israel. When this force proved insufficient, Solomon introduced from ancient Near Eastern custom the corvée, forced-labor gangs conscripted or seized from among free Israelites (1 Sam 8:17). Not only did this destroy the freedom and dignity of those conscripted, but it removed them from the agricultural labor force. As a result, less food was produced, and individual family farms, lacking sufficient labor to make their own land productive enough to meet expenses and taxes, were sold to pay debts.[22] The little people without land, then, became members of a growing proletariat, selling their work at whatever price they could get.

Another source of economic displacement was the store-cities, where grain could be held for speculation at home or abroad and prices fixed at will. Small holders might be wiped out by a single crop failure, or even in an average year be the victims of fixed market prices. They might try to recoup their losses with a loan for the succeeding year, but, once they were on the hook, those who controlled money and the market kept them there until they went bankrupt. Eventually their land would be sold to large landholders who could ride out the market fluctuations.[23]

Thus was the whole economy of Israel changed from an agricultural to a commercial one. Gradually the villages became cities filled with merchants, craftsmen, and the proletariat. Distinction between the rich and the poor became apparent in the sizes and locations of their houses. Once the basis of the economy was changed, dislocations continued to grow into the situations decried by the prophets (see chap. V, below). All of this is the "justification" of the antimonarchic tirade of 1 Samuel 8:11-18.

Instead of the kings being the instruments of Yahweh's justice and deliverance for the people, they had become the sources of systemic injustice in the land. The rest of the Deuteronomic history (2 Sam 8–2 Kings) recounts the reigns of the kings.[24] In each case, it is a story of sin and injustice.[25] The kings of both North and South are unfaithful to the covenant with Yahweh: they allow or even encourage idolatry, they do not enforce Yahweh's laws, and so they become just as grasping and venal as 1 Samuel 8 had foretold. At the end of this history, the Deuteronomic editor of these books can find only two kings to praise—Hezekiah and Josiah, reform kings who returned the people to the true worship of Yahweh and the living of the covenant.

Yet the idea that Yahweh would "be there" in his king persisted in Israel, and hopes for an ideal future king to administer justice sprang from the grim reality of royal injustice. This king would be, of course, of David's line in accordance with Yahweh's covenant (Ps 89:20–38; 132:11–18, especially vv. 15f.). Psalm 2 and Psalm 110 refer to historical kings of Judah, but the reign is extended beyond them to an eschatological rule of the dynasty. The messianic oracles of Isaiah 7, 9, and 11 exalt an ideal king who would truly be Yahweh's instrument of justice for Israel and the world—liberation through human government.[26]

D. SUMMARY

From the beginning of his work in liberating the Hebrews, Yahweh drew men from among the people to be their leaders: Moses, Aaron, and Joshua. Thus liberation was always an interaction between Yahweh and the people themselves exercising their own initiative in pleading their case before the pharaoh, heading out into the desert, spying out the country, engaging the inhabitants in war, conquering the country. This sense of Israel making its own way was heightened as Israel grew to maturity, at first under the judges, then under Saul as the chieftain supreme over Israel, and finally under David as a full-fledged Near Eastern king.

As Israel grew into a greater unity, from tribal league during the conquest to a centralized nation beleaguered from within and without, the dynamics of human liberation called for a central government, and this the Israelites insisted on. This drive to an authority that can administer justice under developed socio-economic circumstances was clearly seen by the inspired writers as a work of God in conjunction with humankind. Henceforward Yahweh would be king over Israel *through* the Davidic king with whom he would make an everlasting covenant. The covenant was made so that Israel might fully participate in its own process of redemption through a government of justice to all its citizens. How this was to be done, how Israel was to become a nation under the majesty of the law, is the subject of the next chapter.

III. Law and Society

The previous chapter indicated that Yahweh is not a God who grants freedom independently of the striving of the people freed. The people ask for a king, push for one, and in the providence of God they are given the ability to rule themselves with one of their own number.[1] But this still might not touch the individual initiative and responsibility of the whole people. It is to this need that the liberator God turns from the beginnings of his covenant with his people, by giving them all a law to *live*.

When Yahweh had led his people out of the house of bondage and had delivered them from the Egyptian army at the Reed Sea and from hunger and thirst with manna, quail, and water from the rock, he led them to Mount Sinai for the greatest deliverance of all. And so God called Moses aside and spoke to him:

> . . . declare this to the sons of Israel, ''You yourselves have seen what I did with the Egyptians, how I carried you on eagle's wings and brought you to myself. From this you know that now, if you obey my voice and hold fast to my covenant, you of all the nations shall be my very own, for all the earth is mine. I will count you a kingdom of priests, a consecrated nation.'' Those are the words you are to speak to the sons of Israel (Ex 19:3–6).

Yahweh proposed to enter into a covenant[2] with the whole nation, a mutual contract, so that he would be their God and they, if they obeyed his voice (contractual obligations), would be his people. And ''all the people answered as one, 'All that Yahweh has said, we will do' '' (Ex 19:8). And so there followed a ritual preparation for the covenant (19:9–25), a theophany on Mount Sinai (19:16–20; 20:18–21), the revelation of the Ten Commandments (20:1–17), the Book of the Covenant (20:22–23:33), and finally the solemn ceremony by which the people ratified this covenant with Yahweh (24:1–18).

All of this material is the product of a long line of oral tradition, and different periods of history are intermingled in the account we now have before us. We must speak briefly of the history of that tradition as well as we can now define it, and then ask what the laws in their present (canonized) form mean to us who read this as God's revealed Word.

A. THE HISTORY OF LAW IN ISRAEL

The Old Testament legal materials—the Decalogue (Ex 20:1–17; 34:10–27; Deut 5:6–22), the Book of the Covenant (Ex 20:22–23:33), the Deuteronomic Code (Deut 12–25), and the Law of Holiness (Lev 17–26)—in the form in which we now have them do not go back to Sinai. The material was stylized and shaped by the needs of the Hebrew community between the time of the desert wanderings and the time of the final editing of the Bible.

There are some scholars who say that there was no law-giving whatsoever on Sinai. Hence, the Book of the Covenant in its present form does not come from a Sinai experience. According to these scholars, the connection of law-giving with Sinai in the Exodus wanderings is a later creation of Hebrew theologians. For proof, they say, consider Deuteronomy 26:5–10, one of Israel's earliest oral creeds: beginning with Abraham, the pious Jew traces God's liberating activity from the Exodus to the possession of Canaan, and nothing is said about laws or about a legal covenant between Yahweh and his people on Mount Sinai. Or read Psalm 105, which rehearses the salvation history of the Hebrews, specifically mentioning covenants with Abraham, Isaac, and Jacob, and the Exodus from Egypt, but without any mention of a legal covenant on Mount Sinai.[3]

Whatever theory one may adopt concerning the giving of the law, it is true that the laws contained in these collections are very old. They reflect tribal customs of nomads (such as blood vengeance) and of early agricultural communities. All this material seems to have been collected before the establishment of the monarchy, for no royal institutions are recorded in the laws (for example, the law courts are not the royal ones, but those of the tribal elders in the city gates). Nor is there any social stratification: the laws reveal no contrast between the nobility and the commoner.

Further, Israelite law seems to consist of two types: apodictic law and case law. The latter, which is common to the ancient Near East, gives definite sanctions for particular types of transgressions: "If anyone does this, he will be punished in such and such a way." Apodictic law is mostly the imperative, without any definite sanction: "Do this," "Don't do that."[4] The fusion of these two kinds of law would have taken place before the time of the monarchy.

This early codification of laws makes us ask just when law began in Israel. In a passage dealing with the people's rebellion against Yahweh in the territory of Kadesh, Exodus 15:25b says, "There it was [at Marah] He charged them with statute and ordinance, there that He put them to the test." So, according to this early tradition, Yahweh does give laws in the desert, but not in the form of a covenant at Sinai. This is in accord with Psalm 105:5, which says that among the liberating marvels of Yahweh were the laws (*mishpatîm*) from his mouth. The same phenomenon is also found in early historical creeds, such as Deuteronomy 6:20–25, where Yahweh gives precepts and statutes and laws.[5] Thus the essence of Yahwism is justice through law: "Strict justice must be your ideal" (Deut 16:20). That law is indeed integral to Yahwism is manifest in much of the legal material itself; see, for example, Exodus 22:20; Leviticus 19:34; and Deuteronomy 10:18f., where the essence of Israel's own liberation from oppression means that the Hebrews must do justice to others. The prophetic literature, too, suggests that law for relieving the injustices of the oppressed is as old as Yahwism itself (see chap. IV, below).

It appears probable, then, that Israel from its birth experience in Egypt understood that Yahweh was a source of just precepts for Israel and that to be a true offspring of Yahweh, Israel must practice justice. The present division of the law into the "Ten Words," which give the basic spirit of Yahwistic religion, and a codex containing more specific laws seems to be part of a desire to manifest Yahweh's passion for justice. I believe that Israel came out of the desert and to the conquest imbued with a sense of law roughly equivalent to the Decalogue and took over secular laws, which the Hebrews infused with their particular religious vision.[6]

This perception that Yahweh demands justice came to be considered the matter of a covenant between Yahweh and his people. And this covenant form was part of a cultic covenant renewal periodically celebrated in Israel. Finally, when Israel learned of the Hittite suzerainty treaties (or something similar), it began to cast some legal traditions in this form—most clearly in Deuteronomy and the Deuteronomic writings.[7]

B. THE LAW IN EXODUS

Whatever the history of legal traditions in Israel, the fact remains that the community finally codified its relation to Yahweh and to one another in the form in which we now have it in the Bible. The book of Exodus as it now exists,[8] then, is God's revealed Word for Israel. It is his invitation and command to Israel to live up to the dimensions of the liberation to which he sets them. It is Yahweh's fatherly love for Israel.

When we look at Exodus, what do we see? The people come to Sinai, where Yahweh had revealed his name to Moses, and now Yahweh continues that revelation of his identity by revealing his concern for justice, making a covenant for justice with his people (Ex 19:3–6). Thus again

Yahweh is the one "there" with them. The people prepare themselves for this holy and transcendent event (19:9–15). Then there is a theophany (Yahweh appears, is manifested) in a thunderstorm (19:16–25), in which Yahweh invites Moses and his brother to come up the mountain.

At this point, Yahweh reveals the Ten Commandments to the whole people (Ex 20:1–17). At the thundering and lightning the people are so afraid that they ask Moses to be an intermediary between themselves and such a God. Thus Yahweh reveals to Moses alone the Book of the Covenant (20:22–23:33). The editor has set the ceremony of the covenant-making between Yahweh and his people (24:1–18) at the end of this block of revelation, thus forming an inclusion with the initial theophany and making Exodus 19–24 a unit.

If that is the present form of the legislation, what is its content? Traditionally the Decalogue has been divided into two sections (the two tablets), the first containing the three or four commandments that list people's duties to God, and the second containing the six or seven that relate people's duties to one another.[9] Is that division justified by the text?

1. The Decalogue

If the "Ten Words" serve as fundamental law, how do the different commandments express fundamental needs of society?

Exodus 20:2. "I am Yahweh your God" is a prologue, introducing Yahweh as the one who has liberated the Hebrews from slavery in Egypt. The introduction is not just to identify Yahweh or to demand credence because of past acts; nor is it to summarize the previous eighteen chapters of the book of Exodus (as Childs suggests in *Exodus,* p. 401). This prologue identifies what follows as of one piece with Yahweh's originating redemptive act. These commands will reveal God's reality and his concerns— liberating ones (for that is his nature), which his people must assume if his liberation is to continue.

Exodus 20:3. "You shall have no gods before me" is the first commandment. The foundation of Hebrew society is the worship of Yahweh alone. At this stage of development, this is no theoretical monotheism; the commandment says, "I am *your* God, and you will worship no others."[10] As we will see in a later chapter, this is the foundation of a just society: Yahweh worship is ethical action for the neighbor, not magical practices, and this is what grounds society.

Exodus 20:4–6. "You shall not make yourself a carved image. . . . " This, the second commandment, bristles with historical difficulties,[11] but our question is, "What does it mean for society in its present form?" Beginning from the explanation in Deuteronomy 4:15ff., the meaning appears to be that Yahweh is revealed in his voice, in commands for the ethical life of his followers. The word for "listening," for "hearing," in Hebrew means "to obey," and so Yahweh's revelation of himself is not in a visible form to be painted or sculpted but in a voice giving a law to be obeyed. To be religious is not to be a figure kneeling before a carved image, but to have a heart obedient to Yahweh's commands.[12]

Exodus 20:7. "You shall not abuse the name of Yahweh." From early times the Lord's name was called on in prayer and prophecy, but misuses of the name remained a continuing threat.[13] What seems to be at stake here is the use of Yahweh's name to swear falsely against the neighbor in law court or in private speech, for thus Yahweh's person would be perverted by turning Yahweh into an instrument of injustice. Again, Yahweh's whole being means justice for humankind.

Exodus 20:8–11. "Remember to keep the Sabbath holy." We have been unable to find the ancient Near Eastern etymology of the word "sabbath," or the origin of the practice of the seventh day as a day of rest.[14] Here in 20:8ff. the main reason adduced for the practice seems to be imitation of Yahweh, who rested on the seventh day in creation. But the list of people who are to rest in v. 10 leads us to believe that the humanitarian motive of Deuteronomy 5:15 lies implicitly just under the surface of this formulation. That would mean that the Sabbath is for people to rest, because they, their slaves, and even their animals simply need a day of rest.

The remaining commandments speak clearly of one's relation to one's fellow man or woman:

Exodus 20:12. "Honor your father and mother" seems intended to keep the aged and infirm parents from being driven out of the home, but it also spills over into keeping peace in the family as the stable unit of society.

Exodus 20:13. "You shall not kill." By the time of this formulation, the commandment prohibits the killing of anyone out of enmity or deceit[15] and so protects the fundamental basis of society, the right of persons to life. No society can exist without this fundamental right being granted to all its members.

Exodus 20:14. "You shall not commit adultery." It is now commonly accepted that a wife was part of the personal property of a Hebrew man and so adultery was more of a crime against his possessions than the rupture of a personal union. However, there are indications that something more than violation of property was at stake in the Hebrew attitude to adultery: the punishment was death (Deut 22:22); it was called "shameful" and was treated with great horror (Gen 20:9; 39:9; and Job 24:14f. links it with murder, etc.). What might be at stake here is something approaching the sanctity of the home and the permanence of the family as the stable unit in society.

Exodus 20:15. "You shall not steal." Perhaps, as Alt has suggested, this originally referred to stealing a man, kidnapping. However, in its present form it prohibits taking anything by stealth. What is protected here is a person's right to the goods of the earth necessary to provide for living and survival, those on which one has imprinted one's own personality by work. Again, no society can exist without some regulation of the use of the world's goods.

Exodus 20:16. "You shall not bear false witness against your neighbor." This was probably originally a prohibition against false accusation of a neighbor (a fellow citizen of the covenant community) in Israel's law courts.[16] Thus it was not originally a prohibition against lying in general. Later prophetic usage (see Hos 4:2) admits lying alongside false swearing in speaking of Israel's covenant obligation, but the formulation in the Decalogue still retains the law-court meaning. Society needs honest administration and procedure, especially in courts of justice, since this is where the oppressed are "saved," "vindicated."

Exodus 20:17. "You shall not covet. . . ." The verb *hāmad* prohibits the interior desire to take another's property,[17] and so the covenant law ends by forbidding not only *actions* that injure the neighbor, but even those *desires* consciously fostered until they lead into the injurious actions. With this commandment we have in a sense passed from what is enforceable in a law court to the interior dispositions upon which society must inevitably be structured.

If we assume that the Decalogue was the fundamental law of the Old Testament, and that therefore it would reveal the substance of what Yahweh wanted of Israel, independently of the Book of the Covenant, what would we discover by this reading?

Yahweh's major preoccupation is not with Israel's proper worship of himself, but rather, that Hebrew do justice to fellow Hebrew (and even to others; cf. 20:10).

a. Only four at most of the commandments deal with people's relation to God:

—The Sabbath observance probably is a humanitarian precept, which allows people and beasts a chance to rest in the midst of a killing week of work (cf. Deut 5:15 as an extension of what already is present in the list of 20:10).

—Even the three commands that deal directly with God can be seen to have a dimension of human justice to fellow human beings: "No other gods" and "no carved image" refer to a rejection of magic and adherence to a religion based on ethical conduct.

—"Not abusing the Name" is at root a plea not to swear falsely in court to prosecute an innocent person.

b. The six commands in the second half of the Decalogue, which have humankind as object, cover major elements of a social ethic:

—A person's right to life (no murder).

—The promotion of the smallest unit of society as a place where one learns love, fidelity, and respect (here the family—commands on adultery, honoring parents).

—A person's right to reputation and justice; involving integrity of speech in law courts (not swearing falsely).

—Protection of a person's possessions (no stealing).

—An ethic which stresses that a person's interior, while not exactly actionable at law, is a decisive factor in what one does in the external forum. The relations of justice described in commandments four through ten are now seen as religious. To do injustice to a person is a crime against God. In short, the Lord has delivered to his people an ethic by which they must take responsibility for their own liberation in society by protecting one another's rights. If they do so, they are his people, and so free; if not, his physical liberation will not have truly freed them.

2. *The Book of the Covenant*

We saw above that the *mishpatîm* were added to the older apodictic material of this law code sometime around 725 B.C. But the question for us is, "What does this law code, which regulated the life of Israel's community after that time, mean in its present form?"

For one thing, placed after the Decalogue, it indicates that the general ethic of the Ten Commandments was not specific enough to regulate a whole society. In short, one of the elements that a society needs which was *not* given in the Decalogue is a code of laws by which a society can be founded and governed. The Book of the Covenant had supplied this defect for a people of the Settlement long before it was collected in the present form, and in its present form it was regulative for subsequent Judaism, and continues so even today.

The exact organization of the law code is not clear, but this can serve as a tentative outline:

a. *Altar Law* (Ex 20:22–26)
b. *Mishpatîm* (case-law for secular needs: Ex 21:1–22:17)
   i. Slave law (21:1–11)
   ii. Capital offenses (21:12–17)
   iii. Laws on bodily injuries (21:18–36)
   iv. Property damage (22:1–17)

c. *Apodictic Material* (from covenant relationship: Ex 22:18–23:19)
   i. Miscellaneous social laws (22:18–31)
   ii. Court procedure (23:1–9)
   iii. The cultic calendar (23:10–19)
d. *Parenetic Epilogue* (Ex 23:20–33)

a. *Altar Law (Ex 20:22–26):* Verses 22–23 link the code to the Sinai theophany and lead into the code by the prohibition of images already given in the Decalogue.[18] The command that the altar is to be made of sod, earth, and field stone (specifically not of dressed stone) seems to be a prohibition of adopting Canaanite altars (especially the step altar of the Canaanite high god) for Israelite worship of Yahweh. The distinctiveness of Yahwistic religion is the cornerstone on which all Israelite law will be based.

b. *Mishpaṭîm (Ex 21:1–22:17):*
   i. Slave law (21:1–11). Is it significant that the civil law of the Book of the Covenant begins with laws that deal with slaves (21:1–11)?[19] Is it possible that this is first because there is here an intersection of property rights and human rights? The "Hebrew" slave probably refers originally to a member of the proletarian class, the group out of which the people of the covenant were formed. If such a man is now enslaved, he must be freed after six years. This means that somehow the man retains some right to freedom, and so is considered a free human being—unlike Aristotle's theory that some men were naturally slaves and had to be so treated by society (*Politics,* I, chap. V). The next clause reinforces this, for a slave can choose, because of his personal relationship with his master or with the wife and family he has in the master's house, to remain a slave. We should probably prefer that the man could have been allowed to take wife and family into freedom, but here Hebrew property rights prevailed. The law is not that humanitarian! Even female slaves, in a society where free women were something of a possession, retain personal rights, the violation of which grants them their freedom.

   ii. Capital offenses (21:12–17). Immediately after slave law we have the only interpolation of apodictic law into the *mishpaṭîm,* the solemn protecting of human right to life in the covenant community. These rights are so sacred that they are sanctioned by the death penalty. In verses 12–14 we have the distinction between murder and manslaughter: asylum cities of refuge were established to deliver the one who had accidentally killed from the retribution of the *gô'ēl,* the avenger of blood. This indicates not only a new quality of mercy in the law, but also a movement to a more civilized mode of justice than the nomadic tribal institution of the avenger. In fact, capital punishment for murder is stronger in Israel than in other ancient

Near Eastern codes. Note that respect for family bonds is so strong that merely cursing one's parents merits the death penalty.

iii. Laws on bodily injuries (21:18–36). Observe that in the first case a man is financially responsible not only for medical costs but also for loss of wages of the one injured. If a pregnant woman is injured in a brawl and a miscarriage results, the one who injured her must pay for the miscarriage, as the judge shall determine.[20] On the other hand, if the woman herself is physically injured, then she must be repaid, "an eye for an eye, a tooth for a tooth," etc. This is the celebrated *lex talionis*.[21] Manslaughter of a slave fits into this body of laws, and not under capital offenses, for the slave is not fully a member of the covenant community. Nevertheless, killing a slave by brutally beating him to death is an offense that must be punished (evidently the judge is to determine the appropriate punishment). This is in spite of the fact that the next verse describes the slave as property.[22] The laws on bodily injuries to slaves are also curious, for they again affirm that the slave has rights and cannot be recompensed even by the *lex talionis,* but must be freed for serious bodily injury. This is impossible to reconcile with a theory that the slave is merely property. Verses 28–30 are traditional ancient Near Eastern law, whereby the owner is responsible for an ox that habitually gores. However, the fact that an owner who has been warned can be responsible to the point of capital punishment is distinctive Hebrew severity in the interest of protecting human life. Whereas other ancient Near Eastern codes compensated by a fine, in Israel human life cannot be compensated by a fine.[23] Verses 31–36 continue the theme of bodily injury to livestock and are nothing more than the customary law of Israel's neighbors.

iv. Property damage (22:1–17). The damage to livestock leads naturally into the destruction and theft of other property. The general principle is that one must make good another's loss for which one is responsible. Two things are worth noting. In verse 3 Israel protects the thief who acts in broad daylight, so that the thief may not be killed. Whereas at night there might be confusion, panic, or anger, in daylight the rights of the thief to life must be respected. No other code so protects the life of the thief. In verse 16 Israel protects unengaged[24] women from seduction by demanding not just that the seducer pay the dowry price for her but that he also marry the girl; the law thus stands by the oppressed woman.[25]

c. Apodictic Material (Ex 22:18–23:19): The collection of *mishpatîm* ends in 22:17, and then a series of laws in apodictic style begins, probably more related to covenant practice.

i. Miscellaneous social laws (22:18–31). Distinctions between ethical, cultic, and social concerns were foreign to Israel, which saw them all as interrelated. Hence laws against sorcery, bestiality, and idolatry could be grouped together (verses 18–20). The sorcerer claimed to interpret and control the future, which belonged solely to Yahweh. Bestiality was not only a shameful practice but may have had roots in Canaanite fertility cults, thus being a turning from the ethical religion of Yahweh.

Verses 21–27 are laws on various forms of oppression of the weak. The stranger or alien was one who lived in the country without being a full citizen, and so lacked the protection of his clan. The widow or orphan lacked the protection of husband and father. The poor lacked the protection of the money that buys power and influence.[26] For all of these, then, Yahweh becomes the protector. The reasons for Israel's concern for the weak are three: Israel knew what it was like to be an alien in Egypt (v. 21); Yahweh is compassionate, that is his nature, and Israel is to imitate Yahweh (v. 27) or suffer God's justice on itself (v. 24); and the covenant with Yahweh rules out exploitation, for Israel must resemble him (v. 25, where Yahweh speaks of "my people"). What is especially interesting is the way Yahweh identifies himself with the leader of the people, probably as the administrator of Yahweh's own justice for his people (v. 28; see chaps. I and II, above).

ii. Court procedure (23:1–9). As we saw in chapter II, the judge was one who delivered the people. This same notion prevails for the elders acting as judges in the city gates. The judicial process is the oppressed citizen's chief chance of liberation, and so anything that perverts that process is especially odious to the God of justice. Verses 1–3 are probably laws for witnesses, who are not to give false reports, pass on rumors, or sell out to those with money, power, influence, or even the tyranny of the majority. Justice must be the sole aim. In verses 4–5 we have the only casuistic passage of this section of the code, dealing with the subject of justice even for the enemy, a theme that occurs also in Hittite laws, though perhaps not with such force.[27] Verses 6–8 are instructions against bribery, more likely addressed to judges. In all, there is an emphasis on justice being done and on a singleminded adherence to justice.

iii. The cultic calendar (23:10–19). The Sabbath year may have had a mythological background, or have arisen from some agricultural practice of fallow fields, but here in Exodus a humanitarian reason is given: that the poor and even wildlife may eat on what spontaneously springs up. (It is presumed that some fields will be fallow producers each year, so the poor always have something to eat.) This humanitarian reason is also behind Sabbath observance: so that people and oxen may have necessary rest. (However, prohibiting even the mention of other gods, v. 13, shows the religious depths of the Sabbath law, too.)

Verses 14–19 recount the E festival calendar, probably the oldest of the calendars of the great feasts of Israel (see Ex 34; Deut 16; Lev 23; Num

28–29).[28] These agricultural feasts have already become attached to historical events in the life of Israel;[29] thus the unleavened bread is attached to the Exodus from Egypt, though there is no explicit mention of Passover. Verses 18–19 are now known to be prohibitions of Canaanite fertility ceremonies.

d. Parenetic Epilogue (Ex 23:20–33): Israelite codes generally end with an exhortation to practice the laws (see Deut 26, followed by blessings for observance and curses for disobedience in chaps. 26–28; Lev 26). Note that here we have promises and warnings relating to possession of the land, but we do not have a reference to the law just given. The redactor probably added the passage to the cultic calendar to end the code. What we have here is general parenesis encompassing two themes: (1) When the Israelites enter Canaan they are to break up the Canaanite religious symbols and make no covenant with them or their gods; (2) if the Israelites remain faithful to Yahweh and do what he says, they will have Yahweh as their ally and he will drive out the nations and give them a kingdom from the Mediterranean to the Euphrates.[30]

Conclusion: If these laws were the only thing we knew about ancient Israel, what could we say of their culture? What advances does the Book of the Covenant make over the Decalogue?

First, we find the same astonishingly small proportion of "purely religious laws" to laws regulating the social relations of people. Of the ninety-two verses of laws in the code, only seventeen (18 percent) are explicitly on Israel's religious (i.e., cultic, obediential) duties to Yahweh.

Second, of those duties to Yahweh (roughly the first three commandments of the Decalogue)—the law of the altar, decorum in cult, laws on sacrifice, the festival calendar, dietary laws—all seem oriented to a recognition that Yahweh is Lord, that there are no other gods for Israel, and that the whole of human life is caught up in service to him (as sacrificing the fruits of the fields and dedicating the firstborn child dedicates all of life to him). The prohibition of idolatry still seems to be central to all religious laws, and this will be seen, as in the Decalogue, to be a movement from magical religion to an ethical religion of service to one's fellow human being.

Third, the code began with religious law (20:22–26) and ended with religious law (23:14–19) to indicate that the whole code is included in the notion of religious obedience to Yahweh; worship of Yahweh surrounds and penetrates all laws governing people's relation to each other in Israel. This confirms the general direction of the Decalogue.[31]

Fourth, of the laws regulating interpersonal relations, laws protecting the rights of slaves occupy first place (21:2–11, 20f.; these twelve verses represent 13 percent of the code). Though they are property, slaves nevertheless are to be treated as persons (but this personalism is unfocused and only emerging).

Fifth, the rest of the laws expand the fundamental concerns of the Decalogue:

a. Protecting the sanctity of human life (the sixth commandment): laws imposing capital punishment for murder and granting asylum for manslaughter (21:12–14) and laws protecting the bodily integrity of humans (21:15–32). These make up twenty-one verses, 23 percent of the code, and so indicate this to be a paramount concern of Israelite law. (Indeed, no society can survive without this concern at the base of its law.)

b. Protecting property rights (the eighth commandment): seventeen verses, or 18 percent of the code. Since people are called to dominion over material things (see chap. IV, below) and to work out their personalities in matter, it is inevitable that laws regarding people's right to material goods are fundamental to any human society.

c. Protecting the family as the smallest unit of society (the fifth and seventh commandments): laws on violation of a virgin (22:16f.), on respect for father and mother (21:15,17).

d. Protecting the integrity of the process toward justice in the law courts (the ninth commandment): 23:1–9, 10 percent of the code.

e. Laws that protect civil government (22:28b) and the proper functioning of the economy (22:10f.) are additions not covered by the Decalogue. An even further extension of Israelite law is the proper protection of the enemy's property (23:4f.).

What moderns accept as purely civil law the Hebrews saw as religious. This was not simply because as a primitive people they could not distinguish religious realms from secular ones, but also because true religion sees the whole of one's life as relating the person to God, even if—as we later suggest—by dynamics that have a natural autonomy apart from the religious sphere.

C. SUMMARY

It is true that if one adds the cultic Decalogue of Exodus 34:17–27 to the law of Exodus 19–24 one raises the proportion of laws directed to worship of Yahweh. This heightened importance of cultic law is also found in the Holiness Code (Lev 17–26) and in the laws scattered throughout the P source, so that these can be said to be almost exclusively religious law. In the Deuteronomic Code (Deut 12–26) we again find a high percentage of civil law, reflecting a later society and couched in a hortatory tone that gives a religious undertone to everything.

Yet our reading of the proportion of person-to-God and person-to-person law in the book of Exodus still reveals a basic tenet of Jewish law. What Yahweh wants as religious worship of himself is justice among people. The material in Exodus 19–24 is a unit which reveals the fundamental nature of Yahwistic religion. What is at stake is the continuation of Yahweh's liberation of the Jews. In a great act of motherly love, Yahweh delivered his people and gave them personality and identity through the liberation from Egypt (see chap. I, above). Yet only if Israel ratifies this by observing a law promoting justice in the community can human liberation come to its mature perfection. It is by an act of fatherly love, giving the government and insisting that Israel promote justice through revealed law, that Yahweh led Israel to complete its own liberation (see also chap. II, above).[32] How Israel reflects this theology back into its previous history and how it carries this out in its subsequent history will be the subject of the next three chapters on liberation in the Old Testament.

IV. Human Origins of Liberation

A. HISTORICAL ETIOLOGY

History has been defined as the grasp of "what was going forward in particular groups at particular places and times."[1] It is the cumulative result, not only of individuals' intentions and executions, but also of the intents and achievements of the group and the nation as a whole. Further, it is the progress or decline due to the individual's or the nation's oversights, mistakes, and failures to act.

Since all of this emerges only in time and is discovered only subsequently by reflective persons putting many pieces together, it is many years, decades, or even centuries later that historians are able to grasp what was going forward as a movement in past history.

What is true of us was no less true of the Hebrews. Even if they had had tape recorders and newspapers it would have been only centuries later that they would have been able to fit together the pieces in a grasp of history. But lacking even these technological benefits, the Hebrews depended on memories of the past, sagas, and legends passed on in tribes and families according to the laws or oral traditions. Only later, when Yahweh had revealed his will to them in the Exodus, were they able to go back and see what had been going forward in their own past as nomads and slaves in Egypt. Moreover, since the evidence was so scanty and so malleable in oral tradition, much of the material was considerably reworked (details added or forgotten, patterns developed, emphasized, etc.) to exemplify the dynamics of salvation history, which Yahweh had by now made clear to them.

One of the names given to this process of reconstruction is "historical etiology,"[2] by which an ancient author sought to explain an experienced situation or event in human affairs by an earlier historical event of which he had no properly historical knowledge. Alonso-Schökel finds this process operative in much Old Testament writing. A number of people are called Semites, and so their origin is traced back to a man named Shem as the father of the race or tribe. Hosea knows the sin of disobedience is universal in Israel, and so he keeps tracing sin in Israel back to an originating sin, the apostasy of the calf-worship at Bethel (1 Kings 12:26–30; cf. Hos 10:5, "Bethaven" as "house of evil").

It is our thesis that this is the process by which the inspired writers of the Old Testament put together most of the material of Genesis. Particularly is this true of Genesis 1–11, containing the prehistory of the whole human race. The method is especially useful in dealing with the story of the fall in Genesis 2–3. Witness Alonso-Schökel:

> An author familiar with the sapiential milieu asks himself: Where does evil come from? He answers: From sin. And where does everybody's sin come from? To answer this, he reflects upon the religious experience of the chosen people, as it appears in sacred traditions oral or written, cultic or non-cultic. This religious world drives him with an ascending force back toward the origin, and he answers: The sin of all men comes from the sin at their origin, from the original pair. That inspired answer he then translates into narrative. For this he employs the classical pattern of salvation-history, with its profound explanation of sin. The sequence is: God's initiative in giving, categorical precept, rebellion, punishment, mercy, and then the continuation of history. The author chose this pattern under the light of inspiration.[3]

Thus it was methodologically correct for us to begin with Exodus and its consequences for Israel (even up to the point of the Deuteronomic salvation-history theme:gift→command→rebellion→punishment→ repentance and covenant renewal→graced prosperity) before taking up the narratives of Genesis. We now turn to the theology of Genesis in an effort to understand at a deeper level what humankind must be liberated from.

B. THE CREATION AND THE FALL

Two great traditions (J and P) reflect on Israel's origins: J sees things from the perspective of human psychology and so anthropomorphizes God. The creation account is placed here as a prelude to J's whole history of humanity's progressive estrangement from God leading up to the liberation from Egypt.[4] It may be that this passage is somewhat later than the J history as a whole (especially if, as Alonso-Schökel suggests, there are developed themes of Wisdom literature in it), yet it must be dated earlier than the second great tradition, the P account, considered at the end of this chapter, since it reached its final form in the fourth century.

1. The Creation (Gen 2:4b–25)

J begins with Yahweh already having created the earth and the heavens, but the earth is not productive without rain and human cultivation. Thus the theme of the Yahwist is not (as in Gen 1) that God creates order out of chaos but that God (with man) replaces barrenness with fruit. In order to do this, Yahweh creates man from the ground: the Hebrew pun *'ādām* (man) from *'ādamāh* (earth) expresses man's organic relation to the earth and also, in view of verse 5, his stewardship over it.[5] What makes *'ādām* different from *'ādamāh* is that Yahweh breathes into him the breath of life (v. 7), making him a living being.[6]

With humankind now created (in first place, almost as the first creature), Yahweh creates the vegetation of the Garden of Eden for him. In the garden (similar to the kind of royal park which only a king could afford in the ancient Near East) is the tree of life (a common Near Eastern symbol) and the tree of the knowledge of good and evil (rarer in the Near East and, in the Old Testament, occurring only here). Given dominion over the earth to make it fruitful (v. 15), humankind is the object of God's love, as the material world is ordered to and for humankind. Indeed, Yahweh gives humans every tree of the garden (v. 16) to be their delight. All of this simply expresses the way God first communicates his love to humans; he does not make his love conditional. However, once the gift of life and the delightful world have been made, then Yahweh asks Adam also to live up to the gift of love in two ways: (*a*) Adam is to till and keep the garden, and so the world's relation to man for its perfection is intimated (see Gen 1:26, 28ff.; Rom 8:19–23, etc.); (*b*) Adam is not to eat of the tree of knowledge of good and evil.

From the temptation (Gen 3:4–5) it appears that such knowledge is not just passive, receptive knowledge, but active knowledge, the establishing of what is good and what is evil, which is proper only to the creator God.[7] Thus, eating the fruit would be a rejection of the role of being God's steward over the world. It would be to supplant God as the giver of gifts. Thus this (covenant) command is not arbitrary, but linked to the Yahwist's whole concept of the relation of world, humanity, and God.

In verses 18–20 J further develops the theme of human dominion. Adam is lord of all creation because he names every animal. (In the ancient Near East, naming means that one has power over the thing named.)[8] Therefore, there·is a hierarchy of creation: earth, plants, animals, and humankind at the top, the first creature. Indeed, the creation of animals is treated as part of God's quest to find someone who can so share with Adam that he is not alone (vv. 18f.). But the perfect helper fit for Adam cannot be found in animals subject to him; it must be someone of the same sovereign nature, who can *con-front* him.[9] Therefore Yahweh casts the man into a deep sleep and forms one of his ribs into a woman and brings her to him. The man's joyful cry of recognition speaks of his contentment: "This at last is bone from my bones, and flesh from my flesh. This is to be called woman, for this was taken from man."[10]

Thus the Yahwist, even at this early stage of Hebrew history (even in the midst of what we saw in chapter III was a severely patriarchal society), affirms an equality of man and woman. As deriving from the man, who is first, she is subordinate, yet she is a strong helper because she can communicate with him in the very nature she derives from his body/person.

Lest we miss the point, the Yahwist points out in verse 24 that it is because of this mutual complementarity in needs and strengths that a man leaves all he would hold dear and would make his life secure (his family) to adhere to his wife to become one body.[11] Out of a need for personal communication (lest man be alone with an aloneness that animals cannot alleviate) the smallest unit of society (family) is created. What is truly extraordinary is that the man's leaving his family is exactly the opposite of Hebrew practice for as long a time as we have any record: it is the wife who leaves her family to go to her husband. What is the meaning, then, of this verse? The Yahwist must be speaking of a psychological leaving and a union so profound as to emphasize the equality of the sexes at a deeper level than we had ever expected.[12]

Finally, J concludes by remarking that nakedness was not a matter of shame, thus indicating that originally man's sexuality was integrated into a personal communion of trust and esteem between man and woman. This idyllic relationship, then, is the Yahwist's final comment on the integrity of Yahweh's whole act of creating in 2:4b–25 and is his correlative to the P account's "And God saw it was good."

2. The Fall (Gen 3:1–24)

If the creation as given by God was good (Gen 1–2), the Yahwist, writing for Hebrew society, still has to explain the origin of evil in the world. This he does with a psychological subtlety far surpassing that of Genesis 2. Within the etiological history of gift—covenant, he has masterfully treated the psychology of temptation and the meaning of sin.

He begins with the serpent, the cleverest of the animals of the garden.[13] The serpent begins by distorting Yahweh's command, saying Yahweh has refused them all the fruit of the garden. Thus the woman is able to enter dialogue, correcting the serpent, being in the right, and defending Yahweh as well. Note, however, that she too exaggerates the command of Yahweh, who never said they could not touch the tree. Now the serpent drops all pretense and uses the ancient motif of God's jealousy in protecting his privilege: if they eat of the fruit they will be like gods, determining good and evil. The dialogue ends; the serpent has said all that is necessary and leaves the woman to deliberate the eternal human temptation, the desire to be God. The description of woman's succumbing is subtle (v. 6): first, she sees the tree as good for food, an appeal to sensual appetite; second, she finds it esthetically pleasing, a more spiritual appeal; and third, she desires it as the object that will produce divinity in her.[14] Presumably it was this last that finally precipitated her into taking the food and eating it.[15]

Then, probably moved by our human desire to have others share our guilt, she gives it to the man, who also eats. Verse 7 indicates that when the man eats, the promise of the serpent is literally fulfilled: their eyes are opened, and where before they had known only good in their nakedness (2:25), now it is a source of shame to them, something to be hidden with fig leaves.

Does this effect in man's attitude to his sexuality indicate the sin was a sexual one? We indicated above that, since Canaanite religion was based on (sexual) fertility, there is an intimate relation between sex and religion in the Hebrew mind. What J really has in mind, however, is not sexual sin (which is probably simply the most obvious instance of powerful desires that humans cannot control), but disobedience to Yahweh's loving covenant command, which is primal sin for a Hebrew. Yahweh had ordered all of creation to humankind, and through humankind all was harmoniously ordered to Yahweh for its perfection (the meaning of Eden). The only command was that men and women were to maintain and cultivate that order. Rejection of Yahweh's command is rejection of man's role as lynch pin in the whole order, and thus destruction of it. The sin is pride in creatures, the blatant *non serviam* ("I will not serve!").

The disorder consequent on rejection of God's design is now depicted. First, there is the disorder in the man's conception of himself (shame at nakedness) and in his interpersonal relation to the woman. Second, association in guilt destroys communion among them: the response of the man upon being questioned by God is to blame God for giving him the woman, and then to blame the woman herself (v. 12). The woman, in turn, cannot face the truth of her guilt, and she blames the serpent (v. 13). Third, all of this leads to an estrangement from God, from whom they now hide (vv. 8, 10). There can be no community among people without an affirmation and living out of God's plan for them. (And once distrust is a part of the fabric of human life it becomes an enticement to react sinfully against others' attempts to control one, leading to a history of sin.)

Since humankind is in fact guilty, as the shame and quarreling manifest, judgment now follows on the three participants (3:14–19): (1) The serpent is condemned to crawl in the dust and to be at constant enmity with men and women.[16] (2) The woman is condemned to pain in childbearing, and yet she will have sexual desire for her husband.[17] The Yahwist uses these as concrete manifestations of the real curse of the woman, her subjection to man ("He shall rule over you"). In this sense the fall is an etiological tale to explain the subjection of woman to man, which the Yahwist found in his own society.[18] (3) The man is condemned to wrestle a living from a recalcitrant earth, which had previously been abundant in its bounty. This constitutes a curse for the earth itself (see Rom 8:20), which no longer fulfills its organic relation to humanity as its head. Moreover, death, which must have always been natural to human beings, is now seen as a symbol of that destruction and disorder that they have sown in all of creation by their sin. Indeed, God's command had sanctioned disobedience with death (2:17), yet after the fall neither Adam nor Eve nor the serpent die. Clearly death is something else, either a dying to that relationship to God which is life, or a physical death that is still in the future.

Indeed, in the next verse (v. 20), J shows the man calling the woman Eve, the mother of the living (another Hebrew pun, relating Eve with living), which means that life goes on.

Finally, the judgments are executed (vv. 22–24) by one of Yahweh's court. Verse 22 creates the problem that Yahweh seems to be a petty tyrant guarding his prerogatives: "See, the man has become like one of us, with his knowledge of good and evil. He must not be allowed to pick from the tree of life, also, and eat some and live forever." Yahweh accepts the words of the serpent: determining good and evil is to be like God. Adam and Eve have attempted that role of deciding which is good and evil, but in so doing they discovered that their determination was not in conformity with reality. The disorder in all their relationships has revealed that they are not the determiners. Yahweh's removal of the tree of life is simply the final congruence of human disorder: since life is life with God, humankind has lost it and must become aware of this fact by a violent separation from the garden and the tree of life.

In sum, J's vision of human origins emphasizes that man and woman have a special communion in the work of cultivation and administering all of creation. This is the gift of Yahweh, who gives of himself (the breath of life) in creation. But such a gift implies also the living out of the implicit relations of the gift. The man refused to live up to his nature and destiny and so enjoy immortality with God. Determining his own way of life has created evil and disorder for himself, his world, his wife, and his relations with God. For this, he and all creation with him were banished from the perfect state of union and bliss God had prepared and were sent to live in a disordered world. It is humankind who has created the evil we find all about us, not God. (And liberation from that evil must begin with a reversal of the irresponsibility of the one who produced it.)

C. THE HISTORY OF SIN

The banishment from the garden indicates that only the first half of the covenant theological scheme has been accomplished (gift→punishment). Genesis 4–11 describes a growing accumulation of sin in the human race until it is hopelessly alienated from itself and from God. Then God takes a hand in human liberation by his participation in salvation history through Abraham and the rest of the patriarchal history (Gen 12–50).

1. Cain and Abel (Gen 4:1–16)

J adds this story immediately to that of the fall. With Cain, the first born, we have the first man living entirely in the conditions of the world as we know it (outside the garden's idyllic bliss)—the first "historical" man.

It may be that this material was originally an etiological saga to explain the origin of the Kenites (see Gen 4:17–26) from Cain. Or it may also have been an exaltation of the seminomadic life of the shepherd over the sedentary life of the farmer (Cain before the crime) or the wandering life of the nomad (Cain after the crime). However, in its present form it is so interconnected with the story of the fall as to be J's theological reflection on humanity's alienation from God.[19] Whereas in Genesis 3 alienation from God effected alienation from self, fellow person, and world, here a crime against one's fellow person is seen to produce alienation from God and world. We have two complementary halves of one and the same theology: sin is an offense against, and alienation from, both God and human society.

Cain is the first born according to normal human reproduction, and becomes a farmer, while his brother Abel becomes a shepherd.[20] They come to offer their own sacrifices according to their own distinctive rituals. We are not told why the Lord accepted Abel's offering and rejected Cain's; that is the Lord's business to decide (see Ex. 33:19b), especially as part of the Yahwist's "younger son" theology. On the other hand, God wrestles with Cain's bad attitude in a fatherly way (vv. 6f.): if he were living morally his sacrifice would have been accepted; if not, then sin (which had been loosed by Adam into creation at large) was lurking like a demon at his door, and Cain had to master it (in order to live well and have his sacrifice accepted).

But Cain succumbed to the demon, the disorder of creation. Taking his brother into the country where no one would see, he killed him. Though Abel's body might have been covered over from human eyes, his blood, soaking into the earth, cried out to Yahweh for vengeance. Yahweh, as the *gó'ēl* for Abel's innocent blood, comes to Cain with the judicial question, "Where is Abel your brother?"[21] Cain responds evasively, "I don't know; am I my brother's keeper?" Yahweh, however, announces that the earth, cursed as a result of the first man's sin (but still ordered to producing for humankind), in receiving Abel's blood, curses Cain. By Yahweh's judgment the earth will not yield to Cain even the fruit among thistles that Adam's progeny can glean. Cain is condemned to the life of a nomad and a fugitive from justice. Cain reflects on the fact that he is now estranged from both God and humanity, and this is more than he can bear. What troubles him most is that others will recognize him as a murderer and kill him first, perhaps even in their own style of blood vengeance. But Yahweh is the protector of life, even of the criminal, and he bestows on Cain a tribal mark, which indicates that sevenfold vengeance will be exacted for his life.[22] Then Cain goes away and dwells in the land of the fugitives (Nod for *nad,* "fugitive"), the desert.

Now, in the midst of a whole theology in which sin and crime are always simultaneously offenses against earth, self, fellow person, and God, the Yahwist answers our question about death, which he had left vague in Genesis 2–3. The death that Adam would die when he ate the fruit (2:17) has come to his descendants. As a result of the disorder unleashed by the prehistoric sin, Cain has put Abel to death, and a human being thus dies the death.[23] Seven times Abel was called Cain's brother, and by this repetition J obviously is saying that we are our brother's keeper (all are our brothers and sisters). Fratricide cries out to Yahweh for vengeance. In this way, J's whole prologue points to the Exodus, where in Exodus 2:23; 3:7 the cry of the oppressed Hebrews arose to God. In answer to the question of whence comes human suffering and death, J is unequivocal: from human malice. And who can deliver us from this malice? Only Yahweh, who is the avenger of all human injustice, will free us from sin, for, left to our own devices, we only increase the malice, as we shall now see in Hebrew history.

2. Noah (Gen 6:1–9:29)[24]

Both J and P traditions are interwoven into this legendary account of God's judgment on human malice.[25] What has begun as the sin of a man has now multiplied to cosmic dimensions, so that even superhuman beings (the sons of God in Gen 6:2–4) are involved in it.[26] Human wickedness had so encompassed the (known) earth (6:5, 11f.) that the Lord was supposed to have been sorry he had created man. And so Yahweh simply decided to let the chaotic forces of water (see section E below) blot out the race. Only Noah, a just man, and his family, together with the (innocent) animals, were spared. When the flood had subsided, Noah led the animals out of the ark and sacrificed to Yahweh as his first act in the new earth. Noah's sacrificial gratitude pleased Yahweh, who made a new covenant with Noah: Yahweh would not again destroy humanity by water, and in return Noah's offspring would have the same dominion over creation as humankind received in Genesis 1:28–30, but they must not eat the blood of animals, nor take the blood of any person.

Yet immediately after this, sin springs up again in Ham's ridicule of his father's drunken nakedness,[27] and extends again over the world through the story of the Tower of Babel.

3. Babel (Gen 11:1–9)

With this story, J has set the stage for Yahweh's intervention in the patriarchal history. Like a cancer, sin again has spread from one man (Noah) out to the world. Again the effort to build a tower stretching to the heavens is interpreted by the Yahwist's God as a proud desire to be like gods. And for their pains Yahweh scatters them over the face of the earth and keeps them divided by their diversity of language. Thus, for the Yahwist, human pride has accounted not only for sin but for the geographical and linguistic divisions of persons against themselves. Such disunity is connected with sin.

D. THE PATRIARCHAL HISTORY

Genesis 11:31ff. describes the migration of Abraham's father toward Canaan; but he stopped halfway, in Haran in farthest northwest Mesopotamia.[28] After the death of Abraham's father, Yahweh spoke to Abraham:

> Leave your country, your family and your father's house, for the land I will show you. I will make you a great nation; I will bless you and make your name so famous that it will be used as a blessing.
> > I will bless those who bless you;
> > I will curse those who slight you.
> > All the tribes of the earth
> > shall bless themselves by you (Gen 12:1–3).

Abraham is asked to leave all he has and all he could hold dear—his country with its customs and even its gods, his family and father's house, which were what offered identity and security to a semi-nomad—and this for a land and a future wrapped in total obscurity. There is only a vague promise that the God who calls him to this will protect him and that he will prosper and be the father of a great nation. All of this occurs at a time when Abraham was already past his prime, and so supposedly not open to new beginnings. Thus God reveals himself as the God coming out of the future, as he would reveal himself to Moses (see chap. I, pp. 4–5, above).

It frequently is said that this promise (formalized as a covenant in Gen 15) is unilateral (as opposed to the bilateral covenant of the law): God asks for no special conduct or observance from Abraham, but he promises that Abraham will prosper if he will but trust God. This statement, however, ignores the fact that Abraham's faith and trust *are* a response, and an enormous one. The promise does not become covenant unless Abraham responds in trust. Paul (Rom 4:1–25) and the author of the Epistle to the Hebrews (11:8–12) understood how enormous was this act of faith, so great that it converted Abraham to a life with God and established the covenant and brought salvation to humankind.[29] Nevertheless, the initiative and actualization of the covenant are in the hands of God as the Lord of history, in which he now is taking a personal part. (Again, the unconditioned nature of God's invitation reminds us of the unconditioned nature of motherly love.)

Strictly speaking, the blessing of Abraham (Gen 12:3) means that he will become so prosperous that other nations will bless themselves by saying, "May you prosper as did Abraham." (Note this meaning of blessing in Zech 8:13.) However, the Hebrew verb can also have a passive meaning, that other nations will receive blessing (salvation) through Abraham (this kind is found in Is 19:24). Since the New Testament (Acts 3:25; Gal 3:8), this latter interpretation has been seen as the deepest meaning of the text. This means that God's salvation history is not just for the Jews, but through them for all people, for God loves all humankind.

The rest of the Abraham story (Gen 12:1–25:18) details the carrying out of this promise/covenant. In 15:1–3 Abraham naturally doubts the credibility of the promise, in view of his lifelong sterility. The promise nevertheless is renewed in verses 4f., and Abraham's trust in verse 6 is called his righteousness, or the justification of his personal relations with Yahweh. Then follows the ritual sacrifice as part of a convenant ceremony (vv. 7–21). Now the covenant explicitly includes the promised land, which the Hebrews will fully possess after the exile in Egypt.[30] In 17:1–27 this covenant is repeated and circumcision is given as the sign of the covenant. In Genesis 18:1–22:24 the promise of progeny is fulfilled in Isaac, even though Abraham's faith is severely tested in the request to sacrifice his son. In this case, again, it is Abraham's faith in God that moves salvation history forward: Isaac is now not merely Abraham's son, but the son of Yahweh, destined in a special way to be the fulfillment of his work in history (21:3–21), and becomes the focal point of the next section of Genesis (25:19–36:43) together with his younger son, Jacob, who supplants Esau (25:22–34).

Finally, the patriarchal history concludes with the story of Joseph (37:1–50:26), who is sold by his brothers into slavery in Egypt. But through God's help he rises to power with the pharaoh and so is ascendent over his older brothers and father (37:5–11) when they must come to Egypt for grain during a famine. Thus Genesis concludes with the Jews as aliens in Egypt (ready to be oppressed), and so the stage is set for the liberation that we studied in chapter I. In all of this, the Old Testament presents us with a consistent plan of God to establish his people in the land of Canaan and to bless all nations in Abraham.

E. THE PRIESTLY CREATION ACCOUNT

After all of the foregoing was written, the Priestly writer came to write his account of creation and set it at the head of the whole Bible as a prologue to all of salvation history. The plan that the J writer had given was set in a new context and given a deeper meaning.

"When God began to create the heavens and the earth, the earth was disorganized and chaotic matter."[31] Our first view of the Old Testament God (Gen 1:1) is as the creator of heaven and earth.[32] However, this is not a metaphysical statement; this is Yahweh's first act of salvation history. Ancient humankind perceived the world as a flux of chaotic, uncontrollable elements, and so to be feared—earthquakes, destructive winds, wild animals, disease, and the evil will of people. The ancients feared especially the chaotic power of water—thunderstorms, heavy crop-destroying rains, floods, even drought. Thus ancient Near Eastern myths conceived of creation as a struggle between the chaotic water powers, pictured as sea serpents or astral forces, and the god who produced order at the end of a titanic struggle. Israelite theology, on the other hand, begins by showing Yahweh liberating the world from the chaotic water powers effortlessly in creation, without any material supplied to him, and without any resistance from other powers.[33] Yet the natural disasters mentioned above continue to plague humankind. (Insurance companies refuse to cover them, since they are "acts of God"!) What then became of the liberation? The author does not address that question until Genesis 2–3, where the Yahwist pins all disorder in the universe on humankind's sin. The ordering at the beginning was liberation; that is the brunt of P's message.

The author has arranged the world of creation into six days, the simpler inanimate creatures being created first, and then the animate world, and finally humanity at the summit.[34] Each "day" has a similar structure: (1) "God said, 'Let there be . . .' " and so, effortlessly, by his mere utterance of a supremely effective word, the various parts of the world came to be: "And so it was." (2) There follows a second stage, the description of what was done, in the terms of the common-sense Hebrew "science" of the day.[35] (3) God calls the new creature by its name, making it what it is (as Adam names the animals as part of the power God gives him in Gen 2:19f.). (4) "And God saw that it was good." Against those mythologies that find the earth and cosmic powers as demonic, or antigods at war with God, P affirms that the cosmos, as coming from the good God and subservient to his good intentions, is good in itself. (Further, in demythologizing creation,[36] Hebrew thought can open the way to an independent scientific study of the world apart from theology, and so to a conception of a dynamic drive to goodness and wholeness in the world, even apart from the order of grace.) (5) Finally, P closes each day with "Evening came and morning came; the —th day." With this five-step invariant scheme, then, the document must have been used in some liturgical setting, celebrating God's (kingly?) rule over the universe. It is clear that the author grounds the Hebrew observance of the Sabbath in God's own practice of resting on the seventh day (2:2–3); this is one of the major teachings of this creation account, an emphasis of the priestly class on Sabbath observance, which would be sharpened up to the time of Jesus.

Let us look more carefully at the creation of man on the sixth day (vv. 26–31). First, land animals and men are created on the same day, thus, as in the J account, teaching the continuity between humankind and the animal world and the whole material creation. Second, however, P abandons the third person imperative he had been using, "Let there be . . . ," and speaks of personal creation, "Let us make man," indicating a personal difference between people and animals. This is further taught by ". . . in our image and likeness." *Selem* ("image") is properly a statue, while *deṃūt* ("likeness") is a less exact and more analogous notion, weakening the first figure. The text seems to say that human dominion over the animals of the earth is a participation in God's own dominion. In order that people might "stand in" (the function of a statue) personally for God in the management of his world, they have to participate in the personal powers of mind and heart that God has. Therefore, it is the function of dominion that is primary, and makes people in God's image: the personal powers are attendant upon that image. In this sense, P's message is the same as J's: people are to manage this world as its summit or head, and so for God and in God's own authority.

When P comes to the second stage of creating people, he locates human imaging of God in different terms: male and female. It is in their sexual fertility ("Be fruitful, multiply, and fill the earth and conquer it"), expressed in both male and female, that humankind images God. This says that God is female as well as male, and tells much about the equality of the sexes.[37]

With this final giving of all creation to human beings to be multiplied and managed in God's name and image, God rests. And so all creation is caught up in a solemn liturgical motion toward God through man and woman.

F. SUMMARY

We have now considered the Torah (the first five books of the Old Testament) and some of the historical writings, and so we can form a foundational picture of the Old Testament God.

God is the creator of a good heaven and earth, liberating the world from the powers of chaos. He gives this world to humankind as the head of creation to manage in his name. Since the manager is personal, God creates woman, imaging another aspect of his own personality, to share everything with the man on an interpersonal level.

But the gift implies a response and the response asked of humankind is to acknowledge its place as mediator between God and the world. This obedience humankind refuses, and in so doing unleashes a miasma of sin on the world: the sin ruptures relations between God and man, man and woman, man and man, and man and world, because one cannot be at enmity with one without being at enmity with the others. The death promised to Adam as a punishment for disobedience breaks out on the first "historical" man, when Cain kills Abel. And God then shows himself as the guarantor of human justice because the blood of oppressed people cries out to him for vengeance. Crimes against men and women are crimes against God and the world, which God will right.[38]

Sin, however, is contagious and spreads over the whole race to Noah and after Noah to Babel. It becomes clear that humankind cannot save itself from sin. It can be saved only if God takes a personal hand in human history by working in and through Abraham.[39] What is asked of Abraham is trust and obedience, a willingness to face the uncertainties of a future under God's guidance alone. Abraham answers this invitation and enters into a covenant with Yahweh for prosperity in a promised land. His descendants eventually migrate to Egypt in search of grain and as aliens are pressed into slavery by the Egyptians.

At this point Yahweh intervenes by revealing himself to Moses as the Lord of history, faithfully present in the future of those who follow him. He enspirits his people and leads them out of slavery in Egypt. He delivers them physically through the Reed Sea and the years in the desert and leads them by the Holy War into conquest of the land that they had been promised in the covenant. All of this was the act of mother love.

But the gifts of creation and liberation must elicit also human free response, cooperation, and responsible action for freedom. And so Yahweh is part of the movement toward national government, in the judges, Saul, and eventually the monarchies of David and Solomon. More importantly, God commands the Hebrews to live up to the measure of justice which is God's by entering into a covenant with them at law. The laws governing their relations to God are mostly aimed at producing justice, love, and peace with their fellow Hebrews. This law extends into the fundamental relationships of any well-ordered society: protection of life, distribution of property, protection of the reproductive and educational unit (family), and promotion of truth and honesty among people. In creating justice in human society, men and women truly manage this world's goods as God's gift and return to the paradisaical world from which sin subtracted them. All of this is the act of God's father love.

Thus the promise and the covenants are God's way of counteracting and overcoming the contagion of sin that humankind has unleashed. That this duel between good and evil persists throughout human history is the theme of the rest of this book.

V. The Prophetic Recall to Justice

A. THE NATURE OF PROPHECY

Generally we consider the prophet as one who predicts the future. In this sense the Greek word *prophētēs* would be derived from *pro* ("before") plus *phēmi* ("speak")—to say something before it happened. However, the Greek verb had previously another meaning: *pro* ("in front of, publicly") plus *phēmi*—to proclaim to the crowd what the god had given one to say, as at the Delphic oracle. Even more significantly for the Old Testament understanding of the word, the Hebrew *nābî'* ("prophet") probably comes from an Akkadian word meaning "the called." So in Hebrew the meaning is of someone called by Yahweh to be his spokesperson, to proclaim Yahweh's message to the people.

There were throughout the ancient Near East (especially in Babylonia and Canaan) individuals who were given the job of speaking for the god, or bands of men who were "ecstatics" and gave their oracles in the throes of divine "possession." One can find evidences of this latter in premonarchic Israel (see 1 Sam 10:5–13; 19:20–24), the "sons of the prophets" (="professional prophets"). Such bands surrounded Elijah and Elisha (2 Kings 2:3–17; 4:1, 38–44; 9:1–10). Nevertheless, though Israelite prophecy had this continuity of form with the Near Eastern culture of its time, its own content eventually caused it to be something unique.

Samuel is, formally, the first Hebrew prophet, but he combined many functions, that of seer (like a Mesopotamian diviner who could find lost animals, 1 Sam 9:9), and of judge, active in the internal and external politics of Israel. It was Elijah who first began to exercise classical Hebrew prophecy in his denunciation of Ahab's sin in 1 Kings 21:17–24. Over the course of Hebrew prophecy this concern with Israel's injustice and sin will come to be dominant and characteristic of Hebrew prophecy (rather than the ecstasy or a vision of the future).

It is true that there must have been some special contact of the prophet with God. The prophets were not simply profoundly reflective religious thinkers, for they never announce their oracles as their own, but usually in the formula, "The Word of the Lord came to me." We do not know whether the experience they had was an ecstatic one or a quieter mystical experience of another Person immense and irresistible, whose word they had to proclaim whether they wanted to or not (see Amos 3:3–8; Jer 20:7–9).

However, it is the ethical content of the message that distinguishes Hebrew prophecy. We have seen something of Yahweh's insistence on social justice as religious obedience (chaps. III and IV, above). During the time of the prophets these laws stressing justice were being preached and elaborated and acted upon in both the North and the South. At this time, for example, the traditions behind Deuteronomy were being formulated.[1] In the eyes of the circle that produced this book, it was simply God's love as free gift that produced the people of the covenant (Deut 4:37; 7:7–15). This gift elicited a response of love from the Hebrews that is manifested in obedience to God's law of justice to one's fellow person (Deut 6:4–9).[2] For example, the Sabbath observance in Deuteronomy 5:15 is now seen as motivated by the Hebrews' love of the oppressed, for they too had been oppressed and needed rest from work in Egypt. (Note also the tone of the laws in 19:1–25:19). Further, if the Hebrews observed the commands, they would find peace and prosperity in the land: "Keep his laws and commandments as I [Moses] give them to you today, so that you and your children may prosper, and live long in the land that Yahweh your God gives you forever" (Deut 4:40). The theme that obedience to the laws produces prosperity recurs in Deuteronomy 5:29, 33; 6:1–3, 18; 7:12–15, etc. Prosperity is explicitly conditioned on observance of the laws ("*if* you obey . . . '') in Deuteronomy 11:13–15; 28:1–14, and that implies that if they do not keep the covenant law they will not prosper, but will be driven out, as in 11:16f.; 28:15–68, etc. That this is the theology of Deuteronomy is made abundantly clear by having the Deuteronomic Code (12–26) end with the ancient formula of the covenant-making:

> Yahweh your God today commands you to observe these laws and customs; you must keep and observe them with all your heart and with all your soul.
>
> You have today made this declaration about Yahweh; that he will be your God, but only if you follow his ways, keep his statutes, his commandments, his ordinances, and listen to his voice. And Yahweh has today made this declaration about you: that you will be his very own people as he promised you, but only if you keep all his commandments; then for praise and renown and honour he will set you high above all the nations he has made, and you will be a people consecrated to Yaweh, as he promised (Deut 26:16–19).

This covenant theology mentioned above (p. 34),[3] which was at work in the law, was also at work in the prophets, so that the law and prophets interacted upon one another. The prophets presume at all times a law oriented to human justice as the context of their preaching. Since that law was unique in the Near East, so is the emphasis on social justice unique to Israelite prophecy. You may search ancient literatures, but you will not find other prophets who spoke to their king as Nathan did to David or Amos to Israel. The Hebrew prophet's experience was of a God so concerned with human social justice and the demands he made on his covenanted people that he was compelled to pour scalding words on his own people's infidelity to the law. If the prophet spoke of the future it was only to foresee medicinal judgment on Israel for infidelity and exploitation of men and women or consolation for the nation that had repented and returned to the law of interhuman justice. Thus the nature of prophecy in Israel was to be the God-given social conscience of Israel.

B. AMOS

The first Hebrew prophet whose writings we have is Amos, a shepherd from Tekoa, just south of Jerusalem. He was active at a time of prosperity and strong national consciousness, probably around 750 B.C., when, under the leadership of Jeroboam II, Israel had reached the summit of its power and a strong Judah was at peace with Israel.

However, the prosperity was achieved at greater disruption of the social order than we saw under Solomon. Added to many of Solomon's expenses, continued by the royal family of Omri, was the outlay required for continual war, both dynastic and foreign. Further, the process of buying up lands had been continued for two hundred years by now and the cities (as we recover them by archeology) showed a clear-cut separation of the luxurious homes of the rich from the hovels of the proletariat in the poorer parts of the city. Amos himself fills in the details: the rich lived not only in houses of dressed stone in cities, but also had summer houses in the country. Their wives reclined on ivory couches, ate lambs and calves specially fattened for their tables, hired muscians for home entertainment, and drank the finest wines. They cared neither for the poor nor for the country itself, but only for their greater luxury. Israelites were sold into slavery, often unjustly in courts where judges were bribed. Since in a small state like Israel only a few could be wealthy, merchants struggled to cheat the farmer and one another with false weights and measures, and large landowners foreclosed on the hard-pressed farmer at the earliest opportunity.[4] The religion of Yahweh, which had stressed the social justice of covenant law, had fallen from its primitive observance and was even threatened by Ahab's syncretism with the Phoenician cult, which had no interest in justice, but only in more fertility from land and flocks.

It is in this atmosphere, then, that Amos opens with oracles against the surrounding nations (1:3–2:16) because of their cruelty in war, slave traffic, desecration of tombs, etc. However, it is against the covenanted people of Judah and Israel that Amos unleashes Yahweh's major threats. Israel is the actual target of Amos' prophetic mission, and so he assails Israel in the last, climactic place:

> . . . because they have sold the virtuous man for silver
> and the poor man for a pair of sandals,
> because they trample on the heads of ordinary people
> and push the poor out of their path,
> because father and son have both resorted to the same girl,
> profaning my holy name,
> because they stretch themselves out by the side of every altar
> on clothes acquired as pledges,
> and drink the wine of the people they have fined
> in the house of their god . . . (Amos 2:6b–8).

Clearly what stirs the wrath of Yahweh is that the rich can either sell a poor person into slavery or can bribe judges to condemn an innocent person. Note that the victim is called a virtuous (righteous, just, *saddîq*) man. Exodus 21 recognized slavery as a fact and tried to control it. Is Amos now making an advance by saying that only the irreligious or only those who fell into debt because of dishonest manipulations should be sold into slavery? More likely Amos is simply reacting to what he sees: hardworking people who have tried to make an honest living from the soil have been manipulated by the system until now their lands and they themselves are sold by the court into slavery. He knows no "economic theory"; he knows only that this is intolerably against Yahweh's plan for Israel. In a word, what is being done may be "legal" by some interpretation of the law, but it is not lawful in terms of the morality Yahweh has given his people.[5] And so Yahweh is going to intervene against the oppressors. The general rule in Israel (v. 7a) is that the rich exploit ordinary people, not just in economics, but even in relationships of love, where a female slave (7b) is forced to become a concubine of both father and son. This is a profanation of Yahweh's holy name.[6]

However, it is verse 8 that contains the ultimate horror: those who have prosecuted the poor and taken their clothes and wine as legal pledges now sacrilegiously bring these extorted possessions into the holy house of the Lord himself![7] In no way could the Israelites have done this—did they not know that the very God whose temple they entered was the one who had driven out the Amorites as oppressors (v. 9) and led in the Israelites as the dispossessed and oppressed (v. 10)? "It is Yahweh [savior of the oppressed] who is speaking!" In fact, the Israelites have even taken the persons consecrated by Yahweh to awaken them to his original justice and tried to pervert and muzzle them,[8] thus denying the role and identity of Yahweh not only in the past but in the present. And so, since they have turned away from Yahweh's law,[9] he will punish them (presumably until they are converted and reawaken to the covenant law, though Amos does not say this here).

The rest of the book is aimed explicitly at Israel, against whom Amos was summoned from his flocks to prophesy (7:14f.). He includes the larger themes of Israel's theology:

1. *Israel's election:* Yahweh has led all the migrations of history (9:7, the Philistines from Caphtor and the Syrians from Kir), for he is Lord of history.[10] Israel's Exodus was one of those movements. What made it special is that Yahweh revealed himself to Israel and made it a special relationship of mutual knowledge. Therefore Israel, in turning from what it knew Yahweh is and does (justice), was especially false to him; and in faithfulness to his personal relationship he must punish Israel: "You alone, of all the families of earth have I acknowledged; therefore it is for all your sins that I mean to punish you" (3:2). The punishment, however, is a part of the election.

2. *A purified remnant* will emerge to inherit the promise: Yahweh has punished them, so far without effect (4:6–11), but now he will make the punishment stick:

> In every public square there will be lamentation,
> in every street wails of "Alas! Alas!"
> Peasants will be called on to lament
> as well as the professional mourners
> and there will be wailing in every vineyard,
> for I am going to pass through you,
> says Yahweh (Amos 5:16f.).

Everything will come to a climax on "the Day of Yahweh":[11]

> Trouble for those who are waiting
> so longingly for the day of Yahweh!
> What will this day of Yahweh mean for you?
> It will mean darkness, not light,
> as when a man escapes a lion's mouth,
> only to meet a bear;
> he enters his house and puts his hand on the wall,
> only for a snake to bite him.

Will not the day of Yahweh be darkness, not light?
It will all be gloom, without a single ray of light (Amos 5:18–20).

The Israelites will be led into captivity:[12]

> Now see, you House of Israel,
> how I am stirring up against you . . .
> a nation that will harry you from the Pass of Hamath
> right down to the wadi of Arabah (Amos 6:14).

> Your wife will be forced to go on the streets,
> your sons and daughters will fall by the sword,
> your land be parcelled out by measuring line,
> and you yourself die on unclean soil
> and Israel will go into exile
> far distant from its own land (Amos 7:17).

In exile, however, they will turn to the Lord, and a remnant will be saved:[13]

> Like a shepherd rescuing a couple of legs
> or a bit of an ear from the lion's mouth,
> so will these sons of Israel be rescued,
> who now loll in Samaria
> on the corner-pillows of their divans (Amos 3:12).

> Yet I am not going to destroy
> the House of Jacob completely. . . .
> I mean to restore the fortunes of my people Israel;
> they will rebuild the ruined cities and live in them,
> plant vineyards and drink their wine,
> dig gardens and eat their produce.
> I will plant them in their own country,
> never to be rooted up again
> out of the land I have given them (Amos 9:8c, 14f.).

3. *False worship* is also attacked by Amos:

> All who swear by Samaria's Ashimah,
> those who swear, "By your god's life, Dan!"
> and, "By your Beloved's life, Beersheba!"
> these shall all fall, never to rise again (Amos 8:13c–14).

It is possible that—as the Jerusalem Bible takes it—this is an indictment of idolatry.[14] However, this is not Amos' ordinary attack on false worship, which centers on trying to offer sacrifice to Yahweh while at the same time ignoring and even transgressing his demands for justice:

> Go to Bethel and sin,
> to Gilgal, and sin your hardest!
> Offer your sacrifices each morning
> and your tithes on the third day,
> burn leavened dough as a sacrifice with praise,
> announce your voluntary offerings, make them public,
> for this is what makes you happy,
> sons of Israel (Amos 4:4–5).

With biting irony, Amos invites the Israelites to their accustomed shrines: "Follow your rituals (tithes, bread, offerings) perfectly, since it makes you happy to observe them. But it will do no good, for you continue to sin, and you mix it with the offerings in such a way that Yahweh has no choice but to punish you [see 4:6]. Your offering is no good." He is more explicit in this celebrated passage:

> I hate and despise your feasts,
> I take no pleasure in your solemn festivals.
> When you offer me holocausts, . . .
> I reject your oblations,
> and refuse to look at your sacrifices of fattened cattle.
> Let me have no more of the din of your chanting,
> no more of your strumming on harps.
> But let justice flow like water,
> and integrity like an unfailing stream (Amos 5:21–24).

Some interpreters have made this and similar prophetic passages into a prohibition of any form of cult, so as to produce only a "worship in spirit and truth" (Jn 4:24). It is agreed today that this is *not* what the prophets meant.[15] Amos here is simply saying that no cult offered to God without a corresponding determination to work for justice can be true worship or be accepted by God. Liturgy is the place where persons acknowledge where they are going in community. If they are failing in political and economic life, there will be failure in their worship. Nevertheless, cult, as rooted in imagination and sensation, has the power to open the person to God's conversion to justice in day-to-day living.

This oracle, then, returns us to the main burden of Amos' prophecy as he exhorts Israel:

> Seek good and not evil
> so that you may live,
> and that Yahweh, God of Sabaoth,
> may really be with you
> as you claim he is (Amos 5:14).

But the exhortation is not fully in earnest; Israel is marked down for judgment because of its luxury and injustice. Amos' vocation is to reveal the grounds for Yahweh's judgment (and so the nature of Yahweh):

4. Amos indicts *Israel's luxury* because it is the result of injustice:[16]

> Listen to this word, you cows of Bashan[17]
> living in the mountain of Samaria,
> oppressing the needy, crushing the poor,
> saying to your husbands, "Bring us something to drink!"
> The Lord Yahweh swears this by his holiness:
> The days are coming to you now
> when you will be dragged out with hooks,
> the very last of you with prongs (Amos 4:1–2).

Perhaps at first those who have profited might be portrayed as simply indifferent to the plight of the poor:

> Lying on ivory beds
> and sprawling on their divans,
> they dine on lambs from the flock,
> and stall-fattened veal;[18]
> they bawl to the sound of the harp,
> they invent new instruments of music like David,
> they drink wine by the bowlful,
> and use the finest oil for anointing themselves,
> but about the ruin of Joseph they do not care at all (Amos 6:4–6).

> I mean to pull down both winter houses and summer houses,
> the houses of ivory will be destroyed,
> the houses of ebony will vanish.
> It is the Lord Yahweh who speaks (Amos 3:15).

But clearly it is injustice that has produced this luxury:

Trouble for those who turn justice into wormwood,
throwing integrity to the ground;
who hate the man dispensing justice at the city gate
and detest those who speak with honesty.
Well then, since you have trampled on the poor man,
extorting levies on his wheat—
those houses you have built of dressed stone,
you will never live in them;
and those precious vineyards you have planted,
you will never drink their wine.
For I know that your crimes are many,
and your sins enormous:
persecutors of the virtuous, blackmailers,
turning away the needy at the city gate (Amos 5:7, 11–12).

It is injustice at the very courts of Israel's law, in the judgments of the elders in city gates, that is most foul. The law was the poor person's only hope, Yahweh's pledge to his people, and now this has been perverted. The acquisitive landowners hate the honest judge, and they get other judges who can be bribed, and so they trample the poor person. First they get the poor to sell their land to repay indebtedness, then they overtax the wheat crop on that land that the poor now only rent. They blackmail, persecute the virtuous, gouge the poor, to get the land clear (v. 12). Soon they will have it, but Yahweh will make sure that they never enjoy it, for he will vindicate justice, even if his judges will not. Though the gates are the focal point, it is in reality Israel's whole economic life that leads the poor person to this final travesty in the gates:

Listen to this, you who trample on the needy
and try to suppress the poor people of the country,
you who say, "When will New Moon be over
so that we can sell our corn,
and sabbath, so that we can market our wheat?
Then by lowering the bushel, raising the shekel,
by swindling and tampering with the scales,
we can buy up the poor for money,
and the needy for a pair of sandals,
and get a price
even for the sweepings of the wheat" (Amos 8:4–6).

Here again we meet the pseudo-piety of the merchants, who observe the holy days (of course, they would not ignore the holy days; was not Yahweh giving them their promised land of wealth?) with thinly veiled impatience to get on with the exploitation of the poor in the markets, which they controlled by stockpiling their grain. Not contented with merely manipulating the market prices, they went a step further and cheated the poor by using a falsified smaller measure for what they sold, and a falsified larger measure for what they bought.[19] Nor did the merchants neglect to sell even the chaff left over from the milling process (doubtless as good grain[20]). In verse 7, Yahweh binds himself by oath to act against these merchants, but to those who know Yahweh, it is superfluous—one knows instinctively that such injustice will be avenged by the avenger of the poor and the oppressed.

In sum, the book of Amos reveals in particular circumstances what we have discovered about Yahweh from the beginning. He has chosen Israel to embody his justice among all people, and he will make that people prosper as long as they observe interhuman justice. When, as in the case of Israel, the whole economic system, from merchant to law courts, is set up to defraud the poor and the weak, Yahweh will intervene, punishing that country through foreign invasion and exile until it eventually returns to the law of justice, which is his covenant, and so to peace and prosperity for all. Yahweh can be no other way.

C. ISAIAH

Ten to twenty years after Amos began his career in Israel, Isaiah ben Amoz and Micah of Moresheth began their prophetic ministries in Judah.[21] Socio-economic change had come early to powerful Israel, with its foreign relations for trade and its greater agricultural potential. It came later and with difficulty to little Judah, an isolated land tortured by steep hills and desert. Judah's chief source of income had been the religious pilgrimages to the Temple,[22] and Jeroboam had substituted shrines at Bethel and Dan to eliminate that. Judah was never fully able to exploit the copper trade of Etzion Geber, nor the mines of the Arabah as Solomon had. However, after Judah reconquered Edom (ca. 760), royal organization began to reshape the country. Diversified industries processed and exported dyes, wine, wool, and olives, possibly under the patronage of Assyria, with whom Judah had allied itself. When the Syro-Ephraimite league (Damascus and Samaria) attacked Judah in 735, Judah's King Ahaz appealed to Assyria for protection, which Assyria offered. However, Ahaz was then forced to Assyrianize the Temple—or he did it to curry favor with Assyria. And so the pure Yahwism of the South was abandoned through syncretism. This abandoning of Yahweh, the God of social ethics, justified what exploitation was going on in the new Judah.

In this environment, Isaiah received his call to prophecy. While in the Temple, he had a vision of the holiness of God:

> In the year of King Uzziah's death I saw the Lord Yahweh seated on a high throne; his train filled the sanctuary; above him stood seraphs, each one with six wings: two to cover its face, two to cover its feet, and two for flying.
>
> And they cried out one to another in this way,
>
> > Holy, holy, holy is Yahweh Sabaoth.
> > His glory fills the whole earth.
>
> The foundations of the threshold shook with the voice of the one who cried out, and the Temple was filled with smoke (Is 6:1–4).

The holiness of God is the central theme running through all of Isaiah's prophecy. On the one hand, it describes the numinous quality of God, which Rudolf Otto called the *mysterium tremendum et fascinans*.[23] On the other hand, it describes the passion for justice, for righteousness, with which Yahweh had stamped himself throughout his dealings with Israel. Therefore Isaiah's first reaction to this encounter with holiness is

> What a wretched state I am in! I am lost,
> for I am a man of unclean lips
> and I live among a people of unclean lips,
> and [yet] my eyes have looked at the King,
> Yahweh Sabaoth.

Then one of the seraphs flew to me, holding in his hand a live coal which he had taken from the altar with a pair of tongs. With this he touched my mouth and said,

> See now, this has touched your lips,
> your sin is taken away,
> your iniquity is purged (Is 6:5–7).

But the extirpation of sin from Israel, to which Isaiah was called, was not to be so easy (cf. 6:9–13). For both kingdoms were replete with injustice, as Isaiah poetically describes:

> My friend had a vineyard
> on a fertile hillside.
> He dug the soil, cleared it of stones,
> and planted choice vines in it.

In the middle he built a tower,
he dug a press there too.
He expected it to yield grapes,
but sour grapes were all that it gave.

And now, inhabitants of Jerusalem
and men of Judah,
I ask you to judge
between my vineyard and me.
What could I have done for my vineyard
that I have not done?
I expected it to yield grapes.
Why did it yield sour grapes instead? . . .
Yes, the vineyard of Yahweh Sabaoth
is the House of Israel,
and the men of Judah
that chosen plant.
He expected justice, but found bloodshed,
integrity, but only a cry of distress (Is 5:1c–4, 7).

The last line contains a poetic play on words: Yahweh has chosen Israel to produce *mishpât,* justice,[24] but it has produced *miśpâh,* bloodshed; he wanted *s^{e}daqâh,* righteousness, and got *s^e'âqâh,* an outcry. This confirms what we have seen all along—the purpose of Yahweh's choice of Israel was to establish interhuman justice.[25] The *sa'aq/za'aq* stem "outcry" is also found in the agonized pleas of victims in Genesis 4:10 (Abel's blood), Exodus 2:23; 3:9; 1 Samuel 9:16 (the oppressed Hebrews); Exodus 22:23 (widows and orphans). Thus this one word "outcry," occurring in all strands of the Old Testament revelation—narrative, legal, and prophetic—manifests Yahweh's nature as the one who hears and delivers the oppressed.

That Yahweh's complaint against the vineyard is specifically over Israel's social injustice is clear from the oracle Isaiah added immediately to the Song of the Vineyard:

Woe to those who add house to house
and join field to field
until everywhere belongs to them
and they are the sole inhabitants of the land.
Yahweh Sabaoth has sworn this in my hearing,
"Many houses shall be brought to ruin,
great and fine, but left untenanted;

ten acres of vineyard will yield only one barrel,
ten bushels of seed will yield only one bushel.''

Woe to those who from early morning
chase after strong drink,
and stay up late at night inflamed with wine.
Nothing but harp and lyre, tambourine and flute,
and wine for their drinking bouts.

Never a thought for the works of Yahweh,
never a glance for what his hands have done.
My people go into exile,
for want of perception;
her dignitaries dying of hunger,
her populace parched with thirst, . . .
for rejecting the law of Yahweh Sabaoth,
and despising the word of the Holy One of Israel.
(Is 5:8–13, 24d; cf. vv. 21–24c; Mic 2:1–5)

In the oracle of Isaiah 5:8–24 we recognize themes already set out by Amos: (1) the indifference of the rich to the plight of the poor and Yahweh's law (vv. 11–12); (2) unjust monopolizing of land, which brings down Yahweh's wrath (8–10); (3) punishment, leading even to exile for the injustice perpetrated. But what is especially characteristic of Isaiah is his title for Yahweh, "the Holy One of Israel" (5:24). With this title he ends the whole oracle, thus suggesting that Yahweh's holiness is what makes all of this unjust activity punishable.[26] That the source of Yahweh's case is lack of justice is made even clearer in his suit (*rîb*) against the elders of Judah:

Yahweh rises from his judgement seat,
he stands up to arraign his people.
Yahweh calls to judgement
the elders and princes of his people:

"You are the ones who destroy the vineyard
and conceal what you have stolen from the poor.
By what right do you crush my people
and grind the faces of the poor?"
It is the Lord Yahweh Sabaoth who speaks (Is 3:13–15).

Again, the first oracle of the book of Isaiah logically enough contains his main themes. It begins with the mournful accusation from Yahweh that Israel has rebelled against him, that "my people understands nothing"

(1:2f.). And what is the rebellion, the lack of knowledge? First, it could be idolatry, turning to other gods, as in the fertility religions mentioned later in the oracle (vv. 29–31 or in 17:9–11). In a fertility cult one attempts, by rites of sympathetic magic, to persuade the fertility god to make fertile the livestock, or to send the rains and the sun at the proper times, so that a harvest may be assured. What is changed is the heart of the god,[27] not the heart of the person. To turn to fertility gods is, then, not to understand true religion. Second, it is not necessary that Israelites turn to other gods to misunderstand: all they need do is in effect turn Yahweh into a magical god, to be placated by sacrifices and incense, by chanting and cult, and ignore his constant commands for the conversion of their hearts to turn to justice—and again they have not understood him. Such is the nature of mouth-worship:

> "What are your endless sacrifices to me?"
> says Yahweh.
> "I am sick of holocausts of rams
> and the fat of calves.
> The blood of bulls and of goats revolts me.
> When you come to present yourselves before me,
> who asked you to trample over my courts?
> Bring me your worthless offerings no more,
> the smoke of them fills me with disgust.
> New Moons, sabbaths, assemblies—
> I cannot endure festival and solemnity. . . .
> When you stretch out your hands,
> I turn my eyes away.
> You may multiply your prayers,
> I shall not listen.
> Your hands are covered with blood,
> wash, make yourselves clean.
>
> Take your wrong-doing out of my sight.
> Cease to do evil.
> Learn to do good, search for justice,
> help the oppressed,
> be just to the orphan,
> plead for the widow" (Is 1:11–17).

We saw this motif in Amos, but nowhere is it more forcefully or clearly stated than here.[28] True understanding of God and true worship of him can be made only by those who hunger and thirst for justice and practice it in their lives. The pious churchgoer who worships on Sunday and exploits (or allows exploitation of) his fellows during the week is not only a fraud, but is an idolator, even if that person is worshiping the one God. That person knows nothing.

Third, not understanding could mean the people's turning to foreign alliances to protect them from foreign invaders. Not only did Ahaz turn to the Assyrians to defend Judah from the Syro-Ephraimite league, but later in Isaiah's career Hezekiah turned to Egypt to help him throw off the Assyrian yoke that Ahaz had taken up. Isaiah inveighs against both alliances.

> You say, "We have made a covenant with Mot [Death],
> and with Sheol we have made a pact.
> The destructive whip, as it goes by, will not catch us,
> for we have made lies our refuge,
> and falsehood our shelter."
>
> That is why the Lord Yahweh says this:
> "See how I lay in Zion a stone of witness,
> a precious cornerstone, a foundation stone:
> The believer shall not stumble.
> And I will make justice the measure,
> integrity the plumb-line."
>   (Is 28:14–18; cf. also 30:1–5, 6–7)

Hezekiah had made an alliance with Egypt, symbolized by the god Death,[29] to escape the destruction that Assyria had wreaked on Israel in 732–722. But this was to know nothing, for Egypt itself was too weak, a "broken reed . . . which pricks and pierces the hand of the man who leans on it" (Is 36:6). Further, it was not to know Yahweh, for making an alliance with a foreign country meant making an alliance with the god of the country.[30] More profoundly, however, it was not to know the true religion of Yahweh, for to live by his law of justice would produce in the land the prosperity and peace that is the only protection against foreign aggression. Thus the law of Yahweh is the cornerstone on which security can be built, justice and integrity the measure of a flourishing society. Once Yahweh's true religion is observed, then Judah will be great. In this sense Yahweh is not only Israel's Rock of salvation but the Lord of history, and so only he is finally effective in saving Israel's remnant (31:1–3).

And that leads us back to the complete sense in which the people know nothing—the one Isaiah adds immediately to Yahweh's accusation in 1:2f.: they have turned from Yahweh to injustice, and this is a violation of Yahweh's holiness, which insists on interhuman justice:

> A sinful nation, a people weighed down with guilt,
> a breed of wrong-doers, perverted sons.

> They have abandoned Yahweh,
> despised the Holy One of Israel,
> they have turned away from him (Is 1:4).

Isaiah spells out this indictment against the women of Jerusalem, dressed in their haute-couture finery while others starve (3:16–24), against priests and false prophets, who babble drunkenly (28:7–13), but especially against the judges who are supposed to administer justice, but who issue tyrannical decrees, cheat the poor, widow, and orphans, to grow wealthy on bribes (10:1–4). This injustice, endemic in the whole people, this wholesale rejection of the law of justice of the Holy One, is what Isaiah means when he says the people do not know Yahweh.

For this, punishment is necessary until Israel repents and a purified remnant returns (Is 1:18–20; 6:12f.; 14:1–2). Here Isaiah introduces a new concept for the glorious future. Whereas it has been the leaders of the people, the judges and kings, who have led Israel in its law-breaking, instead of upholding the law of justice, it will be a new ideal king, a true successor to the promise of Yahweh to David in 2 Sam 7:12–16, who will be an agent of the renewed remnant Israel. Disappointed with the parade of kings in Israel and Judah who have failed to be administrators of the law, who have turned from reliance on Yahweh's covenant to engage in foreign entanglements, Isaiah depicts the ideal king in 32:1–5.

This king is the subject of the famous messianic oracles of Is 6–12. Early in the reign of Ahaz, Isaiah communicated to him oracles that assured him that fidelity to the Lord would deliver his people. As a sign of this, he delivered the famous Immanuel prophecy:

> It is this: the maiden is with child
> and will soon give birth to a son
> whom she will call Immanuel.
> On curds and honey will he feed
> until he knows how to refuse evil
> and choose good.
> For before this child knows how to refuse evil
> and choose good,
> the land whose two kings terrify you
> will be deserted (Is 7:14–16).

That is to say, some woman (probably Ahaz's wife) will soon bear a son (probably Hezekiah, one of two kings praised by the Deuteronomic history for returning the people to true worship of Yahweh). Because of the destruction wrought on Judah by the Syro-Ephraimite league, livestock and harvests will be devastated, and the child will have to live on simple pastoral food. But by the time he is twelve or so, Israel and Syria will be shattered and a new reign will dawn in Judah—under this messiah, anointed king of David's line. He will be king not only for Judah, but for the northern kingdom (Galilee) too (9:1-2):

> For there is a child born for us,
> a son given to us,
> and dominion is laid on his shoulders;
> and this is the name they give him:
> Wonder-Counsellor, Mighty-God,
> Eternal-Father, Prince-of-Peace.
> Wide is his dominion in a peace that has no end,
> for the throne of David
> and for his royal power,
> which he establishes and makes secure
> in justice and integrity.
> From this time onwards and for ever,
> the jealous love of Yahweh Sabaoth will do this (Is 9:6-7).

Note that Yahweh's power is founded on justice and integrity. An even more poetic passage depicting this time of the perfect kingdom of God in Judah is found in Isaiah 11:1-9, where the king, in contrast to Judah's judges, will judge not by appearances, but with integrity. These three oracles make clear that, for Isaiah, the promise of a future everlasting king of David's line who will reign on Yahweh's holy mountain, Mount Zion (where Jerusalem was built), is a more important covenant than the Sinai covenant. The covenant of the law at Sinai plays almost no role in Isaiah. It is Yahweh's identity as King of Judah that makes law and justice so important to Judah, and the ideal king who rules in his stead reigns on Zion because then cult (the Temple in Jerusalem) and kingly power (administration of justice) are joined in Yahweh's perfect kingdom.

Finally, Isaiah indicates that this kingdom is not just for Israel and Judah, but will extend to all nations as well.[31] This was intimated by the fact that Yahweh is the ruler of all nations (he whistles up Assyria like a dog to do his bidding in punishing Israel, 5:26, and he punishes the nations for their injustices in chaps. 13–23). Moreover, in the midst of his vision of the ideal kingdom, which he describes under the symbol of a banquet, there are the Gentiles:

> On this mountain
> Yahweh Sabaoth will prepare for all peoples

> a banquet of rich food, a banquet of fine wines. . . .
> On this mountain he will remove
> the mourning veil covering all peoples,
> and the shroud enwrapping all nations,
> he will destroy Death for ever.
> The Lord Yahweh will wipe away
> the tears from every cheek;
> he will take away his people's shame
> everywhere on earth . . . (Is 25:6–8).

Yahweh's people is still his people, and their perseverance through their punishment will be rewarded by the reestablishment of their kingdom. But it is no selfish victory; as Israel's revelation was not only for itself, now the nations will see the consummation of Yahweh's plan. But how? There is an oracle, quoted also by Micah 4:1–4, which makes this clear:

> In the days to come
> the mountain of the Temple of Yahweh
> shall tower above the mountains
> and be lifted higher than the hills.
> All the nations will stream to it,
> peoples without number will come to it, and they will say:
> "Come, let us go up to the mountain of Yahweh,
> to the Temple of the God of Jacob
> that he may teach us his ways
> so that we may walk in his paths;
> since the law will go out from Zion,
> and the oracle of Yahweh from Jerusalem."
> He will wield authority over the nations
> and adjudicate between many peoples;
> these will hammer their swords into ploughshares,
> their spears into sickles.
> Nation will not lift sword against nation,
> there will be no more training for war (Is 2:2–4).

Note that it is the mountain of the *Temple* (not of the king) that is central here; it is Yahweh's holy presence among his people as justice to which the people come. And they come to learn his ways of conduct, so they might walk in his paths. The law goes out from Yahweh in Zion (undoubtedly through the messianic king, but Yahweh is the real source), and when people observe this, justice comes to the world so that there will be war no more. (Micah concludes the oracle with, "The mouth of Yahweh Sabaoth has spoken it!")

A very late oracle of the Isaian school (19:19–21) extends Yahweh's salvation even to the hated enemy, the Egyptians! The only condition is that they cry out (*sa'aq*) from the midst of oppression to Yahweh, and he will send them a savior. And so the forgiving God, Yahweh, is tender to whoever is oppressed, even former oppressors, for his is always justice delivering the oppressed to justice and peace.

And so the theology that Isaiah has elaborated throughout his career and his book is practically contained in the first two chapters: Yahweh has given his people his law, and they have ignored it. They do not know the nature of true religion, for they turn from Yahweh's command to do justice to each other, and they seek other gods, other alliances, empty cult. Meanwhile, the rich rob the poor through bribes and extortion. For this Judah will be punished until an ideal king of David's line can bring them once again to the practice of the law. In this renewed Israel justice will be done, and the nations of the earth will come to learn Israel's justice from the law of Yahweh himself, and so there will be no more wars and every tear will be wiped away. The Holy One of Israel will see his justice spread throughout the earth which he has made.

D. JEREMIAH

We cannot recapitulate all the history that passed between the time of Isaiah and that of Jeremiah. In brief, the modest religious reform of Hezekiah (715–687) was overturned by Manasseh's (687–642) reintroduction of Assyrian astral deities and Canaanite fertility gods into Judah, which in turn was attacked by Josiah's radical religious reform based on Deuteronomy (640–609).[32] Jeremiah was probably a willing partner, if not a leader, of this reform, which embodied a solemn ceremonial recommitment of the people to covenant law, the destruction of the sanctuaries in the "high places," and centralization of the cult in the Jerusalem Temple where its purity could be controlled.

Politically, Judah had to pay heavy tribute to Assyria through most of the seventh century, and almost all its political alliances were disasters. Thus even the inheritance of a part of Israel's economy after its fall in 722 by no means made Judah prosperous. Pharaoh Neco, after defeating Josiah in 609, appointed Jehoiakim king of Judah, and he paid enormous tribute to Neco, exacted by a tax on the ordinary citizens of the land (2 Kings 23:33f.). Wealth concentrated in Jerusalem, and the countryside declined—a situation Jeremiah attacked. In 605 the Babylonians defeated the Egyptians, and Jeremiah began prophetically advising Judah to submit to Babylon's relatively enlightened rule, which permitted a certain amount of religious and political independence to its vassal states. But Jeremiah was considered a traitor, and the confusion of nationalism and religion that prevailed led to Judah's defeat in 597 and the deportation of its leaders (including the new king, Jehoiakim) to Babylon. The next king, Zedekiah, made the same fatal mistake of revolting against Babylon, and so Jerusalem was sacked in 586, the Temple pillaged, and a second wave of leaders, including Jeremiah (who died shortly after), was deported to Babylon.

In most respects Jeremiah's message is the same as that of his predecessors in prophecy: attack on apostasy from Yahweh (2:13, 20–25; 5:7f.; 7:16–20, etc.), expressed in terms of mouth-worship (7:1–15, 21–26; 9:24ff.; 11:15; 22:13–17; 34:1–22, etc.), reliance on foreign alliances (chaps. 27–28, etc.), violent injustice in the land (5:1–5; 9:1–9, etc.), and the doctrine of punishment, repentance, and the remnant's return (3:14–18, etc.). The student can find all of this in Jeremiah's writings. As representative of his thought, let us take the famous Temple sermon delivered by Jeremiah around 608 B.C. Sennacherib had been defeated at the walls of the Temple in 701, and since then the prevailing belief in Judah was that Yahweh's presence in the Temple made both it and the city immune to foreign attack. Jeremiah attacks this complacent reliance on externals and institutions:

> Put no trust in delusive words like these: This is the sanctuary of Yahweh, the sanctuary of Yahweh, the sanctuary of Yahweh! But if you do amend your behavior and your actions, if you treat each other fairly, if you do not exploit the stranger, the orphan, and the widow (if you do not shed innocent blood in this place), and if you do not follow alien gods, to your own ruin, then here in this place I will stay with you, in the land that long ago I gave to your fathers forever. Yet here you are, trusting in delusive words, to no purpose! Steal, would you, murder, commit adultery, perjure yourselves, burn incense to Baal, follow alien gods that you do not know?—and then come presenting yourselves in this Temple that bears my name, saying: Now we are safe—safe to go on committing all these abominations! Do you take this Temple that bears my name for a robbers' den? I, at any rate, am not blind—it is Yahweh who speaks (Jer 7:4–11; cf. vv. 12–15).

Jeremiah is attacking that false security in institutions of religion that allows us to neglect interhuman justice as the core of our religious observance of God. This was what Yahweh tried to avoid in the famous oracle to David, when he refused to be tied down in a Temple (2 Sam 7:6f.).

Now this understanding that a central institution of Israel's faith is passing away (Jer 7:14), destroyed because of the people's infidelity, is the key to the two new elements in Jeremiah's prophecy. He foresaw that all of Judah's institutions would pass away—the kingship (22:29f.), the Temple (7:14f.), the ark (3:16)—and even that there would be no priestly instruction in the future (31:34). He even understood that Israel's disobedience to the covenant—the covenant of circumcision (Gen 17:9–14; Jer 9:24–26) no less than the Exodus covenant (Jer 11:1–8)—meant that at its heart Israel's relation to God must be restructured:

See, the days are coming—it is Yahweh who speaks—when I will make a new covenant with the House of Israel (and the House of Judah), but not a covenant like the one I made with their ancestors on the day I took them by the hand to bring them out of the land of Egypt. They broke that covenant of mine. . . . No, this is the covenant I will make with the House of Israel when those days arrive. . . . Deep within them I will plant my Law, writing it on their hearts. Then I will be their God and they shall be my people. There will be no further need for neighbour to try to teach neighbour, or brother to say to brother, "Learn to know Yahweh!" No, they will all know me, the least no less than the greatest—it is Yahweh who speaks—since I will forgive their iniquity and never call their sin to mind (Jer 31:31–34).

This vision must have come as a profound shock to Jeremiah himself. He had been raised in a tradition which understood that institutions were part and parcel of Yahweh's relations with Israel (see chaps. II and III, above). And yet now they were to pass away and the remnant's relationship to God would be structured by something within people.[33]

The second aspect of Jeremiah's new vision, however, goes even further. The previous prophets had spoken against the unjust acquisition of riches. But there was a residual feeling that God would reward with wealth in this life the one who served God's law. The very promise to Abraham, the legal codes, the psalms, the Wisdom writings—all contain this theology.[34] Jeremiah attacks this theology at root:

> "Only the poor people," I thought, "behave stupidly,
> because they do not know what Yahweh requires,
> nor the ruling of their God.
> I will approach the men in power and speak to them,
> for these will know what Yahweh requires,
> and the ruling of their God."
> But these, too, had broken the yoke,
> had burst the bonds (Jer 5:4–5).

Jeremiah had not expected the poor farmers to be obeying God's law; their very lack of prosperity showed they were not observers, or they would not be poor.[35] But when Jeremiah discovered that the rich, who presumably were observers (that was why they were rich) were lawbreakers, this shattered not only his human expectations, and the whole covenant obedience→prosperity theology, but also the theology based on the prosperity in the land.[36] In short, everything on which the Jews based their security was potentially shattered by the deepest dimensions of this experience. How to refocus the Jewish vision is the task of postexilic theology, as we shall see in the next chapter.

E. SUMMARY

The prophets as a movement were the social conscience of Israel. They attacked the rich's exploitation of the poor because Yahweh's covenant law demanded not sacrifice but interhuman justice. Therefore the prophets labeled Israel as unfaithful to Yahweh whenever the people refused to do justice to their fellows. The prophets were especially horrified when the Israelites perverted true religion either by turning to the magical rites of the fertility cults or by turning the worship of Yahweh into mere "mouth-worship," unconnected with the human offering of a heart committed to justice. Yet gradually emergent in prophetic theology was the realization that the covenant theology and even the promise of prosperity had to give way in its own fashion to a theology of pure commitment to God in interhuman justice, without any reliance on institutions that froze the relationship into complacency. What became more and more important was the spirit of the laws, the spirit of the promise, the spirit of Yahweh, which lay not in the past but in the future.

VI. Wisdom and the Kingdom of God

This last chapter on the Old Testament will be a grabbag. On the one hand, we want to cover the last major category of Old Testament literature, the Wisdom writings, to see what they have to say about justice. On the other hand, we have been following a generally chronological course through the Old Testament and we want to see what the postexilic prophets say about justice. Further, we want to look briefly at a genre that replaces prophecy in late Judaism—apocalypticism. So this chapter is a *mélange* of different kinds of writings, from different periods of Israelite history.

A. WISDOM LITERATURE

"Wisdom literature" is an umbrella-concept covering many styles of writings, such as instructions on conduct of life, rules of etiquette, and dramatic poetry on the meaning of life or the essence of wisdom. In the ancient Near East there were many collections of works by professional scribes on how to succeed as a courtier or a scribe at court, "how to succeed in business by really trying." This kind of literature assumes that life is very much under control: hard work and diplomacy will produce success and prosperity. The book of Proverbs is a combination of this wisdom of the royal court (and so chaps. 10–22 probably go back as far as the court of Solomon, the traditional source of Israelite Wisdom literature), and other proverbs coined by simple peasants wrestling with the patterns of life ("a stitch in time saves nine"). Clearly the latter come from all periods of Israelite history. Proverbs in its present form probably comes from the fifth century B.C.

Proverbs contains for the most part simple advice on how to get ahead, quite apart from any truly ethical considerations (see 10:4). In fact, even justice or charity to the poor is seen to be inspired by self-interest:

He who gives to the poor shall never want,
he who closes his eyes to them will bear many a curse (Prov 28:27).

Do not denounce a slave to his master,
lest he curse you, and you suffer for it (Prov 30:10; cf. 23:10f.).

Yet the prologue to Proverbs (1:1–7) says the book is to teach genuine ethical conduct ("virtue, justice, and fair dealing," v. 3), and it even roots all its doctrine in fear of the Lord as the beginning of all knowledge (v. 7). Indeed, though such theological themes are not explicitly mentioned, it appears that the theme of following God's law to achieve peace with him and one's fellows (and so prosperity) had some vague influence on the collection as a whole (see 10:22).

> There are six things that Yahweh hates,
>   seven his soul abhors:
> a haughty look, a lying tongue,
>   hands that shed innocent blood,
> a heart that weaves wicked plots,
>   feet that hurry to do evil,
> a false witness who lies with every breath,
>   a man who sows dissension among brothers (Prov 6:16–19).

This ascription of justice to pleasing Yahweh is almost an isolated occurrence in Proverbs, and the vagueness of the crimes is rarely broken by anything as specific as the injustices to which the prophets referred.[1] On the whole, Proverbs is not much of a witness to the Old Testament God's passionate concern for interhuman justice as true religion, but it does see Yahweh as eventually rewarding justice in this life.

Two other books of Old Testament Wisdom literature, Qoheleth and Job, are less the work of collectors and show more unity of composition. Each has a different answer to the riddle of life. The author of Qoheleth (Ecclesiastes, the "Preacher") is considerably less optimistic about simple rules for success in life. He has seen virtuous people poor and criminals rich, and the vagaries of chance often seem to determine which is which. There is the eternal cycle of sun and stars, the round of the seasons, and perhaps a person can plan on that, but what otherwise happens to one simply happens, without explanation. There is a time for throwing stones and a time for gathering them up, but there is no way to know which is which (3:1–8). The old doctrine that God rewards the just in this life and punishes the wicked does not explain the Preacher's experience: he sees the wicked prosper, even to the time of their death. And so he takes refuge in cynicism—there is no making sense of this phenomenal flux. Even contradictions can be maintained: in 3:15 God cares for the persecuted, but in 4:1 there is no one to protect the oppressed. Everything is shadow, illusion, and emptiness (1:1–11), and so "eat, drink, and do your work" is Qoheleth's motto (2:24; 5:17; 8:15; 9:7).

Job, on the other hand, sees the same problem so personally that there can be no retreat to a redoubt of cynicism. He knows that he has committed no crime to merit the loss of children, flocks, and lands. Against the older covenant theology of his three friends, he protests his justice. Since they will not listen, he takes his case to Yahweh himself: "Why does the just man suffer?" And Yahweh gives him a devastating answer in chapter 38: "Do not ask!" That is to say, "If the just man suffers, he ought not to lose what small claim he has to being just by daring to ask the Divinity impertinent questions."[2]

Yet the question is really not impertinent; it is only difficult to answer. On the one hand, the answer ultimately is wrapped up in the mystery of God, and as such is unanswerable. But on the other hand, it may be that given ever new data, people can penetrate closer to an explanation which accords with the mystery. The prophetic covenant theology was one answer that by now was seen to be inadequate, for it flew in the face of human experience. The search for a more adequate explanation in the Old Testament will be a second theme (after the treatment of justice) throughout the rest of this chapter.

B. THE PSALMS

The book of Psalms is sometimes considered a separate category of Wisdom literature. However, these prayers, mostly cultic, cover the whole theology of the Old Testament and a long span of time, which makes them difficult to classify solely as Wisdom literature. They express praise, lament, thanksgiving, trust; some have a stylized form used for ceremonial purposes. Our concern with them here is to see if the theology we have discovered in the Old Testament was really so much a part of the Israelites' grasp of religion as to show up in their prayers.

The psalms certainly reflect Yahweh's passionate commitment to human justice as true religion. Psalm 9, for example, seems to be the thanksgiving of a king of Israel who had fought off foreign aggressors (vv. 3–5).[3] His thanks are expressed to Yahweh as to a king who judges justly (v. 4):

> See, Yahweh is enthroned for ever,
> he sets up his throne for judgement:
> he is going to judge the world with justice,
> and pronounce a true verdict on the nations.
> May Yahweh be a stronghold for the oppressed,
> a stronghold when times are hard.
> Those who acknowledge your name can rely on you,
> you never desert those who seek you, Yahweh (Ps 9:7–10).

And the psalmist adds the reason for this reliance:

> He, the avenger of blood, remembers them,
> he does not ignore the cry of the wretched (Ps 9:12).[4]

Again, Psalm 10, which probably originally formed one psalm with Psalm 9,[5] considers the matter of injustice within Israel. Against the unjust, who must believe that God (whose nature is to do justice) does not see them or will not act, the psalmist cries out to Yahweh:

> Rise, Yahweh, God raise your hand,
> do not forget the poor!
> Why does the wicked man spurn God,
> assuring himself, "He will not make me pay"?
> You yourself have seen the distress and the grief,
> you watch and then take them into your hands;
> the luckless man commits himself to you,
> you, the orphan's certain help (Ps 10:12–14).

The psalm ends on a note of tranquil confidence in such a God:

> Yahweh, you listen to the wants of the humble,
> you bring strength to their hearts,
> you grant them a hearing,
> judging in favour of the orphaned and exploited,
> so that earthborn man may strike fear no longer (Ps 10:17–18).

In other words, to say "Yahweh" is to say "the righter of injustices in human society":

> Yahweh, forever faithful,
> gives justice to those denied it,
> gives food to the hungry,
> gives liberty to prisoners.
> Yahweh restores sight to the blind,
> Yahweh straightens the bent,
> Yahweh protects the stranger,
> he keeps the orphan and widow.
> Yahweh loves the virtuous,
> and frustrates the wicked (Ps 146:7–9; cf. 72:12–14).

The psalmist (103:6) finally rises to the vision that the very nature of

Yahweh is the doing of justice: "Yahweh, who does what is right, is always on the side of the oppressed." And with that statement we see that in prayer Israel affirmed everything that had been revealed to it in history, in law, and in prophecy: Yahweh is always on the side of the oppressed.[6] In fact, the author of that psalm goes on to speak of this nature as revealed to Moses, and paraphrases the words of Exodus 34:6–7: Yahweh is tender and compassionate, slow to anger, most loving, etc. In the midst of all the words in which Yahweh is asked to lash out and vindicate the poor by smashing the oppressor it is good to remember that Yahweh is tender, and his justice is deliverance, not vindictiveness.[7]

Now if this is Yahweh's nature and his action, then his people must be like him, and the psalms carry this theology into human activity. Yahweh stands for justice and so he excoriates Israel's corrupt judges:

> No more mockery of justice,
> no more favouring of the wicked!
> Let the weak and the orphan have justice,
> be fair to the wretched and destitute;
> rescue the weak and needy,
> save them from the clutches of the wicked! (Ps 82:2–4).

And the king who rules in Israel is to be Yahweh's minister of justice:

> God, give your own justice to the king,
> your own righteousness to the royal son,
> so that he may rule your people rightly,
> and your poor with justice (Ps 72:1–2).

And this justice is said explicitly to be alleviation of oppression:

> He will free the poor man who calls to him,
> and those who need help;
> he will have pity on the poor and feeble,
> and save the lives of those in need;
> he will redeem their lives from exploitation and outrage,
> their lives will be precious in his sight (Ps 72:12–14).

Finally, even the ordinary citizen is called to the justice of Yahweh, for that is the meaning of the law he observes. The long Psalm 119, a prosaic encomium of the law, sums it up by saying: "May my tongue recite your promise, since all your commandments are justice " (v. 172). It is, then, in the doing of these commands, which are justice, that Israel is to become truly God's son, and bring peace to earth. When the people as a whole are unjust the psalmist uses the prophetic *rîb* form (see below, p. 174, n. 25) to have Yahweh call them to account:

> Listen, my people, I am speaking:
> Israel, I am giving evidence against you!
> I charge, I indict you to your face,
> I, God, your God.
> I am not finding fault with your sacrifices,
> those holocausts constantly before me; . . . [but that]
> you make friends with a thief as soon as you see one,
> you feel at home with adulterers,
> your mouth is given freely to evil
> and your tongue to inventing lies.
> You sit there, slandering your own brother,
> you malign your own mother's son.
> You do this, and expect me to say nothing?
> Do you really think I am like you? (Ps 50:7–8, 18–21).

Thus the emphasis on justice, repudiation of mouth-worship, and grounding of justice in the holy nature of Yahweh indicate a theology of human conduct in every respect congruent with the message of the prophets (see chap. V, above).

On the question of "justifying" God's punishments or rewards for people, by and large the psalms embody the prophetic covenant theology of retribution: the good prosper in this life and the wicked eventually are punished by losing their false prosperity. This is the basis of psalms of thanksgiving, where the pious thank God for delivery from oppressors, as well as of psalms of petition, where the obedience of the pious serves as the basis for asking for vindication from the surrounding enemies. The doctrine is stated clearly and simply in this so-called "Wisdom Psalm":

> Do not worry about the wicked,
> do not envy those who do wrong.
> Quick as the grass they wither,
> fading like the green in the field.
> Trust in Yahweh and do what is good,
> make your home in the land and live in peace (Ps 37:1–3).

Justice may be slow, but it is inevitable:

> A little longer, and the wicked will be no more,
> search his place well, he will not be there . . . (Ps 37:10).

The slowness may constitute a temptation for the just person to go and do evil, as the beautiful Psalm 73 indicates, but there is truth in Yahweh's way:

> My feet were on the point of stumbling,
> a little further and I should have slipped,
> envying the arrogant as I did,
> and watching the wicked get rich, . . .
> until the day I pierced the mystery
> and saw the end in store for them:
> they are on a slippery slope,
> you put them there,
> you urge them on to ruin,
> until suddenly they fall,
> done for, terrified to death (Ps 73:2–3, 17–19).

When the psalmist speaks of punishment he includes not only the wicked ones themselves, but also their children and descendants in general:

> Those who do wrong will perish once and for all, and the children of the wicked shall be expelled, . . . but sinners shall be destroyed altogether, the descendants of the wicked shall be wiped out (Ps 37:28,38).

This is merely the most devastating punishment of the wicked themselves (see Ps 109:9–14; Sir 41:5–9). In a society that did not believe in a genuine life after death, one's only immortality was in one's children living on, participating in the future life of the community. The community was immortal, not the individual.

However, this formulation was also open to the interpretation that if Yahweh did not catch the evildoers in this life (it is a fact of experience that some wicked die prosperous), then he would catch up with their children. Thus one could explain the apparent violation of the prophetic covenant theology of retribution by saying that the children would lose the wealth, be despicable people, etc. It is possible that such an interpretation could stand behind Sirach 41:5–9 or Wisdom 3:12. Such a theology, in any case, seems to be what is being attacked in Jeremiah 31:29f.:

> In those days people will no longer say:
> "The fathers have eaten unripe grapes;
> the children's teeth are set on edge."
> But each is to die for his own sin.
> Every man who eats unripe grapes is to have his own teeth set on edge.

(See also Ezek 18:1–4, 5–32, where the doctrine is more fully developed.)

Once this possibility of transferred punishment is excluded, then the problem of the wicked who prosper returns. If the lawbreakers wax fat, what has happened to Yahweh's providence for the poor? Is cheating, injustice, exploitation not preferable to living Yahweh's law? The problem of the suffering just person is poignantly expressed:

> My God, my God, why have you deserted me?
> How far from saving me, the words I groan!
> I call all day, my God, but you never answer,
> all night long I call and cannot rest. . . .
> Here am I, now more worm than man,
> scorn of mankind, jest of the people,
> all who see me jeer at me,
> they toss their heads and sneer,
> "He relied on Yahweh, let Yahweh save him!
> If Yahweh is his friend, let him rescue him!" (Ps 22:1–2, 6–8).

Not only does the just man find that the wicked prosper, but they also attack him, condemn him, even jeer at him because he supposes that Yahweh will rescue him. If Yahweh is so powerful and so caring, why do the just ones who call on him not attain deliverance? Yet this man struggles to believe: he knows that Yahweh has delivered his ancestors who trusted in him, and should save him now. If you read the whole psalm you will find that it is part of a thanksgiving ceremony, where a man *has* been delivered from his enemies. He comes into the Temple, recalls verbatim his lament in time of persecution, and recalls that the prayer was answered. Now he is offering his thanksgiving sacrifice to Yahweh, which he had vowed, and he calls the whole community in the Temple to join his hymn of praise to Yahweh the deliverer. Further, he even goes beyond and sees that the whole earth, past, present, and future generations, will praise the Lord who has delivered him and them (vv. 27–31). Although the lament has now been set in a scene of triumph, it is not easy to forget the anguish of the lament (vv. 1–24). Here is no facile theology of secure retribution. For those who have not been delivered the problem remains: is there a reward for those who persevere in the Lord's law in spite of the attacks of the oppressors? And does the intimation in 22:29f. of a triumphant life after death have anything to do with the answer?[8]

C. DEUTERO-ISAIAH[9]

This poet/prophet of the school of Isaiah during the exile resumes many of Isaiah's prophetic themes: (1) It is Yahweh who has punished his people with the Babylonian exile because they have sinned (e.g., Is 42:24); (2) and it is Yahweh who has rescued them when they have repented and turned to him (40:1–2);[10] (3) the remnant, then, is returning (40:3–5; 43:1–7, 19), (4) not just for itself, but for the salvation of all nations (42:1; 49:6). There is also an attack on idolatry throughout, because Yahweh is the creator, *the* (transcendent) God, and that is why he is Lord of history.

However, on the subject of social justice, it appears that Deutero-Isaiah's message of consolation to the returning people is so great that he does not attend to injustice. Not so Trito-Isaiah, who lived during the grinding poverty of the emerging nation that was rebuilding the ruins of Temple and city walls without any resources. He begins his work with "Have a care for justice, act with integrity, for soon my salvation will come and my integrity be manifest" (56:1); "the upright perish and no one cares" (57:1). In fact, third Isaiah castigates the people with the same specifics as did the first Isaiah:

> But your iniquities have made a gulf
> between you and your God, . . .
> your lips utter lies,
> your tongues murmur treachery.
> No one makes just accusations
> or pleads sincerely.
> All rely on nothingness,
> utter falsehood,
> conceive harm and give birth to misery (Is 59:2–4).

Again, the center of the complaint is the injustice done in the courts, where lying accusations are made and upheld. This chiefly legitimates the bloodshed and violence that stain the hands of those who are profiting. Indeed, "anyone who avoids evil is robbed" (59:15) and this means that the just person will necessarily suffer. It is only the Lord who will vindicate the just one, as in 59:17–19.[11]

The Lord will vindicate his oppressed one, Israel; and the foreign nations themselves, the ones who oppressed Israel, will come to serve Israel and there will be a reign of peace:

> Violence will no longer be heard of in your country,
> nor devastation and ruin within your frontiers. . . .
> Your people will all be upright,
> possessing the land for ever (Is 60:18,21).

And this time of peace is announced by the prophet himself:

> The Spirit of the Lord Yahweh has been given to me,
> for Yahweh has anointed me.
> He has sent me to bring good news to the poor,.
> to bind up hearts that are broken;
> to proclaim liberty to captives,
> freedom to those in prison;
> to proclaim a year of favour from Yahweh,
> a day of vengeance for our God . . . (Is 61:1–2).

Indeed, God must begin with justice to the oppressed, or the period of peace will never arrive. When justice begins to be done to the oppressed, the messianic age will begin.

But this means it is not just Yahweh alone who will bring justice; the people, under his guidance, must bring it about with their own justice. That is what underlies the horror of mouth-worship, turning to Yahweh piously for deliverance, while continuing to inflict injustice on the poor:

> They ask me for laws that are just,
> they long for God to draw near:
> "Why should we fast if you never see it,
> why do penance if you never notice?"
> Look, you do business on your fast days,
> you oppress all your workmen;
> look, you quarrel and squabble when you fast
> and strike the poor man with your fist.
> Fasting like yours today
> will never make your voice heard on high.
> Is that the sort of fast that pleases me,
> a truly penitential day for men?
> Hanging your head like a reed,
> lying down on sackcloth and ashes?
> Is that what you call fasting,
> a day acceptable to Yahweh?
> Is not this the sort of fast that pleases me
> —it is the Lord Yahweh who speaks—
> to break unjust fetters
> and undo the thongs of the yoke,
> to let the oppressed go free,
> and break every yoke,
> to share your bread with the hungry,
> and shelter the homeless poor,
> to clothe the man you see to be naked

and not turn from your own kin?
Then will your light shine like the dawn
and your wound be quickly healed over (Is 58:2c–8a).

That is the work of the Lord that will lead to the age of peace, and Trito-Isaiah affirms the whole Old Testament message up to his time, when he insists on the people's commitment to justice.

It is in the theology of retribution, however, that Deutero-Isaiah makes his most distinctive contribution. Embedded in his work are four songs in a highly personal style, written probably toward the end of Deutero-Isaiah's career. They designate a servant who is to bring Yahweh's salvation to the Gentiles. We do not know *who* the Servant is, and it is probable that the descriptions of him are deliberately veiled to avoid a specific identification.[12] What is important in the songs is *how* the Servant brings this justice to humankind.

In the first song (Is 42:1–4), we hear that the Servant has been chosen by the Lord and endowed with his spirit to bring true justice *(mishpāt)* to the nations (42:1). Even the Gentiles who worship idols (and so do not conceive of interhuman justice as constitutive of true religion) are to be brought to Yahweh and so be committed to his justice. How is the Servant to do this?

> He does not cry out or shout aloud,
> or make his voice heard in the streets.
> He does not break the crushed reed,
> nor quench the wavering flame (Is 42:2f.).

It is the gentle way, the nonviolent way. The message is not shouted at the nations. The Servant has consideration even for those who are on their last legs. He will pursue his mission even though he be assailed (v. 3d). This perseverance in the face of opposition is a necessary characteristic of every prophet, but it is going to be especially necessary for the Servant.

The Servant's way is one of discouragement. Although Yahweh has given him a message as sharp as a sword and as piercing as an arrow (49:2), the work of bringing justice goes slowly, and the Servant is discouraged: "I was thinking, 'I have toiled in vain, I have exhausted myself for nothing' " (49:4a); yet Yahweh *is* with him, and *will* make him the light who brings salvation to nations,[13] and so the discouragement is lifted (vv. 4b–5).

It is a way of rejection, shame, and pain. In 50:6 the Servant is physically assaulted by those to whom he delivers his message:[14]

> I offered my back to those who struck me,

> my cheeks to those who tore at my beard;
> I did not cover my face against insult and spittle.

It is Yahweh's presence and help that enables the Servant to endure this and persevere:

> The Lord Yahweh comes to my help,
> so that I am untouched by the insults.
> So, too, I set my face like flint;
> I know I shall not be shamed.
> My vindicator is here at hand.
> Does anyone start proceedings against me? . . .
> The Lord Yahweh is coming to my help,
> who dare condemn me? (Is 50:7–9).

The Servant understands that Yahweh is the guarantor of his message *now*, and that gives him confidence that the message can and must be preached by the servant of the faithful God.

All of this leads to a climax in the fourth Servant song (Is 52:13–53:12), the most remarkable poem in the Old Testament and probably the peak of Old Testament revelation. This is not a song of the Servant himself, who has by now died for his mission (vv. 8f.). The song is composed of Yahweh's announcement of the exaltation of his Servant (52:13–15) and his concluding comment on the career and meaning of the Servant (53:11b–12). Sandwiched between these is the report on the Servant's earthly career by those who observed it with all-too-human eyes (53:1–11a). Before we go further, stop to read the song as a whole with this structure in mind.

The singers report on the life career of the Servant: he grew up as at least an ugly child, if not deformed (53:2). Because of this or because of his mission he was despised in his mature years and rejected by others, "a man of sorrows," one from whom people averted their eyes out of distaste or fear (v. 3).[15] His companions were so wrapped in their selfishness (v. 6) that they even oppressed him (in the sense of economic reprisals complained of by the prophets?) and took him to court, where they got him condemned in spite of his innocence (vv. 7–9). Yet in his death his adversaries became aware that he was the only one not wrapped in his own selfishness. He bore *their* griefs, carried *their* sorrows, and so his very punishment was *for them;* his beatings and death healed them (of their selfishness) (vv. 4ff.). They were awed that a man could be so great (v. 9) that he refused to strike out against them (v. 7) in his own defense. And this has worked a conversion in their lives, so they see justice for the first time.

His knowledge that it is better to suffer injustice than to become a part of it has made them just (v. 11).

And so, because the Servant went to his death without experiencing vindication in this life, but only believing it would happen ultimately, he *is* exalted. In the first place, the honor in which he is now held has granted him an immortality of reputation, even before crowds and kings (52:15). Second, because he made himself a Temple sin-offering for *their* sins, he has seen his offspring (v. 10)—their converted selves? And third, there is an intimation that such a life must bear a personal reward beyond the grave, that his days must be prolonged with the Lord and his offspring (v. 10).[16] This is the meaning of Yahweh's final comment (vv. 11b–12): because the Servant preferred to be despised (taken as a sinner, v. 12d) than selfishly to use the corrupt court to vindicate himself, because he therefore suffered death rather than change (v. 12c) and bore the sins of his tormentors to make intercession for them (12d), Yahweh, the great vindicator, need not crush his enemies (since they are transformed by the servant's justice), but only reward the Servant with the inheritance of the just (12ab).

With this song, then, we come to the penultimate theology of retribution in the Old Testament: a person who accepts pain and rejection and refuses to respond in kind lives the law to perfection and places in the world a contagion of selflessness that converts others. However, to do this one needs a profound faith that a God who could ask for this kind of justice is a God who will vindicate the person who so lives as his servant.

D. WISDOM

The book of Wisdom of Solomon is the book of the Old Testament written last (ca. 70–50 B.C.), probably composed in Alexandria by a Greek-speaking Jew conversant with the Greek culture in which he lived. His purpose was to strengthen the faith of his fellow Jews in Alexandria.[17] Against Greek wisdom he shows that Yahweh's wisdom is comprehensive and superior to that of the Greek world-soul and that Yahweh is the teacher of all virtues that the Greeks could identify.

Our main interest here is to find the last stage of Hebrew retribution theology, which is contained in Wisdom 2:6–3:12. The author begins with the proposition that God is a God of life (1:13f.), and that by practicing justice[18] people enter into that undying life (1:15). The godless people court death by their life (1:16–2:5) and by their "eat, drink, and be merry, for tomorrow we die" philosophy (cf. 2:6–9). In contrast to the profligate rich of prophetic times, who often simply ignored the poor in their rush to consume the goods of their land, these wicked people understand they must oppress the poor to be wealthy, must silence the just person who exposes their atheism and injustice:

> As for the just man who is poor, let us oppress him;
> let us not spare the widow,
> nor respect old age, white-haired with many years.
> Let our strength be the yardstick of virtue,
> since weakness argues its own futility.
> Let us lie in wait for the just man, since he annoys us
> and opposes our way of life,
> reproaches us for our breaches of the law
> and accuses us of playing false to our upbringing.
> He claims to have knowledge of God,
> and calls himself a son of the Lord.
> Before us he stands,
> a reproof to our way of thinking. . . .
> He holds aloof from our doings as though from filth;
> he proclaims the final end of the just as happy
> and boasts of having God for his father.
> Let us see if what he says is true,
> let us observe what kind of end he himself will have.
> If the just man is God's son, God will take his part
> and rescue him from the clutches of his enemies.
> Let us test him with cruelty and with torture,
> and thus explore this gentleness of his
> and put his endurance to the proof.
> Let us condemn him to a shameful death
> since he will be looked after—
> we have his word for it (Wis 2:10–20).

Note here four points: (1) The unjust clearly are not oppressing criminals; they are exploiting poor people honestly trying to scratch out a living; (2) the just man accuses them of injustice and calls that being false to the whole law, their whole upbringing, for the essence of the law is justice; (3) the just man who simply refuses to do their evil works is by that very fact a reproach to them and must be removed; (4) the unjust will try the just man by ordeal. If his view is correct—that is, that justice is rewarded in the end by God—then God has to rescue him from this torture before death. Here is posed the old theory of retribution, that God must reward the virtuous in this life.

The author then contradicts this position of the godless. God has mys-

teriously made humankind imperishable in creating it in his own likeness
(2:21–24). The godless, impious ones are shortsighted:

> But the souls of the just are in the hands of God,
> no torment shall ever touch them.
> In the eyes of the unwise, they did appear to die,
> their going looked like a disaster,
> their leaving us, like annihilation;
> but they are in peace.
> If they experienced punishment as men see it,
> their hope was rich with immortality;
> slight was their affliction, great will their blessings be. . . .
> When the time comes for his visitation they will shine out;
> as sparks run through the stubble, so will they.
> They shall judge nations, rule over peoples,
> and the Lord will be their king for ever. . . .
> But the godless will be duly punished
> for their reasoning . . . (Wis 3:1–9).

It appears that the immortality spoken of here is the immortality of the
soul, a notion taken from the Greeks. There is no resurrection of the body
in Wisdom. Yet at this one stroke the whole problem of retribution has been
moved to a new plane. No longer can one say that justice is unrewarded
because a just person dies poor. All who remained poor because they
refused to oppress others are now seen to be truly children of God, to have
entered into a personal relationship with him that lasts forever. Further,
they will have positions of influence and power in the kingdom of God. The
justice that Yahweh had requested in the law is now seen to be life for men
and women, not only in human society but in his kingdom forever. Thus is
Job, or the suffering Servant who lives justice and delivers its message,
exalted in an everlasting life with God the Father.

E. THE KINGDOM OF GOD AND APOCALYPTIC LITERATURE

The retribution Wisdom spoke of was chiefly concerned with the nagging
problem of individual retribution. Yet it was never Yahweh's intention to
save individuals. He revealed his law and raised kings to heal human
society as a whole, which had, as a whole, been afflicted with the contagion
of sin (Wis 1–4). This was God's reason for calling a people, not an
individual, and the reason for his promise to David of an everlasting
kingdom (2 Sam 7:12–16). That Davidic king was to exercise Yahweh's

own kingship over humankind. In late Old Testament times that rule was called the kingdom of God (this exact title is used only once in the Old Testament, in Wis 10:10). Here "kingdom" is not used in our sense of territory or even number of subjects governed, but in the sense of God's active rule, sovereignty over people and nations. Psalm 103:19, "Yahweh has fixed his throne in the heavens; his throne is over all," stresses the fact that his rule comes from his Lordship in creation. Psalm 145:12f., "Let mankind learn your acts of power and the majestic glory of your sovereignty! Your kingdom is an eternal sovereignty . . . ," roots his kingship in his rule over the salvation history of people. Yet the Old Testament is relatively silent about the kingdom of God; that notion is developed in apocalyptic literature.

Apocalyptic is a genre of literature in which a seer, through the medium of a vision in opened heavens, or the communication of angels in the heavens, receives a revelation of the future, up to the end of the world.[19] At that time there will be a final cataclysmic struggle between the powers of evil (usually allegorically represented by the world powers of contemporary history) and the powers of God. In these latter, the Jewish nation, sometimes under a messianic leader, acts as Yahweh's special instrument of triumph over the world powers, who are thus brought under Yahweh's eternal rule.

The book of Daniel is the only apocalypse in the Old Testament canon. The first six chapters narrate the story of Daniel in Babylon; chapter 7 begins the visions of Daniel. In a vision in his bed, Daniel sees four beasts emerge from the sea, one like a lion with eagle's wings, another like a bear, a third like a leopard with four birds' wings, and the last unlike the others, terrifying and horrible, with ten horns.[20] Then,

> Thrones were set in place
> and one of great age took his seat.
> His robe was white as snow,
> the hair of his head as pure as wool.
> His throne was a blaze of flames,
> its wheels were a burning fire.
> A stream of fire poured out,
> issuing from his presence.
> A thousand thousand waited on him,
> ten thousand times ten thousand stood before him.
> A court was held
> and the books were opened (Dan 7:9–10).

The one of great age is clearly God on his heavenly throne, come to final judgment on the world (note the court and the books; cf. Jer 17:1; Mal 3:16; Rev 20:12). Then the last beast is killed and the others deprived of their power:

> And I saw, coming on the clouds of heaven,
> one like a son of man.
> He came to the one of great age
> and was led into his presence.
> On him was conferred sovereignty, glory and kingship,
> and men of all peoples, nations and languages
> became his servants.
> His sovereignty is an eternal sovereignty
> which shall never pass away,
> nor will his empire ever be destroyed (Dan 7:13–14).

Clearly in the judgment, the beastly worldly powers are replaced by the human kingdom of one like a son of man.[21] But who is the one to exercise this eternal kingdom?[22] Daniel asks this question and hears:

> These four great beasts are four kings who will rise from the earth.
> Those who are granted sovereignty are the saints of the Most High,
> and the kingdom will be theirs for ever (Dan 7:17–18).

In other words, it is the Jewish nation (cf. 7:25) as a whole who will exercise this everlasting kingdom, under the symbol of an individual, as we have seen individuals representing communities throughout the Old Testament writings.

This notion of the kingdom of God undergoes further development in the extracanonical Jewish literature. In the apocalyptic literature the vision of the Day of Yahweh (in Isaiah 24:21–23 and especially in Zechariah 14:6–21) is developed into a view that Israel itself will be exalted over all nations (cf. Assumption of Moses 10:7). Under a messianic king this exaltation will entail political rule over the nations on this earth. The apocryphal Psalms of Solomon look for this messiah:

> Behold, O Lord, and raise up unto them their king, the son of David, at the time in which you see, O God, that he may reign over Israel, your servant. And gird him with strength, that he may shatter unrighteous rulers. . . . And he shall gather a holy people, whom he shall lead in justice, and he shall judge the tribes of the people that has been sanctified by the Lord his God. And he shall not suffer injustice any more in their midst, nor shall there dwell with them any man that

knows wickedness, for he shall know them, that they are all sons of their God. . . . And he shall have the heathen nations to serve him under his yoke . . . so that nations shall come from the ends of the earth to see his glory, and see the glory of the Lord, with which God glorified her. And he shall be a just king, taught of God, over them, and there shall be no unrighteousness in his days in their midst (The Psalms of Solomon 17:23–38; see also The Sibylline Oracles 3:46–50, both in R. H. Charles, *The Apocrypha and Pseudepigrapha of the Old Testament,* Oxford: Clarendon, 1913).

Notice how strongly the passage stresses that the purpose of Yahweh's final kingdom on earth under the Messiah is to establish justice among all people. It is the completion of Jeremiah's new covenant, where all will be taught justice by God himself. Here, in the figure of the Messiah, the apocalyptic joins the prophetic literature's quest for the ideal king who will administer justice to Israel and the nations (see chap. V, above), as well as the worshiping community's thirst for the just king (see chap. II, above; see also Pss 45:1–9; 72:1–20) and the Wisdom literature's conception of the role of the king as promoter of justice (Wis 6:1–12).

In the rabbinic literature of the earliest Christian era, the kingdom of heaven means the interior acceptance of the authority of God as revealed in the Torah. The rabbis prayed that the kingdom would come, that the nations would accept this revealed law and live it—and so Yahweh would establish justice on earth. This combination of the nationalistic political messianic expectation and the interior kingdom is the background of the words "messiah" and "kingdom of God" used in the New Testament when God sends his Son to establish justice on earth.

F. SUMMARY

In the conclusion of chapter IV we summarized the revelation of the Old Testament in the law and the historical books. God had created a world good in its natural dynamisms with its component creatures ordered to their perfection in him through one another and especially through men and women. That was God's first act of liberation. But humankind refused that order, and in so doing introduced conflict and disorder between creatures, between man and man, between man and woman, and between humankind and God. Left to itself, humankind was susceptible to the contagion of sin, where selfishness provoked selfishness and sin spread to the whole world. To remedy this, Yahweh raised up his own people who trusted him, and when they were oppressed he delivered them from oppression and into their own land where they could live in union with him. That was the second stage of liberation. However, Yahweh's liberation was not simply a physical one in which he took the initiative, but one in which he encouraged and fostered the people's own attempts to produce justice through human government and law. The "religious law" he gave his people stressed that interhuman justice under God is true religion and is the way to the order and peace that had been lost in the world through sin. That was the third phase of liberation.

In chapter V we saw that the prophets everywhere presupposed that Israel had been called to holiness in the observance of the law. Wherever the people had fallen short of that observance of justice, which is Yahweh's nature and will for his people, the prophets castigated the people and foretold punishment until Israel was converted. Especially did they abhor "mouth-worship" (giving cultic worship to Yahweh in an attempt to obtain prosperity from him while living the kind of life that denied prosperity to the many). Such oppressors can obtain nothing from God.

In chapter VI we have seen that the Israelite community at prayer presumed that their God was a God of justice, who would reward people according to their practice of justice. When this rule of retribution did not appear to be occurring in this life, the community broke through to an idea of retribution after death in a glorious life with God for the just. In any case, since God was justice, those who lived lives of justice would find him. Further, it appears that a life of justice, lived to bring peace to earth, is a redemptive life for people. By our own sufferings in the cause of justice, we can bear the sins of others and heal their wounds. In spite of all the sin and pain we see about us, God has pledged that he will bring in his kingdom of justice and peace and the nations will share in that banquet. How the messianic king and Israel will be the agents of that justice is not clear, but as the Old Testament closes we await that kingdom in trust that his will shall be done.

VII. The Kingdom Come

A. THE COMPOSITION OF THE NEW TESTAMENT

Tracing the composition of the New Testament poses many of the same problems we encountered in tracing the origins of the Old Testament. The disciples probably had been expecting Jesus to usher in a final kingdom of peace right up to the time he died and even, when they had accepted his resurrection, immediately after. "Lord, is it at this time that you are going to restore the kingdom to Israel?" (Acts 1:6). (As we will see, they had plenty of reason for this expectation.) Consequently, they had not been gathering a book, a Gospel, a collection of the Lord's preachings to pass on to a community of followers after his ascension. If there had been warnings from Jesus that the community would have to be his witnesses over a long period of time,[1] they would have been ignored in favor of those statements that the kingdom was soon to arrive.

The process of composing the Gospels ("gospel" means "good news") was, then, long and laborious. At first the disciples made a simple proclamation[2] that centered mostly on God's unexpected exaltation of a man killed as a criminal. This was an approval that stamped his as the way of life for all humankind. But as men and women came to believe in this message (Acts 2:41 speaks of about three thousand coming to faith and baptism in response to Peter's maiden speech), they naturally began to seek more elaboration of Jesus' life and teaching and its implication for their own lives. Then the disciples began to collect stories about Jesus' works and recollect his words about his disciples' future style of life. The pressure of the community's questions about this lifestyle forced most of the recollection and shaped the material of the accounts. Thus the charge of Jews and Romans that Jesus had been a criminal would have provoked stories from Jesus' own life affirming his law-abiding nature, for example, his affirmation that everyone must pay taxes to the civil government (Mk 12:13–17; Mt 22:15–22; Lk 20:20–26).[3] The Christians' question of whether or not they had to obey the Mosaic law would have had to be researched in Jesus' own words and practice. Jewish Christians (converts from Judaism) would have probably remembered best Jesus' words that retained their beloved law (cf. Mt 5:17–19). Gentile Christians, who had not previously known or practiced that law, would have remembered those phrases that freed Christians from the observance of the old law (Mk 7:1–23; Mt 7:12; 12:1–8,11). The necessity of the community's finding some way of celebrating its identity as God's family would have led to the celebration of a covenant meal patterned on the last supper Jesus shared with his friends (Mk 14:22–25 and parallels). It was the preaching, the ethical concerns, and the sacramental life of the community, that is to say, its own life-situation,[4] that determined which stories from Jesus' life would be recalled and how they would be recounted.

Thus there is a long period of oral tradition before the Gospels actually came to be written down (similar to the long period of oral tradition before the legal and narrative materials of the Old Testament were written). Perhaps Luke 1:1–4 reflects this when it distinguishes eyewitnesses of Jesus' life, servants of the word (early preachers of Jesus' words and deeds), those who wrote connected narratives (the written sources of the Gospels), and finally the evangelist himself, whose work was a result of considerable human research and artistic genius.

Thus the Gospels are the result of a long process, and the words of Jesus were filtered through the disciples' selective memory before they came to be written as the Word of God. If they are the result of this human process, how can they be the revealed Word of God? Again we recall our first chapter: when God reveals to humans, he must do so in a way that humans can understand, and so by human process. It is clear from the New Testament itself that we do not have all of Jesus' revelation in the Gospels: "There were many other things that Jesus did; if all were written down, the world itself, I suppose, would not hold all the books that would have to be written" (Jn 21:25). Yet the process of selecting these was not entirely human:

> I have said these things to you
> while still with you;
> but the Advocate, the Holy Spirit,
> whom my Father will send in my name,
> will teach you everything
> and remind you of all I have said to you (Jn 14:25f.).

It was, then, the Spirit's guidance of the early community that enabled them to find those stories, and those formulations of the stories, that are the Word of God for us.

Finally, this long process of development means that the Gospels are not the earliest theologies of the New Testament. All of Paul's letters were written before the Gospels were fixed in their final form. Yet the Gospels retain theological perspectives that are often earlier than Paul's. Therefore it is difficult to set out, in a nontechnical book, the chronological development of doctrine within the New Testament. Consequently, the next four chapters will have more a thematic and topical structure and development than the chronological development we attempted to follow in the first six chapters of the book.

B. THE NEWNESS OF THE NEW TESTAMENT

Jürgen Moltmann, the principal proponent of the theology of hope, likes to point out that the emphasis on the "new" in the New Testament is in striking contrast to Greek philosophy's view of everything as past event recurring over and over in history.[5] We saw that Yahweh revealed himself to Israel as the God of the future, who would "be there" in Israel's history. However, when Israel had arrived in the promised land, had set up its government and legal structure, it thought it had arrived. The kingdom *had* come, and there was nothing more to look forward to in the future. The thrust for achieving interhuman justice was blunted, and the country stagnated in patterns of gross social injustice. In spite of the thunderings of the prophets, it was only the Babylonian exile, where Israel's government and autonomous exercise of the law were destroyed, that brought about a renewed hope for a future of justice and peace. The Jews conceived of this as a future messianic kingdom: a new kingdom with a new messianic king, in a new covenant.

If the New Testament is a fulfillment of these promises, how does it avoid settling into the stagnation of an achieved state, as Israel did under the monarchy? Would not this change the nature of God from a God of the future to a God of the present?

First, there is no doubt that the New Testament community considered itself both the fulfillment of the Old Testament and also something new. Our recollections of the earliest Christian teachings, the sermons of Acts, reveal the theme of fulfillment:

This [the outpouring of the Spirit on Pentecost] is what the prophet spoke of . . . [and he goes on to cite Joel 3:1–5 as what was fulfilled] (Acts 2:16).

. . . it was impossible for Christ to be held in its [death's] power since, as David says of him [citing Ps 16:8–11] . . . (Acts 2:25).

. . . this was the way God carried out what he had foretold, when he said through all his prophets that his Christ would suffer (Acts 3:18).

It is to him [Jesus] that all prophets bear witness (Acts 10:43).

This fulfillment of Old Testament prophecy will be developed in greater detail throughout these chapters.

That the Christ event is something new is seen in Jesus' own description of his way as a new wine (Mk 2:22). Early Christian theology considers him the new Adam (1 Cor 15:45), the new man (Eph 2:15), who gives a new commandment (1 Jn 2:7f.), as the mediator of a new covenant (Lk 22:20; 1 Cor 11:25; 2 Cor 3:6; Heb 8:8). In Christ the Christians form a new creature (2 Cor 5:17; Gal 6:15), and so they sing a new song (Rev 5:9). Jesus brings in a new Jerusalem (Rev 3:12), a new heaven and a new earth (Rev 21:1), so that God can say, "Behold I make everything new" (Rev 21:5). Is this new thing the ultimate, so that we can be said to have arrived at the final kingdom and can rest? Or are we still oriented to a future in which God becomes more and more in humankind?

C. THE KINGDOM OF GOD

In chapter VI we saw that there was, in some indeterminate way, to be a kingdom of God on earth in the last stage of history. Now Jesus came preaching that in him the kingdom of God had come:

After John had been arrested, Jesus went into Galilee. There he proclaimed the Good News from God: "The time has come," he said, "and the kingdom of God has come. Repent, and believe the Good News" (Mk 1:14f.).[6]

Further, this sense that the final, awaited kingdom of God had arrived in Jesus' own person is developed in Matthew. After Jesus has cast out the demon from a blind and mute man,[7] the Pharisees accuse him of using Beelzebub, the prince of devils, to cast out the demon. Jesus refutes them by a complex logic, and then says, "But if it is through the Spirit of God that I cast devils out, then know that the kingdom of God has overtaken you" (Mt 12:28; cf. Lk 11:20). The reference to the Spirit means that Jesus is the servant of Yahweh, anointed with the Spirit, since Matthew had cited this very passage from Isaiah 42:1–4 only a few verses previous to the story of the demoniac (see Mt 12:18–21). Thus Jesus' casting out of the demons is the overthrow of the power of evil and the ushering in of the reign of justice and peace for which the nations themselves are hoping. The kingdom has already come.[8]

However, the Gospel stories also contain a second view of the kingdom: it has not come yet, but is coming soon. After Jesus lays down the conditions of discipleship, he says, "I tell you solemnly, there are some standing here who will not taste death before they see the kingdom of God has come with power" (Mk 9:1). This second view, that the kingdom is coming completely in the lifetime of the disciples themselves, can be taken in two ways. First, it can mean that the final judgment on history spoken of in Daniel 7 is about to take place. Before the disciples die, the Son of man will come in glory to judge the nations; history will end and the eternal reign of the saints of the Most High will begin. This seems to be the meaning of the passage in Mark 9:1, for it is joined immediately to a passage (Mk 8:38) which says the Son of man is coming in the glory of his Father with the holy angels (apocalyptic imagery for the end of time). This expectation seemed also to have been Paul's early theology, so that his churches came to expect Christ's imminent return as judge.[9]

On the other hand, as day followed day, year after year, and that generation of disciples died without the Lord's returning, the Spirit aided human experience to understand that the Lord's return was not imminent. Rather, the Day of the Lord (the Parousia) was in the indeterminate future, a final guarantee of the worth of this life. Yet the word of the Lord had been true: the kingdom *had* come in the lifetime of the disciples, as the church filled with the Spirit. Matthew, again, is the most explicit about this. He divides the kingdom of heaven (as a Jew calls it) into the *kingdom of the Father,* which is to come at the end of time as the final eschatological kingdom, and the *kingdom of the Son of man,* which is the kingdom now present in the Spirit-filled community. Thus Jesus, after giving the parable of the seeds and weeds (Mt 13:24–30), explains it this way:

> The sower of the good seed is the Son of Man. The field is the world; the good seed is the subjects of the kingdom; the darnel [weeds], the subjects of the evil one; the enemy who sowed them, the devil; the harvest is the end of the world; the reapers are the angels. Well then, just as the darnel is gathered up and burnt in the fire, so will it be at the end of time. The Son of Man will send his angels and they will gather out of his kingdom all things that provoke offences and all who do evil, and throw them into the blazing furnace, where there will be weeping and grinding of teeth. Then the virtuous will shine like the sun in the kingdom of their Father (Mt 13:38–43).[10]

That is to say, the kingdom of the Son of man will be composed of both good and evil, as is the Christian church. At the final judgment, the good will be accepted into the final and complete kingdom of the Father, but in the meantime the church is in fact a stage of the kingdom of God. (The same message is contained in the parable of the dragnet in Mt 13:47–50.)

This seems also to be what Luke means by the kingdom of God: the presence of the Spirit and the living of Jesus' words in the Christian community. In Luke 22:16, Jesus says he will not eat the passover with the disciples again until it is fulfilled in the kingdom of God, and then he proceeds to inaugurate the Eucharist, which the church ever after celebrates as its passover with him. The meal Jesus celebrates with the disciples at Emmaus (Lk 24:30) is a Eucharist,[11] indicating that the kingdom has already come in Jesus' resurrection.

Clearly if the first interpretation of the imminent coming of the kingdom is maintained, then that expectation was never fulfilled. If the second interpretation is the one that accords with the facts, then do we have a fulfillment of the kingdom of God so complete in the church that the future orientation of revelation is gone?

There is a third series of texts on the kingdom in the synoptic Gospels. This series speaks of the kingdom as a future reality, coming only at the end of time. This kind of reference to the kingdom is found in Jesus' apocalyptic discourse in all three synoptic Gospels (Mk 13:24–27; Mt 24:29–31; Lk 21:24–28). Jesus speaks of the great messianic banquet of Isaiah 25 as taking place in the kingdom of the Father:

And I tell you that many will come from east and west to take their places with Abraham and Isaac and Jacob at the feast in the kingdom of heaven, but the subjects of the kingdom will be turned out into the dark, where there will be weeping . . . (Mt 8:11; cf. Lk 13:28f.).

This is evidently the same as the kingdom of the Father in Matthew 13:43. It is as the future judge that Jesus identifies himself in the trial before the Sanhedrin: ". . . you will see the Son of Man seated at the right hand of the Power and coming with the clouds of heaven" (Mk 14:62; cf. Mt 26:64). Note that the Son of man will soon ("from now on" in Matthew) be seated at the right hand of the Power (of God), but will be coming on the heavenly clouds to judge (where "coming" refers to a future activity).

Thus, in answer to our question, the Old Testament promises of an eternal kingdom *are* fulfilled in the New Testament: (1) in the historical person and works of Jesus of Nazareth, and (2) in the presence of the Spirit in the work of the early community. Yet even the community is not a perfect exercise of God's perfect justice and peace, and so it is but part of the dynamic movement to the perfect kingdom conceived of as a feast at the end of time. The kingdom of God announced and achieved by Jesus is like a mustard seed, planted in Jesus' own lifetime (Mk 4:1–34) and growing until the harvest at the end of time. Thus Jesus does bring in the kingdom in which people are freed for justice and peace, but only imperfectly, moving progressively to perfect justice only in the kingdom's final fullness. God is still "out there," ahead of us, to be met in the future.

D. THE MESSIAH

In many late Jewish expectations the final kingdom of God was to be brought in by a messiah, an anointed king of David's line.[12] It is to this line of thought that Peter is alluding in Acts 2:36, "God has made this Jesus whom you crucified both Lord and Christ," where Christ is the Greek translation for Hebrew *mâshîah*. It is clear that the whole New Testament considers Jesus to be this promised messiah, as the word *christos* is used 529 times in the New Testament, in every stratum of tradition and by every author. But the way in which the messiah is conceived by the New Testament is astonishing, and of crucial importance for any understanding of how God liberates humankind in the kingdom.

1. The Title "Messiah"

Whereas from earliest times (Acts 2:36) Jesus is called the Christ, and Paul even used the title as Jesus' proper name (see Rom 5:6,8, etc.), Jesus almost never uses the title of himself and seems even to avoid it. Thus the word *christos* is used fifty-five times in the Gospels (and *messias* twice in John), and yet Jesus uses it of himself only three times. In the synoptic Gospels (judged to be closer to the picture of the historical Jesus than is the highly theological John), only in his post-resurrection appearances to disciples does Jesus refer to himself as the messiah by saying the Old Testament indicated that the Christ had to suffer (Lk 24:26, 46). Otherwise the Jesus of the synoptics responds evasively when others ask him if he is the messiah (Mk 14:61 and parallels; Mk 15:2 and parallels; Mk 8:27ff. and parallels).[13] Only in John 4:25 does Jesus volunteer the information that he is the messiah. Other Johannine passages are close to an affirmation (Jn 10:25f.; and 17:3, although this is clearly not the historical Jesus speaking, but Johannine theology). In fact, in Mark Jesus actually forbids demons and disciples to speak of him as the messiah or as a wonderworker (1:25,34,44; 3:12; 5:43; 8:30; 9:9; etc.).

How does one explain this evasiveness? Wilhelm Wrede, at the turn of the century, thought it had two sources: (1) Jesus had not been aware that he was the messiah, and so never used the title; (2) the primitive church, who by then saw that Jesus was the promised messiah, had to explain why the Jews who were awaiting the messiah had not accepted Jesus as the Christ; they did so by writing into the Gospels the "messianic secret" whereby Jesus avoided the title and refused to let others use it. This theory has the difficulty of explaining how Jesus came to be charged as king of the Jews (Mk 15:2 and parallels). Yet clearly Wrede had discovered a central point of Marcan theology in the "secret." Can there be another explanation of that data?

I would suggest that Jesus historically did not use the title. Yet this does not necessarily mean he was not aware of himself as messiah. Indeed, his preferred title for himself, the Son of man, was charged with messianic implications.[14] Probably by Jesus' own time the title "messiah" had come to have such heavily nationalistic and political implications (as for a Davidic king who would evict foreign rulers, e.g., the Romans, and establish an independent theocratic rule of Israel) that Jesus avoided the title because it would not serve to illustrate what he meant to do.

2. The Title "Son of Man"

The situation is reversed when one comes to "Son of Man." This title is used eighty-one times in the Gospels,[15] but only once in the rest of the New Testament (Acts 7:56). All of these Gospel uses occur on the lips of Jesus himself; the title is never used by others of Jesus.[16] Jesus seems to use the title of himself in three general categories. He refers to:

a. his human condition of lowliness, poverty, suffering, and dying:

> The Son of Man came eating and drinking and they say "Look, a glutton and a drunkard . . ." (Mt 11:19; cf. Lk 7:34).

> Jesus replied, "Foxes have lairs and the birds of the air nests but the Son of Man has nowhere to lay his head" (Mt 8:20; cf. Lk 9:58).

> "The Son of Man will be delivered into the hands of men; they will put him to death, and three days after he has been put to death he will rise again" (Mk 9:31f. and parallels).

b. his messianic powers and messianic mission:

> "But to prove to you that the Son of Man has authority on earth to forgive sins . . ." (Mk 2:10 and parallels).

> ". . . so the Son of Man is master even of the Sabbath" (Mk 2:28 and parallels).

> "The sower of good seed is the Son of Man" (Mt 13:37).

c. his apocalyptic coming in glory to judge the earth:

> "And then they will see the Son of Man coming in the clouds with great power and glory . . ." (Mk 13:26 and parallels).

> "Are you the Christ," he said, "the Son of the Blessed One?" "I am," said Jesus, "and you will see the Son of Man seated at the right hand of the Power and coming with the clouds of heaven" (Mk 14:62 and parallels).

In short, what had been an apocalyptic figure (Dan 7:13) has now been reshaped in the Gospel tradition to become a personal title for Jesus in all aspects of his career. Critics dispute whether the historical Jesus actually used the title in all three of these categories.[17] It appears that *in the forms in which these sayings now occur* they are the theological formulations of the early church. Nevertheless, I think the most likely explanation for the Gospel traditions' reserving all uses to Jesus' own lips is that it *was* his favorite title for himself. Since it was not a popular messianic title, it avoided all the misconceptions that "messiah" caused, and yet referred to a mysterious function in the coming eternal kingdom. In exactly what way Jesus understood the title himself is too subtle an investigation for us now, and it is not quite the point. The point is that the early church's understanding of Jesus' usage is God's revealed Word for us now, and that is what we must study if we are to understand the message of the New Testament on liberation.

What is most astonishing (and, I think, most central to the New Testament message) is Jesus' use of a glorious apocalyptic title for his work as the Suffering Servant.[18] Thus, at the center of Mark's Gospel[19] Jesus three times predicts that he is going to Jerusalem to suffer and die as the Son of Man. Look at the first example:

> Peter spoke up and said to him, "You are the Christ." And he gave them strict orders not to tell anyone about him.
> And he began to teach them that the Son of Man was destined to suffer grievously, to be rejected by the elders and the chief priests and the scribes, and to be put to death, and after three days to rise again, and he said all this quite openly (Mk 8:29–32).

Note that Jesus here seems to accept the title "Messiah" from his disciples, but he charges them not to tell anyone else and immediately proceeds to tell them what kind of a messiah he is—a Son of Man who suffers, is put to death, and rises again. The pattern is that of the servant of Yahweh who suffers and so is exalted, rises to great heights (Is 52:13). In fact, the Son of Man's rising from the dead (Mk 9:9) is the fulfillment of the Servant's being delivered from death (Is 53:10f.). This same teaching, under the same title, is repeated in Mark 9:30-32 and 10:32-34,[20] and the whole section is summed up by the great statement of the Servant motif in Mark 10:45: "For the Son of Man came not to be served, but to serve, and give his life as a ransom for many."[21]

It is in this context of one who takes on all suffering and humiliation to bring true justice to the nations (Is 42:1) that all of Jesus' statements about his lowly condition can be read: "Foxes have lairs and the birds of the air have nests, but the Son of Man has nowhere to lay his head" (Mt 8:20).[22] Indeed, Matthew 8:17 cites Isaiah 53:4, "he took our sicknesses away and carried our diseases for us," to say that Jesus' whole healing ministry was the work of the Servant. Matthew is even more explicit in 12:18-21, where he quotes most of the first song of the Servant (Is 42:1-4) to give the theological meaning of Jesus' ministry of healing in 12:9-14, 22-32. This latter passage announces that the kingdom of God has come, that it is present in the healing ministry of Jesus as the Servant. Thus John 12:28, citing Isaiah 52:15c, "Who could believe what we have heard," etc. (referring originally to the Servant's total life of suffering), applies it to the whole of Jesus' wonderworking as a sign of who he was. Jesus' whole life, and not just his suffering in the passion, was to be understood as the work of the Servant of Yahweh.

But it is his passion especially that is the fulfillment of the prophecies of the Servant's work:

—Isaiah 49:1: God pronounced his name while he was still in his mother's womb, before he was born (Lk 1:31).

—50:6: he offered his back to those who beat him (Mk 15:15 and parallels).

—50:6: his face was spat upon (Mt 26:67; 27:30).

—50:6: he was mocked (Mt 26:67; 27:31; Mk 15:29-32 and parallels).

—53:5: he was pierced for our faults (Jn 19:31-37).

—53:7: he never opened his mouth, like a lamb led to the slaughter (Mt 26:63; Jn 19:9;[23] Acts 8:32f. explicitly cites Is 53:7f.).

—53:8: by force and by law he was taken (Mk 14:43-52 and parallels).

—53:9: there was no perjury in his mouth (1 Pet 2:22).

—53:10: his life offered in atonement produces a long life (Jn 12:24).

—53:12: he let himself be taken for a sinner (Lk 22:37).

—52:15: [the crowds] will see something never told (Rom 15:21).

Thus there can be no doubt that the climax of Jesus' life—his death—is conceived of by New Testament theology after the model of the suffering Servant. Now, like the Servant's, this suffering is vicariously redemptive for other people: Isaiah 53:5–6 described the servant as "pierced through for our faults, crushed for our sins; Yahweh burdened him with the sins of all of us." The New Testament describes Jesus' own death as *for our sins:*

> . . . who was handed over for our sins and raised for our justification (Rom 4:25; cf. Gal 1:3–4).

> For our sake God made the sinless one into sin (2 Cor 5:21).

> . . . who sacrificed himself as a ransom for them all (1 Tim 2:6).

> God dealt with sin by sending his own Son in a body as physical as any sinful body, and in that body God condemned sin (Rom 8:3).

> [Christ] innocent though he was, had died once for sins, died for the guilty (1 Pet 3:18).

In fact, 1 Peter describes Jesus' whole passion under the theological symbolism of the suffering Servant's fourth song:

> This, in fact, is what you were called to do, because Christ suffered for you and left an example for you to follow the way he took. He had not done anything wrong, and *there had been no perjury in his mouth.* He was insulted and did not retaliate with insults; when he was tortured he made no threats but he put his trust in the righteous judge. He was *bearing our faults* in his own body on the cross, so that we might die to our faults and live for holiness; *through his wounds you have been healed.* You had *gone astray like sheep,* but now you have come back to the shepherd and guardian of your souls (1 Pet 2:21–24).

Thus our inquiry into Jesus' place in the kingdom of God that he preached has discovered that the New Testament considered him the messiah who brought in the kingdom growing among us. Yet Jesus did not refer to himself as the messiah, preferring instead the more obscure, apocalyptic title "Son of Man," which he, however, transformed into a title for the one who was the suffering Servant of Yahweh spoken of by Isaiah. Through his healing ministry and especially his passion, he suffered to bring justice into the world, and so died for our sins. As a result, he is raised to God's right hand, triumphant.

What we have seen briefly of Jesus' wonderworking and of his passion is true of his preaching ministry, too. The early church's preaching considered that the Good News began with Jesus' baptism by John (Acts 1:22;

10:37, ". . . he began in Galilee after John had been preaching baptism. God had anointed him with the Holy Spirit . . ."). And that anointing itself was conceived after the model of the Servant, for the words spoken immediately after the baptism reflect, with slight changes, the opening words of the Servant's first song: "Here is my servant, . . . my chosen one in whom my soul delights" (Is 42:1):

> As soon as Jesus was baptised, he came up from the water, and suddenly the heavens opened and he saw the Spirit of God descending like a dove and coming down on him. And a voice spoke from heaven, "This is my Son,[24] the Beloved; my favour rests on him" (Mt 3:16f.).

Not only are the words similar, but the descent of the Spirit is the fulfillment of Isaiah 42:1b: "I have endowed him with my Spirit, that he may bring true justice to the nation." Thus Jesus, like the Servant, is anointed for his mission of justice; in the baptism he already accepts his role as the Servant. Luke especially brings this out. The Spirit received at baptism is the same one that leads him into the desert temptations (Lk 4:1), whose power is in his Galilean preaching (4:14), and to whom Jesus refers in his inaugural speech in the synagogue at Nazareth:

> Unrolling the scroll he found the place where it is written:
> "The spirit of the Lord has been given me,
> for he has anointed me.
> He has sent me to bring the good news to the poor,
> to proclaim liberty to captives
> and to the blind new sight,
> to set the downtrodden free,
> to proclaim the Lord's year of favour"
>
> (Lk 4:17–19; citing Is 61:1f.).

Thus, as Third Isaiah had considered his own call to be an extension of the spirit of Second Isaiah's Servant,[25] so Jesus takes up Third Isaiah's servant function of bringing justice to those imprisoned. You can find this mission to sinners and the poor throughout all the Gospels, but Luke makes it especially obvious by using the same phraseology in two passages: (1) When John the Baptist sends messengers to ask if Jesus is the one who is to come, this is the sign Jesus gives of his inauguration of the kingdom: "The blind see again, the lame walk, lepers are cleansed, the deaf hear, the dead are raised to life, the Good News is proclaimed to the poor" (Lk 7:22). And (2) In giving instructions to his host, Jesus said, ". . . When you have a party, invite the poor, the crippled, the lame, the blind . . . " (Lk 14:13).

Thus, not only in the manner of his death, but throughout his life, Jesus fulfilled the prophecies of the Servant in the Isaian school. Therefore he is called the Servant in the early preaching of Acts 3:13, 26; 4:27,30. The Scriptures most often spoken of as fulfilled are those referring to the Servant (see Lk 18:31; 24:26,46; 1 Cor 13:3–5, etc.).

And so it is fitting that on the night before he died Jesus gathered his disciples for a grand ritual act in which he summed up his life and the death upon which he was entering—a last will and testament for us:

> . . . Then he took a cup, and when he had returned thanks he gave it to them. "Drink all of you from this," he said, "for this is my blood, the blood of the covenant, which is to be poured out for many for the forgiveness of sins" (Mt 26:27f.).

Jesus at the end of his life pulls together two great Old Testament prophecies: (1) Jeremiah's prophecy (31:31ff.) that God would establish a new covenant with humanity, now seen as the covenant of a man pouring out his own blood for his fellows, surely an act to change our hearts of stone to tender hearts of flesh (cf. Ezek 36:26f.). Note that in Isaiah 42:6, the Servant himself is called a covenant of the people! (2) The motif of the servant songs that the servant will bring about universal salvation (Is 42:6; 49:6; 53:12), and his death (blood) will be a ransom for sins (Is 53:8,11; "by his sufferings shall my servant justify *many,* taking their faults on himself").

E. THE SAVIOR

If Jesus was the promised messiah leading in the kingdom of God through his work as the suffering Servant, then he is Yahweh's instrument of salvation for humankind. He is the savior. It remains true that as God the Father was the savior of Israel and of individual Jews in the Old Testament, so he remains the savior throughout the New Testament (Lk 1:47; 1 Tim 1:1, 2:3; 4:10; Tit 3:4f.). But it was according to his plan that Jesus suffer as man, and in so doing become our savior (Lk 18:31; 24:26, 46; Acts 3:18; 4:28; etc.). Thus Jesus' life mission is summed up by his name—*Yēshû'a,* Jesus, "Yahweh saves"—given him "because he is the one who is to save his people from their sins" (Mt 1:21). The Samaritans call him the Savior of the World (Jn 4:42), the early church preached him as savior (Acts 5:31; 13:23), and the early and late letters also so considered him (Phil 3:20; 2 Tim 1:10; Tit 2:13; 2 Pet 1:1, 11; 1 Jn 4:14).

What, then, is this salvation that humanity has attained in Jesus, the liberation that humankind has been seeking? This will be the theme of the remaining chapters of this book. Here we sketch only briefly the summary statements about salvation given in the New Testament.

Negatively considered (what Jesus frees us *from*), salvation consists first in our being freed from physical ills, which themselves are a result of sin.[26] Second, and most important, Jesus saves us from sin (Mt 1:21; 1 Tim 1:15), especially through his forgiveness (Lk 1:77; 7:49f.). Third, Jesus thus saves us from death, in two ways: (1) from physical death, insofar as he has transcended death and has risen in a new life, which he shares with us (Rom 6:8; 2 Cor 4:14; Phil 3:10f.; 2 Tim 2:11; 1 Cor 15); (2) from spiritual death, the effect of sin in us (2 Cor 7:10; Jas 5:20), which is described as God's condemnation, or wrath (Lk 19:10; Rom 5:9; 1 Cor 5:5; 1 Thess 1:10). This is salvation also from "this perverse generation" (Acts 2:40) now.

Positively considered (what Jesus frees us *for*), the Christian is freed for *life,* which is (1) a new quality of existence in freedom and goodness now (Col 1:13; Eph 2:5), and (2) a pledge of an eternal life of glory to come (Rom 8:24; 2 Tim 2:10; cf. Mk 10:17–31 and parallels). Further, this life can be considered a life of love, generosity, selflessness, truth, hope, etc., in the kingdom of God, which is the Christian community. It is the "how" of this that we investigate in the next chapters.

F. SUMMARY

In chapter II we saw that when God wanted to liberate his people he began by helping them to establish a kingdom in Canaan. But that kingdom was not an adequate reflection of his holiness, and so he sent his son in human flesh to bring about a kingdom of justice and peace. Like the Old Testament kingdom, the new kingdom of God was established under a Davidic king, the long-awaited messiah. Yet this messiah was not the powerful monarch of a nation-state; he was the Son of Man, a Servant of God who established his kingdom among men and women by pouring out his life for humankind. By his vicarious suffering we are healed, saved from evil of all kinds—physical, moral, and social.

Again, however, the question arises: how are we in our freedom to participate in that salvation, make it our own? In the Old Testament the Jews participated by observing laws that were to lead to justice and peace in the kingdom. The next two chapters will investigate what should be the human response to God's initiative in Christ.

VIII. Incorporation into Christ

A. SALVATION IS ONE

In the Old Testament, when Yahweh had determined to save human beings, he did not save them as individuals. Rather, he entered into covenant arrangements with whole peoples. A person who wanted to be saved became a member of the people saved through the covenant. In order to make his salvation ever more securely present to individuals, Yahweh expressed his will with ever greater specificity and exactness by entering into covenants with a steadily decreasing number of people. Thus, with Noah, Yahweh entered into a covenant with all, but a covenant that revealed very little of his demands (Gen 6:18; 9:8–17). He entered into a more demanding covenant with the Semites in Abraham (Gen 15:7–21; 17:9f.), into a covenant with elaborate legal demands with the Jews under Moses (Ex 19–24), and finally into a covenant for the eternal kingdom with David's line (2 Sam 7).[1]

This decreasing movement comes to a halt in the one man Jesus of Nazareth. For this one man is himself the covenant. As the Epistle to the Hebrews points out, he is the perfect high priest because in him God and humanity are one. Therefore he is the perfect mediator (1 Tim 2:5) of the new covenant (Heb 8:6). In him the pre-existing divine Word (Jn 1:1–18), *the* Son, took flesh (Jn 1:14), and dwelt with humanity, a man like us tempted in every way, but without sin (Heb 4:15). He is the perfect revelation of the unseen God (Jn 1:18). Because in this one man God's fullness resides, the decreasing covenant movement reverses itself and in him explodes to include all people, so that Jew and Greek, male and female, master and slave (Gal 3:28) are one in him, and in him one with God. Thus the pattern of the Old Testament is both continued and reversed: (1) Only one man is saved, and if you want to be saved you must be united to him; (2) this reduction, however, to one man is not exclusive but inclusive, so that in him the covenant extends to all men and women.

In order to understand our process of liberation in him, we must first come to understand how we all become one in him.

1. The Body of Christ

The Gospel tradition shows a Jesus eager to form men and women in union with himself and with the Father. In describing himself under the figures of the gate of the sheepfold and the good shepherd (Jn 10:1–15), Jesus says, ". . . and there will be only one flock, and one shepherd" (10:16). That he means to accomplish this by a physical and metaphysical union is indicated by his figure of the vine:

> As a branch cannot bear fruit by itself,
> but must remain part of the vine,
> neither can you unless you remain in me.
> I am the vine,
> you are the branches.
> Whoever remains in me, with me in him,
> bears fruit in plenty;
> for cut off from me you can do nothing (Jn 15:4–5).

Jesus' knowledge that "I am in the Father and the Father is in me" (Jn 14:10) is the basis of his great prayer for unity with his disciples:

> Holy Father,
> keep those you have given me true to your name,
> so that they may be one like us. . . .
> May they all be one.
> Father may they be one in us,
> as you are in me and I am in you (Jn 17:11, 21).

Not only was this Jesus' desire, but in fact he accomplished this union with us in his own body, first in his death: "Jesus was to die for the nation—and not for the nation only, but to gather together in unity the scattered children of God" (Jn 11:51f.). And before this, on the night when he was betrayed for his death, he celebrated a last meal with his disciples, which summed up what his life had been and what his death was to mean:

Now as they were eating, Jesus took some bread, and when he had said the blessing he broke it and gave it to the disciples. "Take it and eat," he said, "this is my body." Then he took a cup, and when he had returned thanks he gave it to them. "Drink all of you from this," he said, "For this is my blood, the blood of the covenant, which is to be poured out for many for the forgiveness of sins" (Mt 26:26–28).

Thus does Jesus establish a new covenant (cf. Jer 31) in blood, as the old covenant had been made in blood (Ex 24:6f.). That he meant the eating of his body and drinking of his blood to make a union between himself and his disciples is indicated by the long discourse on the bread of life in John 6 (especially vv. 41–63), which gives the theology of that eucharistic union:

> Anyone who does eat my flesh and drink my blood
> has eternal life,
> and I shall raise him up on the last day.
> For my flesh is real food
> and my blood is real drink.
> He who eats my flesh and drinks my blood
> lives in me and I live in him.
> As I, who am sent by the living Father,
> myself draw life from the Father,
> so whoever eats me will draw life from me (Jn 6:54–57).[2]

This doctrine of humankind's physical union with Christ comes to full expression principally in Pauline theology. In one of the earliest writings of the New Testament, the first letter to the Corinthian community (ca. A.D. 54–57), St. Paul gives his first large-scale development of the church as the body of Christ. The problem of his Corinthian community was one of factions and disunity. On the one hand, different elements in the church thought themselves superior to other elements because they had been converted or baptized by a "superior" apostle, like Apollos, Cephas, the Jesus party, or Paul (1 Cor 1:10–16). On the other hand, some thought themselves more enlightened or superior because they had the "superior" charisms of prophecy, of healing, etc. (1 Cor 12–14). Paul's solution is to stress (1) the Christian principle of the cross as not seeking superiority or exaltation over anyone else (1 Cor 1:17–4:21), and so leading to the bond of love (1 Cor 13), and (2) the basic unity that all of them have in the body of Christ (1 Cor 12):

> Just as a human body, though it is made up of many parts, is a single unity because all these parts, though many, make one body, so it is with Christ. In the one Spirit we were all baptised, Jews as well as Greeks, slaves as well as citizens, and one Spirit was given to all to drink.
> Nor is the body to be identified with any one of its many parts (1 Cor 12:12–14).[3]

Paul then goes on to argue by analogy (1 Cor 12:15–26) that the principle of organicity (diversity of function of members of the body) means that all those with different gifts in the body of Christ have that diversity in service of one another in the whole body:

> Now you together are Christ's body, but each of you is a different part of it. In the Church, God has given the first place to apostles, the second to prophets. . . . Are all of them apostles, or all of them prophets, or all of them teachers? (1 Cor 12:27ff.).

All of them have their individual parts to play in building up the whole body, and their honor and glory come from their integration into that whole glorious body of Christ.

The exact understanding of this powerful image is a problem for theology.[4] But whether one takes the message in its most literal or most metaphorical sense, it is clear that Paul is stressing the ontological union with Christ, which every Christian has through baptism in the Spirit. Thus the resurrection that Jesus has attained in his own body is already present in effect to the individual Christian.[5]

2. The Cosmic Christ

Indeed the very physicalness of the imagery of the body leads the later Paul of the epistles to the Colossians (ca. 61?) and Ephesians (ca. 63–64?)[6] to the notion that the physical body of Christ is the physical organ of the whole material cosmos. Already in 1 Corinthians 15:20 Christ was described as not just risen himself, but the first fruits of all who belong to him. Thus he turns over himself and the kingdom formed in him to his Father, "that God may be all in all" (1 Cor 15:49). In the later epistles this union with Christ is seen to apply to the whole material world, since the Word has truly become flesh, matter.

That this risen body of Christ is the goal and destiny not just of all men and women, but of the whole material cosmos, is first seen in Colossians. Paul concludes his thanksgiving for the community at Colossae with a phrase similar to what we saw in 1 Corinthians:

> . . . he has taken us out of the power of darkness and created a place for us in the kingdom of the Son that he loves, and in him we gain our freedom [redemption], the forgiveness of our sins (Col 1:13f.).

Then Paul integrated into his argument an early Christian hymn, which celebrates the pre-existence of the Son, his work as creator and unifier, and his destiny as the goal of the cosmos:[7]

> He is the image of the unseen God,
> and the first-born of all creation,
> for in him were created
> all things in heaven and on earth:
> everything visible and everything invisible,
> Thrones, Dominations, Sovereignties, Powers—
> all things were created
> through him and for him.
> Before anything was created, he existed,
> and he holds all things in unity.
> Now the Church is his body,
> he is its head.
> As he is the Beginning,
> he was first to be born from the dead,
> so that he should be first in every way;
> because God wanted all perfection [fullness, *plērōma*]
> to be found in him,
> and all things to be reconciled through him and for him,
> everything in heaven and everything on earth,
> when he made peace
> by his death on the cross (Col 1:15–20).

Clearly we are speaking of the incarnate Son of God (v. 13) as the first-born creature, Jesus Christ. Yet the same incarnate Son served as the model and location or center (v. 16, "in him") in which all creation came to be. In fact, as the image of God (v. 15a) he was the creator (v. 16c, "through him") of all, even the angelic and spiritual world, and is the end or terminus of all creation (v. 16c, "into him"). But this is not simply a past act; he *now* is the organic center of all creation, holding all things in unity (v. 17).[8] Explicitly he does this because his risen body is the church, to which he gives life and direction as its head (v. 18a). It is through his function as image that we are created, but it is nevertheless through his human death and resurrection that we are reconciled, and everything finds unity and reconciliation with God (vv. 18–20).[9]

Note, however, that the body of Christ is not simply the cosmos, but the church, the place where the present Christ exercises his rule over the cosmos.[10] The church is the instrument by which and in which the cosmos comes to union with its principle of creation and last end, the body/person of the whole Christ. In this way the church inchoately embodies the cosmos in the same way it inchoately embodies the kingdom of God. In both cases, the church is a servant, bringing a future, more perfect reality into being.

These ideas are developed further in the opening "hymn" of Ephesians 1:3–14. Here, though the idea of a pre-existent Christ as head of everything occurs, the focus is less on the cosmos and more on God's predestination of Christians in Christ. It is in the prayer that Paul adjoins to this hymn that the cosmic dimension and its relation to the church reappears. As a result of Christ's resurrection he sits at the right hand of the Father, above all the invisible creatures of the world (v. 21). Thus he rules over everything (v. 22) by virtue of being "the head of the Church, which is his body, the fullness of him who fills the whole creation" (Eph 1:22–23). The church, as body of Christ, in Paul's thought corresponds to the *plērōma* ("fullness") of which the Gnostics spoke.[11]

The church as body of Christ is, then, the fullness of the created world, spiritual and material. Paul is not explicit about the relationship between church and cosmos, but it appears that Christ now is explicitly and consciously honored as head by the church as his body, and at the end of time the whole world will, in and through his body, come to acknowledge him as its head. This takes place through the actions of the church: "This may be a wicked age, but your lives should redeem it" (Eph 5:16).

In both Colossians and Ephesians our redemption, or freedom, was spoken of as the forgiveness of sins. Outcast humankind, from the time of Adam alienated from God and one another, now in unity with Christ as adopted sons and daughters of the one Father (and so brothers and sisters), are united to the Father. Christ himself died for sins on the cross (Gal 3:10–14; Rom 5:6), and by this death cleansed his whole body united with him:

> . . . just as Christ loved the Church and sacrificed himself for her to make her holy. He made her clean by washing her in water with a word, so that when he took her to himself she would be glorious, with no speck or wrinkle or anything like that, but holy and faultless (Eph 5:25–27).

Thus, through our baptismal union with Christ, we too are freed from sin and united to the Father as adopted children. Thus do we also enter into his salvation, as personally one with his death and resurrection through our baptism into his risen body. Somehow the cosmos is saved through its growing union with that body through the church, and so the whole of creation comes to union with the Father.

Now, in Romans, we study the implications of this for our own conduct of life.

B. STAGES OF MORAL DEVELOPMENT

Before we come to Paul, however, it will be good to consider the different stages through which each person and each culture passes in its growth to full humanity.[12] When this is understood, the genius of Paul's description of the Christian life will be much clearer.

1. The Instinctual Level

At this level children cannot reason for themselves what is good for them. And so society, through the parents, rears children with taboos, prohibitions, and commands, which are sanctioned by physical punishments and rewards. Thus *law* comes not from within the person, but from outside the person. The individual assumes this pressure from society and turns it into a feeling of obligation; but the *obligation* is somehow still experienced as alien to the individual, and so, increasingly, is experienced with ambivalence.[13] At this level *guilt* and *sin* reside in the material transgression of some prohibition or taboo, producing a blind feeling of having offended some order.[14] *Contrition,* then, is not a desire to reform, but a desire to escape punishment as the consequence of the transgression, usually through a system of formulas, or, in religion, magical rites. For Catholics, *confession* can be the magical system, which, when done according to the prescribed ritual, releases from punishment.

2. The Moral Level

We begin to recognize our autonomy as persons, as people who by powers of reason, will, and feeling, can actualize ourselves as spirits in the world. Our dignity is seen as residing in our achieving free and authentic self-development in communion with our fellows and with God as Absolute Person.[15] Actions now are seen as right because they contribute to self-development in community.[16] *Law* now is not extrinsic, but the interior law of personal growth, and *obligation* is what a person's freedom owes itself in being faithful to one's drive to authentic self-development. *Conscience* emerges as the power of discriminating what will promote development.[17] *Sin* is infidelity to our authentic unfolding, and *guilt* is the realization of it. *Contrition* and *confession* are now conversion to further development and the fixing of the resolution through communal ritual and reinforcement.

3. The Religious Level

Here growth occurs not through self-development, but through self-donation to the lover, especially the Absolutely Personal Lover who is God. Development does not come from within by a calculated process, but by a risky leap of faith in which one commits oneself to the beloved and draws virtue from that person. Development is not of two individuals, but of a union that enriches the partners beyond their abilities to achieve alone. Now *law* is an invitation to yield in love, to "let go" to person and God, which results in the divinization of human persons. *Obligation* becomes vocation. *Conscience* is discernment of what the Spirit is urging subtly, in a choice among diverse goods. *Guilt* and *sin* are saying No to love. *Contrition* and *confession* are the fulfillment of desire to re-enter dialogue and communion with God and other people.

In summary, when we talk about a person's moral development, we see growth from mechanical, physical, ritual observance of law because it is imposed, to observance of law because it is seen and affirmed as instrument of personal growth, to self-donation and service beyond all the requirements of law because the love of God and others pulls one beyond calculated self-interest. What is true of individuals is true of cultures, too, so that in law and religion a culture passes from taboo to the Spirit-filled community of believers.[18]

C. PERSONAL LIBERATION ACCORDING TO ST. PAUL

The discussion of Christian freedom arises in Pauline thought from specific circumstances. Paul had evangelized the predominantly Gentile communities of Galatia, probably on his second missionary journey (ca. 49–52). After he had left the area, some "Judaizers" entered the community, so called because they persuaded the Galatians to submit to circumcision and the prescriptions of the Mosaic law in order to inherit truly the salvation of Christ, who had said, "Salvation comes from the Jews" (Jn 4:22).[19] When Paul heard of his community's lapse into Mosaic observances, he wrote them a wrathful letter in which he replaced his normal thanksgiving for the faith and charity of the community with a stinging rebuke (Gal 1:6–10). The doctrinal section of the letter (chaps. 3–4) shows that the law has no positive function in the moral life of a Christian, for it is faith in Christ that justifies a Christian (2:16). The letter, written under the pressure of so much emotion and making extensive use of elliptical rabbinic argumentation, is an extraordinarily difficult one to understand, and probably was not well understood by the Galatians.

Therefore, a couple of years later Paul composed a tranquil doctrinal exposition of the same theme of the relation of faith and law, Gentile and Jew, as a letter introducing himself to the Roman community, which he was about to visit for the first time. This letter will best serve as our understanding of Christian freedom as effect of Christ's salvation.

The doctrinal section of Romans seems composed on the following outline:

A. Through the gospel of Jesus Christ the justice of God justifies the person of faith (1:16–4:25):
   1. The theme announced: The gospel is source of salvation (1:16f.).
   2. Without the gospel, God's wrath is on all people (1:18–3:20):
      a. on the pagans (1:18–32)
      b. on the Jews (2:1–3:20)
   3. The theme illustrated: In the old law Abraham was justified by faith, not by observance of law (4:1–25).
B. The love of God assures salvation to the Christian justified by faith (5:1–8:30):
   1. The theme announced: The reconciled Christian will be saved in hope (5:1–11).
   2. The new Christian life brings a threefold liberation (5:12–7:25):
      a. freedom from death and sin (5:12–21)
      b. freedom from self through union with Christ (6:1–23)
      c. freedom from law (7:1–25)
   3. Positively, the Christian life is lived in the Spirit (3:1–30).
C. This plan of salvation does not contradict God's promises to Israel (9:1–11:36).

Paul begins by showing that both pagans trying to follow God's revelation in their consciences (Rom 2:14f.) and Jews trying to follow it in their law, insofar as they rely on their human striving alone, fall short of the justice to which God has destined them. This indicates the insufficiency not only of the taboo stage of morality, but even of the second, reasoned stage. Only Abraham (Gen 15:6; see pp. 41f., above) is justified, and that by his raw belief that God would save him. This belief was a radical personal commitment to a God of the future, beyond any attempt to reason out what such a God had done, or would do. Therefore, it is at the third, or religious stage of morality that humanity is truly justified, made right. Paul ends this first section with a transition to the New Testament God of faith:

> . . . our faith too will be "considered" if we believe in him who raised Jesus our Lord from the dead, Jesus who was put to death for our sins and raised to life to justify us (Rom 4:24f.).

In Paul's theology, God first loved us (Rom 5:7): even while we were sinners, estranged from him by the accumulation of evil in our human history, he sent his Christ to die for our sins (5:6–8). Jesus came in a physical body (Gal 4:4), subject in that human body/person to the historical contagion of sin since Adam:

God dealt with sin by sending his own Son in a body as physical as any sinful body, and in that body God condemned sin. He did this in order that the Law's just demands might be satisfied in us . . . (Rom 8:3f.).

The interpretation of this passage had already been given in Galatians 3:10–14. There Paul explained that the law itself said, "Cursed be everyone who does not persevere in observing everything prescribed in the book of the Law" (Deut 27:26). No one has observed the law perfectly, and so everyone has been cursed. Now Christ, as the perfect man, obedient to death, took on himself that curse, and died under it, thus fulfilling the law completely. As a sign that Jesus had taken the curse, Paul cites Deuteronomy 21:23, "Cursed be everyone who is hanged on a tree."[20] Thus, Jesus' death on the cross expiated the sins of humanity, ended the curse of the law, freed from the law, and opened salvation also to the Gentiles, who did not observe the law. While humankind was in its infancy, the law was its guide and teacher; when Jesus, the mature man of perfect obedience, arrived, the law was outdated and was replaced by the covenant of faith in Jesus. In his perfect act of obedience, then, Jesus as man was reconciled to God, and through him we too are reconciled (Rom 5:9–11). This was the great act of mother love, totally unmerited on our part. It is the radical, total self-giving love of a God who is always pouring himself out for humankind, in creation and in redemption through history.[21]

We are reconciled because through our baptism we have been united to Jesus' own death and resurrection, and so share his new risen life (Rom 6:1–11). Baptism was mostly by immersion in the early church. The candidate waded into the waters and was immersed under them. Going under the waters symbolized dying and going into the tomb with Christ (Rom 6:4). The symbolic act, however, actually united the Christian baptized in Christ's death with his risen body. At the moment of death the Spirit was given to the candidate, who rose from the waters as a member of the risen body of the Lord. This is the union Paul had spoken of in 1 Corinthians 15, and would speak of in Colossians 1:5–14 (see section A of this chapter). As Christ's death had destroyed sin, so the Christian is dead to sin, reconciled to God, and, as a spiritual person, has a new direction for life (Rom 8:5–11).

In the lapidary expression of Romans 4:25, Jesus "was put to death for our sins, and was raised for our justification." By dying, he released us from selfishness, sin, death, and the law (Rom 5–7), and by rising he gave us the Spirit, life in him (Rom 8).

Christ's Spirit makes us (adopted) children of the Father, for we are identified with *the* Son, Jesus Christ. The union is so real that we can use his unique way of addressing God as "Daddy" (Rom 8:14–16).[22]

Clearly we are now talking about the kind of personal relationships that signal the third level of moral development, the religious. There is no way we can make a calculated, reasoned response to a God who so loves us that he sent his Son to die for us. There is no way we can be face to face in prayer with the Son who was crucified for us ("who loved me and sacrificed himself for me," Gal 2:20) without our heart reacting. That kind of Father and Son are an invitation to the depths of love where we are drawn out of ourselves, "let go" to the fullness of humanity and being. Through this leap of faith we enter into that union with the Beloved that makes two become one; we become the Christ we love. Becoming that child of that Father is the risk of faith by which we let go to a God who asks more and more of us in the model of the suffering Servant of humankind.

Therefore in this identification with the risen Christ who is free of the limitations of death and sin, we are free from sin and death (Rom 5:12–21). In Romans 5:12–14 Paul elaborates the Christian doctrine that came to be called "original sin."[23] He recalls that in Genesis 3–4 Sin (personified as an actor in Paul's thought) entered the world, and so Death came to all people. Physical death is the sign of spiritual death (sin) ruling over all. From the time of Adam his selfishness provoked a reaction of selfishness in another, until self-seeking became a way of life, and so death-dealing was a contagion over the whole world. When Christ entered the world, however, as the one who would not succumb to this contagion, who refused to do evil for evil, but would rather lay down his life than reject the truth of his Father's vision for humankind, then another contagion came into the world. Those who take the risk of faith in that style of life, who enter through faith and the Spirit into identification with that Light which is Life, are freed from sin and death. As they themselves exercise that freedom of the Servant's way of life, with their selfishness healed by love, they foster and promote that contagion of goodness in the world that overcomes the contagion of sin still remaining from Adam:

> The results of the gift also outweigh the results of one man's sin: . . . If it is certain that death reigned over everyone as the consequence of one man's fall, it is even more certain that one man, Jesus Christ, will cause everyone to reign in life who receives the free gift that he does not deserve, of being made righteous . . . (Rom 5: 16–17).[24]

Thus we are, by the love of Christ to which we surrender, healed of our selfishness, free from it. We are, through faith and baptism, "dead to sin, but alive to God in Christ Jesus" (Rom 6:11). Casting ourselves into the love of the Father expressed in Christ's flesh, we transcend our neurotic concern to protect ourselves, protect our well-being in a hostile world. Free from self-clinging, we give ourselves to the justice and peace that Christ promotes in our world:

> . . . you must not let any part of your body turn into an unholy weapon fighting on the side of sin; you should, instead, offer yourselves to God, and consider yourselves dead men brought back to life; you should make every part of your body into a weapon fighting on the side of God; and then sin will no longer dominate your life, since you are living by grace and not by law (Rom 6:13f.; cf. 6:15–19).

Finally, Paul speaks of the Christian's being free even from the law. We have to realize what a shock this must have been to the Jewish Christians Paul was addressing. For them the law was God's Holy Word, and there was no reason whatsoever to think that it would be supplanted: the whole covenant was based on it, and God is faithful to his promises. Yet that is what Paul is saying:

> . . . you, my brothers, who through the body of Christ are now dead to the Law, can now give yourselves to another husband, to him who rose from the dead to make us productive for God (Rom 7:4).

The argument, as we developed it on pages 110–11, is that Jesus died to all the conditions of humankind, including the old covenant with its law. Therefore we, who are one body with Christ, died to the old law in the sinful body and are now free to enter into the new covenant with Christ in his risen body.

> Before our conversion our sinful passions, quite unsubdued by the Law, fertilised our bodies to make them give birth to death. But now we are rid of the Law, freed by death from our imprisonment, free to serve in the new spiritual way and not the old way of a written law (Rom 7:5–6; cf. Gal 2:15f.).

For most of us, trained in a religion of the Ten Commandments, this radical freedom from law produces anxiety. How am I to know what to do? Where do I find the boundary between liberty and license? If all may do as they please, can we have a community, a society, a church? How do I know where I stand with God?

It is true that for most of us the Ten Commandments were a clear guideline of our relationship with God. For Catholics there were the further specifications of definite precepts of the church. You could tell a Catholic because he or she observed abstinence from meat on Friday. Not only did this identify one for other people, it gave oneself a sense of identity. Today when all structures that identify us are changing so rapidly, when there is so little security in our world, we are even more eager to hang on to structures that "locate" us, give us the security of knowing how we stand with God and other people. Yet Paul takes the law away from us. Why does he do it, and how can this be liberating? He does it because (1) the law often gets in our way of doing the good, and (2) it is not part of the level of religious morality by which a person is saved.

In the first place, we need only look at the Pharisees of the Gospels. They were the good people, the ones who observed the laws so as to give reverent obedience to God. Yet this often kept them from being open, self-sacrificing, loving to others. For example:

Matthew 9:10–13: The Pharisees, according to Jewish law, would prohibit Jesus from eating with tax collectors and sinners. Yet these were the very people who most needed Jesus' friendship and mother love, so they could be converted to God. The Pharisees followed the law, but people died in the process.

Matthew 12:1–8: The Pharisees, according to their interpretation of work on the Sabbath (harvesting), prohibited Jesus' disciples from satisfying their hunger with food the law granted them. Jesus replied that there are needs greater than the law, that the Pharisees are not attuned to the love of God behind the law.

Luke 13:10–17: The synagogue official prohibited people from coming to be cured on the Sabbath (which is "work" for Jesus). Jesus shows that even the observant Jews themselves set the law aside when urgent needs are on them. And so do we all—all the time. (From early times the church has interpreted the commandment prohibiting stealing in such a way that it is possible for a person in desperate need to steal, or for a person in danger of death to kill another person. But this is to say that there is a deeper principle of morality than the law, that we can go beyond the law in favor of urgent and proper self-love.)

Paul merely ratified Jesus' own practice: when the law keeps us from doing the more loving thing for the other, we are freed from that law. We cannot use church law to keep us from loving relations with sinners, from helping those in need because we have religious duties to perform, or because of danger of "scandal" to the church. There is a great deal of the Pharisee in all of us, as there was in Peter, too. In Galatians 2:11–14 Paul tells how Peter used to violate Jewish law to eat with the Gentiles in Antioch, to express his friendship and love for them. But when official

Christians with a strong orientation to observance of Jewish law arrived, Peter went back to his observance of the law. Paul accused him of not only abandoning the Gentiles, but forcing them thereby to observe the very law that had proved a burden to Peter himself. The Gentiles were free from the law; why saddle them with it? Thus the law had kept Peter from doing the good he earlier had done spontaneously in the Spirit. And so Paul concluded:

> If you love your fellow men you have carried out your obligations. All the commandments: You shall not commit adultery, you shall not kill, you shall not steal, you shall not covet, and so on, are summed up in this single command: You must love your neighbour as yourself. Love is the one thing that cannot hurt your neighbour; that is why it is the answer to every one of the commandments (Rom 13:8–10).

Second, the law is not proper to Christians because it tends to keep them on the first two levels of moral development. We have this tendency to measure out our response to God according to what he demands of us. By doing this we are safe; he cannot lay a glove on us.[25] We can, however, fall into the nonreligious aberration of the scrupulous—conceiving God as a person harshly insistent on the letter of the law being observed, to a minuteness of detail that drives us to obsession. Yet love, as we saw, is a risk, a going beyond, a casting of oneself into love that has no measure. Only the one who conceives of God as an infinite invitation to love of himself and humankind really is relating to God. This is scary: how much can I give, not how much must I do? The one who takes this infinite invitation seriously understands Paul's injunction to "work out your salvation in fear and trembling" (Phil 2:12). Only the one who is free from law and entrusting self personally to God in loving action is liberated and free to grow in Christ's divinized humanity.

Is there, then, no function for law in Christianity? There is no positive function. Paul does grant it a negative function. It still serves as a guide for us who fall short of the highest levels of human morality. For us who are still sinners, it catches us up, calls our consciences to account, makes us aware of our sin (see Rom 7:7–13). In reality, none but the greatest saints are free from the law in all aspects of their lives. Ordinarily our union with God in Christ is not so complete that we are free in all aspects of our human conduct. Human growth is ordinarily irregular; we move to advanced stages of growth in some areas of our conduct, while lagging at an infantile stage in others. And so most of us need law to affirm values in those parts of our lives where we actually are still in the first stages of morality. We hope that we shall come to pass through observance of the law, to go beyond that law to the law of the Spirit. But in the meantime, as Paul's disciple points out,

> . . . laws are not framed for people who are good. On the contrary, they are for criminals and revolutionaries [i.e., the rebellious], for the irreligious and the wicked . . . (1 Tim 1:9f.).

What do we do with our anxiety over what is right conduct? How do we keep this liberty from becoming license, a "do what you want" morality? Paul saw that this was *the* problem for his moral teaching, just as legalism and scrupulosity were the perversion of the law-abider:

> My brothers, you were called, as you know, to liberty; but be careful, or this liberty will provide an opening for self-indulgence. Serve one another, rather, in works of love, since the whole of the Law is summarized in a single command: Love your neighbour as yourself (Gal 5:13f.).

It is when we are doing works of love for the neighbor, not protecting our own interests, that we know we are Christians. Jesus himself had given this as the sign of the Christian's distinctive morality:

> If anyone wants to be a follower of mine let him renounce himself and take up his cross and follow me (Mk 8:34).

> For the Son of Man . . . did not come to be served but to serve, and to give his life as a ransom for many (Mk 10:45).

> By this love you have for one another,
> everyone will know that you are my disciples (Jn 13:35).

Paul now spells out some indicators of this self-giving level of morality:

> . . . If you are guided by the Spirit you will be in no danger of yielding to self-indulgence, since self-indulgence is the opposite of the Spirit. . . . If you are led by the Spirit, no law can touch you. When self-indulgence is at work the results are obvious: fornication, gross indecency and sexual irresponsibility, idolatry and sorcery, feuds and wrangling, jealousy, bad temper and quarrels; . . . What the Spirit brings is very different: love, joy, peace, patience, kindness, good-

ness, trustfulness, gentleness and self-control. There can be no law against things like that, of course (Gal 5:16–24).

And so, in the last analysis, it is the discernment of the Spirit in one who has cast aside the self-indulgence of the old person that is determinative for the new person risen in Christ. What has happened is the new covenant, by which our hearts of stone have been replaced by hearts of flesh (Ezek 36:26). Our loving union with Christ changes our desires so that we are really free from selfishness and sin, and so beyond law. It is as a black Pentecostalist preacher recently said to a friend of mine: "I am free; I can do anything I want. It's just that all my wants have been changed!"

D. THE HOPE OF SALVATION

Yet, in spite of the justification in faith that grants us freedom now, we are still not saved.[26] Our final salvation is still ahead of us, when we finally ratify Christ's obedient death by our own submission to death and pass into Christ's complete salvation. In the meantime, we feel in ourselves that conflict between self and Spirit that Paul speaks of:

> In fact, this seems to be the rule, that every single time I want to do good it is something evil that comes to hand. In my inmost self I dearly love God's Law, but I can see that my body follows a different law that battles against the law which my reason dictates. This is what makes me a prisoner of that law of sin which lives inside my body.
> What a wretched man I am! Who will rescue me from this body doomed to death? Thanks be to God through Jesus Christ our Lord! (Rom 7:21–24).

It is Jesus Christ who saves us, by giving us the Spirit. And the Spirit is a contagion of good that combats the contagion of evil, which we have from the time of Adam. Romans 8 goes on to speak of this positive element in our midst, which saves not only us but our world.

Not only ourselves but all creation moves toward this salvation. As Adam's sin had effected a rupture between God, people, and world, so the work of the Spirit in the body of Christ reunites all three and leads them to perfect unity:

> The whole creation is eagerly waiting for God to reveal his sons. Creation was subjected to futility, not through its own fault, but through the work of him who so subjected it. But creation still retains

the hope of being freed, like us, from its slavery to decadence, to enjoy the same freedom and glory as the children of God. From the beginning till now the entire creation, as we know, has been groaning in one great act of giving birth, and not only creation, but all of us who possess the first-fruits of the Spirit, we too groan inwardly as we wait for our bodies to be set free. For we must be content to hope that we shall be saved . . . (Rom 8:19–24).

E. SUMMARY

In this last passage, from Romans 8, is summed up much of the revelation we have studied up to this point. All creation has been ordered to God through humankind. It has been unable to attain its purpose because men and women have historically been unwilling to be stewards of its bounty for one another. (There is here a basis for a theology of ecology.) Yet in Christ as the perfect human being, God's perfect Servant/steward, creation is once again oriented through humankind to God. The perfect attainment of God in Christ's risen body (note the cosmic Christ of Colossians) is still in the future, when Christ hands over his kingdom to the Father (1 Cor 15); this is the foundation for a theology of hope. As humans we are responsible to enter into that perfect stewardship of Christ. This we do, not by following a series of laws, but by a personal commitment of faith by which we enter a personal covenant of love of God in Christ's own Spirit. By surrendering to the Spirit in prayer (Rom 8:26f.) and in works (Rom 8:28), we live out Christ's own relationship to his Father, and can address God with his familiar "Abba." This relationship of love, really beyond all contract, makes us brothers and sisters of one another, and so constitutes our hope for salvation for all our world. We, too, can cry out with Paul:

For I am certain of this: neither death nor life, no angel, no prince, nothing that exists, nothing still to come, not any power, or height or depth, nor any created thing, can ever come between us and the love of God made visible in Christ Jesus our Lord (Rom 8:38f.).

IX. The Christian Response(ability)

We saw in the chapters on the Old Testament that liberation was twofold: the physical liberation from Egypt as God's mother love for humankind, and the moral liberation under law in which God's father love brought Israel up to the human level of assuming its own responsibility to make itself free. The two chapters on the New Testament dealt mostly with God's mother love in liberating humankind in Jesus Christ. He came preaching the ultimate kingdom of God, embodied it in his own work as the suffering servant of Yahweh, and, by rising and giving us the Spirit, bound us to himself as the One Redeemed Humankind. Inevitably, however, we ask: what is our responsibility in this liberation?

In the preceding chapter we saw that our response was not to be conceived as a living of the old law, or any law. Our personal liberation in the Spirit freed us from law and urged us to go beyond law in faith and self-forgetting love for human beings and God. Yet it is true that we tend to find such an injunction vague and confusing. Thus we saw that Paul was eventually constrained to lay down *some* guidelines for discernment of right and wrong in his own communities. The movement to make Christian conduct more specific continued in the early church and came to a head in the communities of Matthew and James. We now turn to these to see what the fullness of Christian revelation in the Bible says about a person's response.[1]

A. THE SERMON ON THE MOUNT

This sermon of Jesus is recorded in two places in the Gospels, in Matthew 5:1–7:27 and in Luke 6:20–49. When we compare the two versions, we find that Matthew has included much more material (especially on the law) in his Sermon on the Mount than Luke has in his Sermon on the Plain. Clearly one (or probably both) has doctored the original, or traditional, sermon to give his community emphases they needed.[2] Nevertheless, there are enough points in common to cause many interpreters to believe that there was probably a sermon of the Lord made up of beatitudes (Mt 5:3–12; Lk 5:20–23), commands on love of neighbor (Mt 5:38–48; Lk 6:27–36), and on not judging others (Mt 7:1–5; Lk 6:37–42), the Golden Rule

(Mt 7:12; Lk 6:31), and a concluding parable exhorting one to "do" the commands (Mt 7:15–27; Lk 6:43–49). At any rate, whatever the original words of Jesus, it is clear that both Matthew and Luke placed these words at the beginning of their Gospels as inaugural speeches of Jesus, to set his message and goal as a brief unit before the Christian reader. We will study each of these, then, to determine what the New Testament gives us as the law of the Christian life.

1. The Sermon on the Mount (Mt 5:1–7:27)

If we are to judge from its concern with questions of the old law, Matthew's Gospel seems to be addressed to a Judeo-Christian community, that is, one with background in and reverence for Jewish traditions. This may account for Matthew's locating the sermon on the mountain, as on a new Sinai on which Moses gives his new law of the Christian dispensation.[3] If Matthew's readers, however, were looking for a new law, they got a law of a different sort. The beatitudes hardly read like legal commands:

How happy are the poor in spirit:
theirs is the kingdom of heaven.
Happy the gentle:
they shall have the earth for their heritage.
Happy those who mourn:
they shall be comforted.
Happy those who hunger and thirst for what is right [justice]:
they shall be satisfied.
Happy the merciful:
they shall have mercy shown them.
Happy the pure in heart:
they shall see God.
Happy the peacemakers:
they shall be called sons of God.
Happy those who are persecuted in the cause of right:
theirs is the kingdom of heaven.
Happy are you when people abuse you and persecute you and speak
all kinds of calumny against you on my account. Rejoice and be glad,
for your reward will be great in heaven; this is how they persecuted
the prophets before you (Mt 5:3–12).

The beatitude is, strictly speaking, a form of speech used in Wisdom literature. It is not a legal pronouncement, but sets down the ideals by which men and women are to live if they want to attain to the richness of human life. However, the beatitudes of Old Testament Wisdom literature are often practical platitudes about how to get ahead. These beatitudes are wildly different: they speak of the happiness experienced or to be enjoyed by those who have not got ahead in this world—the poor in spirit,[4] the gentle, the mourners, those who hunger and thirst for justice[5] because it is still not present, the persecuted, etc. Therefore, what Matthew seems to have done is to present Jesus as the new Moses,[6] now attempting to give a new law, but confounding the expectations of his readers by beginning not with legal material, but with paradoxical Wisdom sayings.

Further, Jesus goes on to say (Mt 5:13–16) that the disciples who take their direction from these beatitudes are the salt of the earth and the light of the world. The paradoxical beatitudes are not to be taken as merely ideals; they must be carried into practice if the world is to be transformed. Therefore, like law, they are dealing with real persons' conduct in the real world. Indeed, they are to be taken as the fulfillment of the old law, which Matthew's hearers had, as Jews, firmly fixed in their minds and hearts as God's revealed Word to them (5:17–20). This emerges first from the fact that Jesus does not intend to abolish the law but to complete it (5:17), and yet to produce virtue deeper than that of the scribes and Pharisees (5:20).[7] And second, the whole section of the antitheses (5:20–48)[8] is cast in the form of (legal) alternatives to formulations of the old law. Clearly, Jesus is giving rules for Christian conduct: "You have heard it said to our ancestors, 'You shall not murder.' . . . But I say to you[9] that anyone who is angry with his brother will be liable to judgment." And Jesus goes on to five more antitheses:

The Old Law	*Jesus' New Law*
You shall not commit adultery (5:27)	You shall not look at a woman lustfully (5:28)
You must give a divorced woman a certificate of divorce (5:31)	You shall not divorce (5:32)
You shall not swear falsely (5:33)	You shall not swear at all (5:34)
[No more than] an eye for an eye and a tooth for a tooth (5:38)	You shall not retaliate at all (5:39)
You shall love your neighbor and hate your enemy (5:43)	You shall love your enemy (5:44)

When you think about it, these are enormously difficult laws. Never to be angry, never to have lustful thoughts, to have such integrity of speech and action that one never has to back up a statement with an oath, and can remain faithful to one partner until death, not to retaliate with violence for prior violence, even to love the enemy who persecutes one—this is a standard of conduct far beyond what the world observes. It looks like the impossible dream. And yet, Jesus is dead earnest about these commands, as is indicated by the hyperbolic statement, "If your right eye causes you to sin, tear it out and throw it away; it is better to lose one member than to have your whole body thrown into hell" (Mt 5:29). Further, the sermon ends, as do some law codes of the Old Testament, with an injunction not merely to proclaim adherence to the Lord (Mt 7:21ff.), but to do these commands (7:24–27) or destruction will ensue. Can any of us, then, keep such radical demands? Perhaps a look at Luke's version will give us a clue as to how we are to take Jesus' demands.

2. The Sermon on the Plain (Lk 6:20–49)

Luke's version also begins with beatitudes: blessed are the poor, the hungry, the mourning, and those hated and excommunicated (Lk 6:20–23). Note, however, that Luke's version is even more this-worldly, real, than Matthew's: the poor are not the poor in spirit, but simply the materially destitute; the hungry not those who hunger and thirst for justice, but those without food; the mourners are those who cry out in pain. Luke clarifies this by dropping the other four beatitudes and adding "curses" on those in conditions of ease in this life: woe to the rich, the satiated, those who laugh and rejoice, those in good favor and reputation among people. Indeed, the paradox of Jesus' values (as opposed to those of the world) is sharpened in Luke, and this reinforces Luke's general theology that Jesus came as the Servant to overturn unjust human systems:

> The Spirit of the Lord has been given to me,
> for he has anointed me.
> He has sent me to bring the good news to the poor,
> to proclaim liberty to captives
> and to the blind new sight,
> to set the downtrodden free,
> to proclaim the Lord's year of favour (Lk 4:18f., quoting Is 61:1f.).

Luke's sermon then omits the material on the law (Mt 5:17–20), as well as the legal form of the antitheses (Mt 5:20–48), as of little importance for his Gentile Christian community, and gives Jesus' ethical teaching in the form of diverse injunctions (Lk 6:27–49), which may be reduced to four general commands: love all; give all; forgive all; judge only self.[10] Note that whereas Matthew built his injunctions to a climax in the great law of loving one's enemies, Luke begins Jesus' commands with that one (6:27) and has the rest of the sermon explicate that one command.

Yet the demands are no less radical than those of Matthew's sermon. Compare, for example, the moral demands of John the Baptist's preaching (which set a high ethical standard) with those of Jesus in the sermon:

John (Lk 3:10–14)	*Jesus (Lk 6:20–49)*
He who has two coats, let him share with him who has none (3:11)	Give to the one stealing your coat your shirt as well (6:29f.)
Collect no more than is your due (3:13)	Do not ask a return of your loan; make it into pure gift (6:34f.)
Rob no one by violence (3:14)	Offer the other cheek to the person striking you (6:29)

In every respect, Jesus is making demands on his disciples that go beyond the bounds of reason, that even violate our sense of justice. How can we simply let people take advantage of us, violate us, welsh on loans? Unless we look at the outrageous character of these demands, we will never discover what Jesus intended in his preaching. Let us ask ourselves honestly if we can do these things, or even if anyone has ever done them or could do them. If this is Christian law, how can such oppressive and unreal demands be liberating?

B. THE INTERPRETATION OF THE SERMON

Faced with the mysterious character of this "law," Christian theologians have resorted, essentially, to four major ways of understanding it, namely, the three categories considered below, plus the so-called interim ethics of Albert Schweitzer:[11]

1. *As law,* which the Christian is bound to fulfill. This interpretation takes seriously all the legal resonances of Matthew's setting and literary forms, and it reflects the seriousness of Jesus' exhortation that disciples must *do* these things. Yet against this interpretation is the radical content of the sermon. For law is an ordinance of reason setting out the *minimal* observances necessary to promote the common good of a society.[12] But the demands of the sermon call for *maximum* observance. The sermon does not forbid the most egregious acts of revenge, but prohibits *all* retaliation, no matter how urgent the cause. Further, the sermon prohibits even interior dispositions (lustful thoughts), which are not actionable at law. Thus

the sermon is asking for a level of human conduct that will evoke from men and women the peak ethical observance of which they are capable. In short, it simply does not make sense to call "Give your coat to the one suing you for your shirt" *law,* because we are not dealing with minimal actionable standards of conduct.

2. *As an unrealizable ideal,* which provokes a sense of the mercy of God. This, the classic Lutheran position, attends to the maximal nature of the commands. Jesus is laying out the standards of conduct that faith-filled Christians would measure themselves against. But our poor human nature always falls short of these demands and so comes to a profound awareness of its own sinfulness. Hence Pharisaism is overcome because we *cannot* observe the law. Out of the depths of our sinful misery, then, we cry out to God, who, in his mercy, justifies us because of our faith in his saving of us sinners.

However, this interpretation does not seem to take seriously enough the Lord's demands that we *do* this law, and the warning that if we do not *do* it, we will be destroyed. Hence, it does not seem to see the sermon as proposing a transformed style of life, which in turn would transform the world and so advance the kingdom of God.[13]

3. *As gospel,* good news of the realizable ideal. Jesus, in this view, lays down standards that are realizable and are realized by the one who enters into the faith/love relationship with God and human beings characterized by the religious level of morality (see chap. VIII, above). Thus, because the kingdom has already come to birth in Jesus, he is able to live the life of the Sermon. He holds up to his disciples the possibility that if they enter into his relationship of profound faith and love with the Father, they too will find this spiritual power spilling over into acts of altruistic love of neighbor far beyond what seems possible to human nature. The living out of this new dynamic is the establishment of a community of believers whose shared beliefs and actions transform the anticommunity of selfishness.

This personal relationship of love is central to living the Sermon. It is what makes the Christian ethic religious, rather than one of stoic principle. The reason we can be converted to giving ourselves to others is that we are sons and daughters of a loving God who is totally outpouring love for us. We become so captivated by his beauty and enriched by his bounty that we become generous by a kind of connaturality with him. Earlier (p. 23) we said, "Yahweh worship is ethical action for the neighbor." From the standpoint of law, the statement is true, but it tells only part of the story. The Hebrews who were really religious obeyed the laws because they were so in love with their transcendent God that they could be free of self-interest and so do justice to their fellow Hebrews. (Read Psalm 1 and you will find a person not so much in love with the laws as with the Author of his life and that of his community.) Religious morality, as being in love with God and so doing works of justice for our fellow human beings, is intensified in the New Testament when God becomes visible in the human flesh of Jesus of Nazareth and is incarnated in our brothers and sisters. This message will be developed in section D of this chapter.

This interpretation seems to do more justice to both facets of the sermon. It takes seriously the fact that the content of the sermon calls for actions beyond the capacity of our present selfish human natures: we are asked for a maximum that we cannot pharisaically achieve by stoic resolve. And yet, the actions can and must be done by the disciples: transformed conduct is essential to the disciples' bringing in the kingdom.

C. THE ESSENCE OF THE SERMON

We have already touched on one of the essential qualities of the sermon: its *maximalization*. It is *not law* calling for observation, but *gospel* asking for the peak of human authenticity, while at the same time proclaiming that such actions *are available* in Jesus' loving relationship to the Father, shared with the disciples.[14] (That is why Matthew's sermon moves from the antitheses into the prayer of the Our Father, Mt 6:5–18.) Consequently, it is because God, through Jesus, is asking for maximum human virtue that the community of Christian believers can be a leaven in the world, bringing the kingdom to completion among people. However, Matthew does not seem to stress as much as Paul that this maximum is possible only at the third level of religious morality by the power of the Holy Spirit given us.

A second essential quality of the sermon is its *interiorization*. We saw (chap. III) that the decalogue itself prohibited coveting, yet it appeared there (see p. 167, n. 17) that *hāmad* refers to the kind of desire that carried over into action. But in Matthew 5:28 Jesus is talking about lust precisely as apart from any action. Thus, if the sermon is to bring peace among humans, we must start from our own interior peace springing from interior harmony.[15]

A third essential quality of the sermon is its *conversion to the neighbor*. We saw that the religious law of the Old Testament consisted mostly of regulations of interhuman justice. If we look at the beatitudes and the antitheses of the Sermon on the Mount, we find at their root a concern to do justice to one's fellow human beings. This is obvious in an injunction like, "Love your enemy, pray for those who persecute you." It is also true of statements like "Blessed are the poor," "Blessed are those who mourn." "Happy the poor." One who looks, for example, at the theology of poverty in Luke can see two motives for being poor:

1. Asceticism[16]

Riches clog the spirit and keep it from discerning God as central to one's life. Luke 12:13–21 gives a parable of a rich man who keeps on amassing wealth for an easy life without consideration of God's coming. When he dies, his foolishness is made manifest. Instead, Jesus enjoins on us "being rich towards God" (Lk 12:21). But what could that mean? It seems tied up with the second motive for poverty.

2. Justice or Charity

By means of the pivot-word "treasure" (Lk 12:21, 33, and only in these two places in Luke), Luke seems to indicate that selling what one has and giving alms (to the poor) is what builds up an "unfailing treasure in heaven" (12:33), and so is "being rich towards God" (12:21). This second motive is predominant in Luke's theology; see Luke 16:9, "Make friends for yourself with the mammon of iniquity [=money], so that when it runs out, they [the ones you have befriended with your justice and charity] may receive you into the eternal dwellings." Further, this seems to have been the way of the early church, which practiced a form of primitive communism:

> The faithful all lived together and owned everything in common; they sold their goods and possessions and shared the proceeds among themselves according to what each one needed (Acts 2:44f.).

Indeed, this seems to have been the reason for the efficacy of the early Christian preaching, according to Acts 4:32–35.[17] Thus poverty is not merely ascetical by casting off what distracts. By giving to those less fortunate than ourselves, we become poor, and so subject to the beatitude "Blessed are the poor," for our sensitivity has not only united us to our brothers and sisters but also to God.[18]

Something similar could be said of the mourners. Only when we care enough about others to be vulnerable to crying and mourning for their misfortune are we truly human and alive. Again the Lord—who, unasked, grieves for the widow (Lk 7:11–16), needs the companionship of his disciples (Mt 26:38–41) and mourns for Lazarus whom he loves (Jn 11:35f.)—serves as the model of the Sermon.

By extending this analysis to all the elements of the Sermon, one can see how and why Jesus is able to sum it all up by the Golden Rule: "So always treat others as you would like them to treat you; that is the meaning of the Law and the Prophets" (Mt 7:12). Further, this emphasis on interhuman justice sums up the Gospel of Matthew as a whole, for at the end of Jesus' last discourse in the Gospel comes his famous description of the Last Judgment, where the motive for judgment on the success or failure of every human life is "Whatsoever you did to one of these, my least brethren, you did unto me" (25:40). Thus does conversion to the neighbor come to be seen as the rule of Christian conduct, not only in the Sermon on the Mount, but in the whole of Matthew's Gospel.

Finally, we conclude this section with two cautions from the Sermon about the process of conversion to the neighbor. The ethic of total giving to the other, even to the point of nonretaliation for violence, does not mean that Christians should be doormats, passive and inert before all injustice. The life of Jesus himself is the interpretation of the demands of the Sermon. On the one occasion in the Gospels when Jesus was struck on the cheek (Jn 18:22) he did not turn the other cheek in servile submission, but rather challenged his attacker: "If what I said was wrong, point it out; if it was right, why do you hit me?" (18:23). Being a doormat is *not* conversion to neighbor; the doormat does not care enough about the neighbor to face him or her in honesty and challenge what sin is doing to that person. Real conversion to neighbor demands that we try every nonoppressive means to convert the opponents of justice from their oppressive ways, which oppress themselves, too. Doing to others as you would have them do unto you means that the oppressor must be challenged and converted; that is what we all really desire for ourselves. Choosing nonviolent means of challenging injustice demands more ingenuity and more persistence and more heroism, but in the long run it will succeed because it cares not only for the victims of oppression but for the persons of the oppressors themselves.

In the second place, the Sermon is a whole. That is, we cannot just choose one of the elements and ignore the others. If we decide to accumulate the goods of this world, even at the price of impoverishing others, it will do us no good to practice nonviolence. Of course we will be robbed. Nonviolent resistance can work, in individuals and in nations, only when Christians are openhanded with their goods, faithful to their words, and so forth—in short, doing all that the Sermon asks for the good of the neighbor.

D. LOVE OF NEIGHBOR IN THE REST OF THE NEW TESTAMENT

This interpretation of Christian responsibility is corroborated by the writings of John and James.

1. The Johannine Literature

a. The Gospel of John speaks of a union of God the Father with his Son Jesus, and, through him, with all who believe in Jesus and accept him (1:12). In Jesus' last discourse, he says this union will occur for all those who keep his commandments (Jn 14:15–24, especially, vv. 15, 21, 23). Yet when one searches for these "commandments" throughout Jn, only one can be found: "I give you a new commandment, that you love one another; just as I have loved you, you also must love one another" (Jn 13:34).[19] Indeed, this love of one another (not of God) will reveal Jesus' disciples as his: "By this will all know you are my disciples—if you love one another" (13:35). Note here the advance Jesus has made over his summary of Old Testament law (Mk 12:30; Mt 22:37ff.; Lk 10:27). Whereas the Old Testament had said you must love your neighbor as yourself, Jesus now says Christians must love their neighbors as Jesus had loved them—by laying down their very lives for the neighbor (Jn 15:12f.). The suffering Servant has become the norm of Christian morality.

b. The first Letter of John,[20] written to combat a docetist Christianity,[21] has as its theme the fact that salvation has come in the flesh of Jesus, and as a result of this salvation that Christians share, they must love one another. The letter stresses the same single commandment as the Gospel: "This is not a new commandment that I am writing to tell you, but an old commandment that you were given from the beginning" (2:7). We can be sure we are in life only if we love our brothers (cf. 3:14).

In the fourth chapter we find the kernel of John's message: God is love (4:8). And if we are to be sons and daughters of that Father, we too must love, "Let us love one another since love comes from God and everyone who loves is begotten by God, because God is love" (4:7–8). In fact, John lines up his argument in such a way that we are led to think that our religious response to God's love ought to be to love God, but the response, really, is that we must love one another:

> God's love for us was revealed
> when God sent into the world his only Son
> so that we could have life through him;
> this is the love I mean:
> not our love for God,
> but God's love for us when he sent his Son
> to be the sacrifice that takes our sins away.
> My dear people,
> since God has loved us so much,
> we too should love one another (1 Jn 4:9–11).

Note that God's love precedes, as mother love, enabling us to respond to the command of father love that we must love one another. This is reiterated:

We are to love, then, because he loved us first.
Anyone who says,
"I love God,"
and hates his brother, is a liar,
since a man who does not love the brother he can see
cannot love God, whom he has never seen.
So this is the commandment that he has given us,
that anyone who loves God must also love his brother (1 Jn 4:19–21).

This love is not empty, a pious exhortation. It calls for action in the flesh, a sharing of our worldly goods, which will make us poor:

> If a man who was rich enough in this world's goods
> saw that one of his brothers was in need,
> but closed his heart to him,
> how could the love of God be living in him?
> My children,
> our love is not to be just words or mere talk,
> but something real and active (1 Jn 3:17–18).

And so the Johannine writings add up to the same message as that of Paul and the Jesus of the synoptic Gospels: true Christian love is a spontaneous response to the Father, who has first loved us. The response is to love the brother and sister, especially in sharing one's worldly goods with the one in need, and so entering into the poverty that makes one happy.

2. The Letter of James[22]

This is more a homily than a letter. Its main purpose seems to be to present an ethical code that will measure up to the demands of living in the present world and still be valid long into the future. It grows out of a Christian parenetic tradition built on the words of Jesus; see 5:12, which reflects Jesus' own words on not swearing (recorded in Mt 5:34f.). The main thrust of the letter's ethics is, again, the service of the poor:

> Pure, unspoilt religion, in the eyes of God our Father is this: coming to the help of orphans and widows when they need it, and keeping oneself uncontaminated by the world (Jas 1:27).

And neither is this a general rule without immediate application, for James applies it to the rich and poor classes within his own community:

My brothers, do not try to combine faith in Jesus Christ, our glorified Lord, with the making of distinctions between classes of people. Now suppose a man comes into your synagogue, beautifully dressed and with a gold ring on, and at the same time a poor man comes in, in shabby clothes, and you take notice of the well-dressed man, and say, "Come this way to the best seats"; then you tell the poor man, "Stand over there" or "You can sit on the floor by my foot-rest." Can't you see that you have used two different standards in your mind, and turned yourselves into judges, and corrupt judges at that? (Jas 2:1–4).[23]

On the contrary, blessed are the poor:

Listen, my dear brothers: it was those who are poor according to the world that God chose, to be rich in faith and to be the heirs to the kingdom which he promised to those who love him (Jas 2:5).

Again, Christians have a chance to become or to remain poor precisely by using perishable worldly goods (1:10f.) to attend to the needs of the poor:

If one of the brothers or one of the sisters is in need of clothes and has not enough food to live on, and one of you says to them, "I wish you well; keep yourself warm and eat plenty," without giving them these bare necessities of life, then what good is that? Faith is like that: if good works do not go with it, it is quite dead (Jas 2:15–16).

Otherwise they fall heir to the woe that Luke's Jesus proclaimed to the rich:

Now an answer for the rich. Start crying, weep for the miseries that are coming to you. Your wealth is all rotting, your clothes are all eaten up by moths. All your gold and your silver are corroding away, and the same corrosion will be your own sentence, and eat into your body. . . . On earth you have had a life of comfort and luxury; in the time of slaughter you went on eating to your heart's content. It was you who condemned the innocent and killed them; they offered you no resistance (Jas 5:1–3, 5–6; cf. Lk 6:24; 12:16–21; 16:19–31; etc.).

And so James reinforces the same ethical message we have seen throughout the New Testament: this world's goods must be used to alleviate the miseries of the poor. This is *the* religious response, and it will keep us in the happiness promised the poor.

E. SUMMARY

In the final analysis, the ethical message of the New Testament (its "law," so to speak) is similar to that of the Old Testament: what God wants is interhuman justice. The New Testament advances on the Old Testament message by speaking of the love of a Father given to us in his Son Jesus, who gave us his own death as a model for the kind of love we should have for one another. Our response to this love is to be converted to the neighbor so totally, beginning from the spontaneous desires of our heart, that we share all of this world's goods with those who are poor. In this way we incarnate the suffering Servant in our world and really enter into that community in poverty that makes us blessedly happy and brings justice to those less fortunate than we. This message, we shall now see, is the *only* salvation for our world.[24]

X. Will It Work—Utopia or Eutopia?

In the preceding chapter we outlined a plan to bring justice to the world through maximal conversion to the neighbor. The "commands" there studied seemed to ask for a level of human commitment that was beyond human attainment, an impossible ideal. Yet the Lord made our very salvation as Christians depend on the attainment. We saw that this was possible only through the power of the kingdom in us, the love of Jesus Christ flooding our hearts (through the Spirit, which has been given us, Rom 5:5) and healing interiorly our selfishness. This level of conduct actually has been verified in our human history, not just by the Son, but by countless heroes of our faith whom we call saints, whether canonized or not.[1] However, there is a further difficulty with the agenda given by Christ and his disciples: even if we could follow the example of Jesus, is such living practical for our world? Will it work? Is it an ethic we can use to transform our world today? And if it does work, how can we explain the way it works? This chapter is a brief attempt (the sketchiest in the whole book!) to deal with these questions in a preliminary and rudimentary way. We begin by the structure of our world as it has come to be historically.

A. THE CONTAGION OF EVIL

We saw in chapter IV that there was a history of sin in our world. Paul, in Romans 5, finds that "sin reigned over all from Adam to Moses" and that it constitutes an actor on the stage of life. Sin is larger than the guilt of anyone, a miasma from which only Christ was able to free us.[2] In chapter IX (and also n. 23, p. 183) we suggested that sin is structured into our world and this constitutes the original sin spoken of in Rom 5:12–14; this section will elaborate that hypothesis.

It is the very nature of sin for us to prefer short-term personal solutions over long-term social ones. In other words, we choose that good immediately present to us, rather than find that which is gratifying in the long run by creating a society in which we can live in peace.

We make such short-term choices not solely out of the freedom of our will seeking self-gratification, but also because the short-term choices of others have historically structured a society in which short-term choices are held out as the conventional wisdom of the day. For we do not create the society in which we are raised: its dynamics are already present, and its values given us as we mature.[3] There is a certain "objectivity" of the social world as it has already been created by our ancestors in our particular society. It is "there," and we must fit into it. First there are the expectations of our contemporaries: social pressure will influence what we can do. Second, the way these contemporaries understand the dynamics of the world given them by ancestors is assumed to be all there is to know about the world. "That's the way things are (have been) done," and so there is no other. What is known in our society becomes what is knowable, period. And in order to institutionalize the choices and structures of the society so that all will follow them, that society will develop a metaphysics and theology to legitimate its procedures.[4] Citizens are socialized by the example of elders and by education based on the metaphysics and theological legitimation of the society until they do spontaneously what their world does.

Thus we can grow up in a society where certain selfish patterns are taken for granted as part of the ontological and moral structure of the world. These structures limit our freedom to act morally and responsibly; they are original sin, and we are from birth a part of it. For an example, take the structure of racism in the southern states of the United States. First blacks were slaves, less than human because owned. To justify the economic gain the white landowners had from them, blacks were considered, ontologically, slaves and, theologically, descended from Ham, made by God a slave of his brothers (Gen 9:25). In that society a white restaurant owner wishing to serve a black would have to contend with the contempt and ostracism of his white "brothers," their anger, violence, and economic reprisals against his business for overturning their profitable economic system, perhaps even the thundering of the church against his "unnatural" morality. And so he would have been constrained to practice racial prejudice out of peril to his life, and it would have taken heroic virtue to act against the dynamics of his world. (Indeed, Catholic moral theology would not have "forced" him to act against these norms if such an act would have imperiled his life or livelihood!) And so such a man would have taken the action that would provide short-term advantage for himself, rather than the heroic breaking of society's unjust pattern, which would provide long-term justice for his world.

These external structures are internalized as biases in the individuals and groups of the society.[5] Individuals growing up find their own shortcuts to surviving in the world. Perhaps a girl finds that when cornered about some act she has done, crying affords an easy way out. She may grow into "adulthood" and continue this practice with her husband, when what is needed is an honest facing of faults and responsibilities. The child's solution is really no longer acceptable, but she can refuse to recognize the new demand on her person and grow.[6] In our society this ruse has become unacceptable, and so this individual bias is fragile and can be broken down by a harsh enough response by her husband or others, leading her to face the inadequacy of her response.

On the other hand, if all society or a large group in it were to accept as fact and theory that women cannot be responsible or rational, and so crying is the acceptable way for women to cope with conflict, then group bias would reinforce her individual bias and make it difficult for her husband or others to break it down. Group bias is, then, tougher, more resistant to reversal, change, growth. We recognize group bias in the American work ethic, in racial prejudice, in actions of interest groups, social classes, etc.

Where society can structure into its members a group bias enshrining short-term solutions to human problems, a sinful social structure occurs, and sin is an objective actor in the whole human process. Thus, when both rich and poor accept as ultimate truth that the only reason for poverty is the laziness of the poor, a situation where the rich can *legally* exploit the poor is tenable. The rich necessarily get richer and the poor poorer, and nothing can be done about it. And so injustice will be in the air that people breathe, and one kind of exploitation will have no redress except the immediate retaliation of the few bold enough to turn to crime. Eventually the whole society will seethe with injustice. Therefore,

> an irrational element has been introduced into the social situation. This element is destructive: destructive of coherence, of meaning, of well-being, perhaps even of life. But once it is there, it will provoke not a reversal of the irrational but an accumulation of the irrational. For if there were a circle of trust among all men, then the situation in which each found himself would call for an open, loving, generous response. But once that circle is broken, once the earliest structures are those of contest, and distrust and domination, then the situation invites each person to respond defensively. The roles we are taught are meant not only to channel our contribution to society, they are meant to help us to protect ourselves. We learn early to act on the basis of our own biased insights into a situation—a bias towards protecting our own personal interests. This in turn further skews the subsequent situation, provoking others to still further defensive action.[7]

We do not mean to say that there is no personal responsibility in this sinful situation. Eventually we become dimly aware that in this world we are becoming progressively isolated, alienated from our fellows, unhappy, and distrustful. When we become aware, but refuse to pursue that awareness to analysis and solution and, rather, continue in the pattern of the destructive relationships of the sinful social structures, then the sin is personally ours, and we recapitulate and augment the sinful objective structure. We do mean to point out, however, that the dynamics of the world in which we live have a certain specious rationality as presented to us in our society, and that a kind of heroism is involved in breaking the structure and forming another one. How does the Sermon on the Mount realistically address itself to bringing justice and peace into such a complex structure of sin?

B. THE PRACTICALITY OF THE SERMON'S ETHIC

There are two main charges leveled against the Sermon as Christian ethic: (1) It was never intended as a worked-out ethic, but as a fundamental spiritual attitude. The working out of an ethic would arrive at forms of conduct more feasible and practical than (and even at times opposed to) the attitudes of the Sermon. (2) The Sermon may have been a sufficient ethic for Jesus' agrarian society in first-century Palestine, but it cannot work in the power politics of our present industrial society. And so it must be modified by an ethic for today.

There are many variations of the first position. Albert Schweitzer saw Jesus as an apocalyptic preacher convinced that the world and its social structures were coming to an immediate end. Therefore the Sermon embodied "interim ethics"—what to do until the end arrived. Injunctions to turn the other cheek, which would be the death of institutions, made sense in such an apocalyptic situation, since the institutions were dying anyway. But now that Jesus has been proved wrong and social structures go on in human history, a real ethic is needed. Another variation sees Jesus as dealing with spiritual matters, not social ones. He tried to get persons to make a religious response to God and fellow humans, but this has to be supplemented by a genuine ethic that enters into the concrete existential world made up of ambiguous and complicated issues and helps us make better choices.[8]

The second position likewise has many possibilities. On the one hand, Jesus lived in a simple agrarian economy, and his radical personalization of all ethical problems was possible in a village sociology where knowing everyone is possible. Jesus, therefore, had no intention of developing an ethic for complex national and international organizations. On the other hand, Jesus' rural society did exist as part of the Roman empire, whether governed by Herod, the procurators of Judea, or the governor of Syria, and so a part of a complex socio-economic political structure. Yet neither Jesus nor his disciples in the early church had any power within, or control over, these larger structures. Consequently, they could be only a faithful minority witnessing to the integrity of personal relationships as over against structures. They had no responsibilities for the structures.[9]

Those who argue either of these cases maintain that Jesus' fundamental attitudes have to be broadened, sometimes even overturned by an ethic for our day, which would begin from an analysis from other sciences (socio-economic, political, psychological, philosophical) of the world in which we live. This is not the position, remember, of enemies of the gospel, but of committed Christians. What have we to say about this?

In the first place, everyone must admit that Jesus' "ethic" does address itself to individuals in their own existential relationships, and that this ethic is most clearly effective in a simple society built on direct personal relationships. And so one must admit that this ethic was not directly addressed to the complexities of society even in the early church's own days, to say nothing of the complexities introduced in our own time by modern science: the bomb, contraceptives, economic dependency structures, parliamentary log-rolling, etc. Therefore those basic attitudes must clearly be elaborated by other principles to form an adequate Christian ethic for our day.

In the second place, however, it is one thing to build from the same fundamental principles into a more adequate ethic in a new situation, and another to structure an ethic around entirely different principles so that the basis of ethics is changed. This latter is what has happened in the history of Christian thought. For example, let us take the Christian just-war theory. Clearly the gospel speaks of nonviolent turning of the other cheek, and this ethic was asserted by Augustine for the individual Christian. However, when Augustine spoke of the duties of the monarch, these included the duty of defending the peace of the state, even by war, an opinion in which Aquinas concurred.[10] In the sixteenth century Vitoria and Suarez developed the theory that war was not intrinsically evil, and therefore could be legitimate or just on the following conditions: (1) It must be waged by lawful authority; (2) the cause must be just (a defensive war or aggressive war to redress the infringement of some right); (3) peace must be attainable by no other means; (4) the war must be waged and the peace imposed with moderation.[11] Pius XII and John XXIII have since withdrawn wars of aggression, no matter how just, from this theory's justifications of contemporary war. In the same line of reasoning as these arguments about the rights of the state, Catholic moralists came to develop the right of the individual Christian to kill an unjust aggressor in self-defense. And so, eventually, the church has come to compromise the gospel ethic even on the level of individual responsibility. The new ethic is based not on the gospel call to self-sacrificing justice as an act of faith and love, but solely on the use of human reason in calculating the relations of rights and duties.

In the third place, such compromise with the gospel is perfectly understandable: we do it all the time. We do it in fulfillment of contracts, in foreclosing a mortgage on a hard-pressed family who temporarily cannot meet payments, or when a husband whose wife leaves him for another man decides the contract is voided and remarries. We do it simply to stay alive, as when a university compromises its principles to curry favor with wealthy benefactors who can keep it going. And we do it even when we have to engage in activities we know are wrong, as when we cut corners on promised services to customers because it is the only way to stay competitive, or when we lie under oath in court as the only way to defeat a case built on a structure of lies. What is happening, then, is that the Sermon is inviting us to the highest levels of human integrity, but we are still on the level of rational morality (see the preceding chaps. VIII and IX), calculating our actions not on the principle of self-sacrificing love, but on that of enlightened self-interest. That problem is compounded in institutions, where even the few who are converted to love of neighbor must make their decisions together with the majority who act, at best, out of self-interest, if not out of greed. And so, in a hostile and grasping world, we, as individuals and institutions, feel we must compromise the gospel ethic if we are to survive, and we make the enlightened self-interest that originated with the Greeks the basis of our ethical systems.

But in the fourth place, such compromise is totally ineffective in liberating our world from recurring patterns of injustice. One need only ask what war was ever prevented by the use of the just war theory? Anyone can easily discover in present fact or past history reasons for the drive to war. Even in a war that seemed to Americans as black and white as the war against racist and totalitarian Nazism, there were not lacking German bishops and other clergy to bless the German war effort.

Such reasoning need not be sophisticated. You can observe the contagion of violence in any schoolyard fight. First one boy jostles another, and the latter responds with a jab of the elbow: one encroachment invites a "just" retaliation by the other. And then the first, whose originating action was either accidental, or caused by a feeling that he previously had been put down and must get even, now feels himself "unjustly" attacked by the other boy's response, and so escalates his original provocation. And so it goes, back and forth, until there is a full-scale war. Even if the schoolyard supervisor intervenes and imposes peace, it will not last if "injustices" continue to smolder in each boy until the next opportunity for conflict arises. Acting according to the perceived justice of enlightened self-interest cannot be the principle by which the conflict will be overcome, for each will inevitably perceive his cause as just.

Let us take an example from the institutional level in our society: the American penal system. Words like "penitentiary" and "reformatory" attest to the fact that the original intention of prisons was to be a place where criminals could reflect on their crimes, repent, do penance, and return to society as whole persons in a whole society. That is still our expressed desire (awakened especially in the nineteenth and twentieth centuries), yet the literature on prisons today attests that there is very little practical commitment to effective rehabilitation programs in the prisons. In fact, the real motivation behind our imprisoning criminals seems to be protective and vindicative.[12]

If we get in touch with our own feelings with regard to criminals, we may find deep down this motive: "I want my family to be protected; lock them up so that my wife won't be raped, my children mugged, my house robbed, etc." Again, this is very reasonable, and very human, but it will not touch the criminals. What it says, in effect, is that I come first, and I really don't care about the criminals, as long as they do not have access to injuring me. In fact, most of us do not want to go anywhere near a prison, perhaps on the subterranean motivation that if we do not come to know criminals as persons we will not be disturbed by the way society handles them.

The second motive, as I said, is vindicative: "The criminal has offended against society such and such an amount, and now must repay such and such an amount, in order to return society to a just balance." Thus we cast up different amounts of punishment for misdemeanors and felonies, according to the magnitude of the crime, and we measure this out to each offender. The person and needs of the offender are rarely considered; it is a question of restoring objective balance. Again in this situation we do not aim at the conversion of the criminal, but at the restoration of some abstract order.[13]

I submit that neither on the one-to-one level, nor on the institutional level of courts, prisons, wars and imposed peace, does the self-protecting concern of enlightened self-interest effect the conversion of neighbor and society. Only when I am touched first by someone else's love, given a sense of self-worth, am I able to grow into one who loves justice and does justice to my fellow human beings. Only a society concerned enough to put the criminal's personal worth above the risk incurred by self can help the offender to return justice and love to that society. In terms we have used throughout the book, one must first experience mother love before father love can elicit a response that is human and loving in return. Any ethic that ignores the ethic of the Sermon, based on self-sacrificing conversion to the neighbor, and builds instead on rational self-interest cannot bring peace and justice to society. Thus, we must turn to the Sermon again as embodying the only hope for long-range justice in our world.

C. OUTOPIA OR EUTOPIA?

There are many utopian thinkers who say that if people would only be converted to their fellow human beings, if they shared justly the goods of this earth, a tranquil society would result. The history of such thinking antedates the New Testament; it goes back to Plato and Aristotle, but it reaches its peak expression in Thomas More's classic *Utopia*.[14] More conceived of an ideal commonwealth as a city of the future serving as a model for all humankind. Thus his was no idle fancy seeking a return to a primitive paradise or a previous golden age,[15] but a bold plan for the possibility of ethical renewal of a whole society. More based his hopes on a communism for the whole nation, equality of men and women (indeed, the whole nation approaches a casteless democracy), the pre-eminence of learning, and the connection between goodness and religion. Utopian thinkers since his day have aimed at producing in the ideal society of the future the full satisfaction of human wants, a happy labor or a rich leisure, equality throughout the society, effortless virtue making discretionary authority unneeded or able to be minimally exercised by all, and so a harmony in society leading to perpetual peace. In our day utopian thinking is mostly the province of Marxists, building from Marx's own vision of a classless society built on the principle, "From each according to his ability, to each according to his needs."

If the principle of the Golden Rule, treating others as you would want to be treated, is the mainspring of perfect society, why is the Sermon, or Christianity, or even religion, so necessary? The Sermon is necessary because its principle of love of neighbor is not, as in utopian thought, an *ideal* principle, but a *real* one. Utopian thought fixes on a future state and looks at the principles of conduct already operating in an already perfect society. But such utopias do not now exist; they are *nowhere*.[16] It is true that in an ideal society virtue might be (more) effortless. If I lived in a society where everyone gave to me according to my needs and asked no more than what I could deliver, I might be able to love everyone. If I came first in their considerations, I would be free to make them first in mine. But this is *not* the real world. We live in a world where people are trained from childhood to look out for themselves first and foremost: "If you do not take care of number one, no one else will." We live in a world where people manipulate others for their own psychological security, where the rules of business ethics demand that we exploit one another,[17] and where such conduct elicits from the one wronged a response of revenge. We all recognize that not only are these the dynamics of the real world, but they are structured patterns of our world, influencing us to do likewise. In short, we live in a world of sinful social structures. Yet Jesus, in the sermon, does not ask us to love in the utopian world; he asks us to be converted to one another in this real world, *now!*

Jesus knew that one generous act would not convert a world structured in evil. That is why the sermon makes it clear that those who practice Jesus' way of life will be taken advantage of, persecuted:

> Happy are you when people abuse you and persecute you and speak
> all kinds of calumny against you on my account. . . . This is how they
> persecuted the prophets before you (Mt 5:11f.).

Jesus, following in the line of thought of Wisdom 2:10–20, knew that just
persons can expect that their very goodness will be a threat to others and
will provoke exploitation and persecution. That is what happened to Jesus,
and he assured us we could expect the same. Therefore, the most realistic
words of the New Testament are these: "Love your enemies, and pray for
those who persecute you" (Mt 5:44). Nor is this a question of a temporary
persecution. It is probable that we, like the suffering servant of Isaiah
52:13–53:12, or Jesus himself, shall die before we see such selfless love
working the conversion of our enemies. Thus we live entirely on faith that
the cross will issue in the resurrection, not only for our individual selves,
but also for the world, the kingdom coming.

In short, we are not talking about reasoned self-interest. Jesus has
already indicated that this is not enough: "For if you love those who love
you, what right have you to claim any credit? . . . Even the tax collectors
do as much, don't they?" (Mt 5:46). Such love does not convert the other,
and the world continues its accustomed ways. Further, the New Testament
tells us over and over that we do not have, of our own natural resources, the
power to love like this.[18] It was necessary that God's own love enter into
our human history and be the Actor destroying sin and raising us to new
power to love. And so the Word became flesh, and "this has taught us what
love is, that he gave up his life for us" (1 Jn 3:16). And so if we commit
ourselves in faith to him and his style of love we shall receive his Spirit of
love (Rom 5:5) and be able to love our fellows. Thus it is only on the
dynamics of the third stage of morality, where we are caught up by the love
of the Father, Son, and Spirit, God's antecedent mother love, that we can
be committed to our brothers and sisters for whom Jesus dies in a way that
converts them. Jesus' call to believe, to have faith in his Father and his own
revealing way of life, is no light matter: our own existence and the peace
and justice of our world is at stake.

In the last analysis it all comes down to the individual. I cannot wait for
others to take the first step. Indeed, that seems to be the meaning of the
Sermon's prohibition of my judging others; as long as I can wait for the
pope, or the bishops, or my wife to move, then I do not have to move. But
the Sermon tells us not to judge (by) them: I am summoned to bring in the
kingdom by my own faith working for justice through the Spirit of Jesus,
and it is my responsibility to respond, no matter where the others are.[19]
Christ's love must so awaken in me his thirst for justice that independently
of others' self-seeking ethics and the sinful structures of the world that will
avenge themselves on me, I will lay down my life for the sister or brother,

with only faith in Jesus' resurrection that this will be a step to the conversion of enemies and the whole world. This love, then, is salvation (1) for me personally, (2) for communities and institutions, and (3) for our world.

1. When I have arrived at that point of power in my own life, then I am in *eutopia,* the "good place" (Greek *eu,* "well" plus *topos,* "place") of the kingdom of God "within me." I am *saved*—saved in the first instance from my own selfish addiction to the accumulation and consumption of the material things that Madison Avenue makes the center of my being. If I consider that my goods belong to all humankind, through God's disposition of them, then I cannot be anxious if someone else might steal them[20] or I might not get an abundance of them. Instead of conversion to *my* goods, which is really alienation from my deepest desire to enter communion with men and women, my giving of these goods symbolizes and effects my entering into community with them.[21] Thus I am freed, in the second instance, from my loneliness and alienation from human society.

I am saved, in the third instance, from my own guilt and sinfulness. In realizing how far short of the ethic of the kingdom I fall, I can become prey to guilt feelings that make me indulge myself even more in the goods of this world. But the Lord frees me from that by loving me even in my selfishness and weakness, and so through both mother love and father love leads me into freedom to *be* for others. I am even freed, in the fourth place, from the indifference or cruelty of others, for, having made up my mind that my justice will be an affront to them, I expect and so am willing to accept their taunts, persecution, even their maiming or killing me. And I am even freed from my own hatred of such people, for I see them as conditioned to take the short-cut solution to my challenge of the sinful structures in which we live. Thus I am trying to attend to the deeper dynamic of the long-term conversion to the other, which is deepest and best in them, and which I have sure hope will emerge if I remain faithful.

At the end I am released into a life of peace, hope, even joy: "Happy are . . . ." I am at peace, for I am doing what I individually can do in this mess to bring integrity and peace to our world. My conscience does not trouble me, even if the ills to which I see my neighbor subjected do haunt me. I am not a Pollyanna: I realize that the struggle to which the Christian is committed is fierce, but I do believe that the Christ who is operative in our world through the *logos* in which it was created will eventually return the kingdom to his Father,[22] and in this I have hope. At least in my own conversion I see that the world has grown closer to the kingdom. If *I* can be touched, so can the multitude of other individuals who have God's *logos* working for justice in them. In some way, time is on the side of God's kingdom. If at this moment I see signs of life present in my striving, then I can celebrate Christ's resurrection among us. If now I see regression and defeat, then I can celebrate that death of his which was the seed falling into the ground to bring forth life, and my depression is tempered by hope for a resurrected future kingdom.

2. A person living such a life committed to his fellow human beings not grudgingly, but full of joy in the present and hope for the future, inevitably exercises a fascination and attraction for his or her contemporaries. That person's *logos* calls out to the deepest desires in them, and they join the person in spirit and work. So it was with the prophets, with Christ himself, and so with Benedict, Francis of Assisi, Ignatius of Loyola, Roger Schutz of Taizé, and all holy men and women up to Dorothy Day and Mother Teresa. Therefore the *eutopia* of the individual becomes by contagion a *eutopia* for a group or religious community. Further, we are now talking about real community, for the dynamics central to such group organization are conversion to and sharing with the neighbor. In this way is realized, against the world anticommunity's contagion of selfishness, a countervailing force of selfless community. Liberation begins to approach the structural level. As the individual's goodness leavens the group, so the contagious goodness of the community is more visible to the larger world, and leavens it. In short, we have a dynamic of expanding circles of effectiveness:

CHURCH   **STATE**

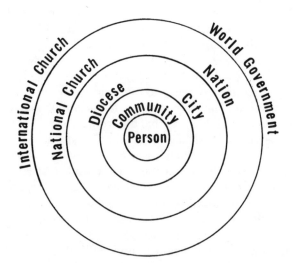

However, it must be admitted that individual prophets, without institutional bonds tying them down, are singularly free to live and spread charism. But once that charism is structured in a group, its wine is diluted. Different persons in the community have different views of practical applications of the originating vision, and so a common denominator must be sought.[23] Thus Francis's poverty came out of his personal charism. When it was shared with a group of Franciscans who had different individual personalities and gifts, some compromises were made so that all could participate. Yet Franciscans as a community did more to make contact with and convert Francis's world than he could have done by himself. When his world (say, city government) caught the message from his community, it had to deal with people less touched by the charism, and so made further compromises to incarnate a Franciscan detachment in governmental structures, where the whole populace's style of living would be ameliorated. This dialectic between prophet and institution is a constant in human history.[24] Far from being lamentable, it is a fact of life that has its own benefit: the prophet speaks and passes on; the enduring community and structured institution ameliorates the life of the whole.[25]

We spoke earlier of the individual's faith being the only guarantee that that person's message and life would be vindicated (and that perhaps only after death!). However, human faith is such that it must be shown to be reasonable.[26] As the prophets experience in their own lives that they are coming to justice and peace in their own person, they have the suspicion that their message is real, from God. But as their charism is seen to be attractive to others, drawing them to community, and so effective in their lives, converting them to self-giving love of neighbor, prophets begin to see that the mysterious message is not subjective; it is God's deliverance for the larger human society. Finally, as they come to see that not only does it work, but it is the only solution to the problem of evil as it exists in our world, then that faith commitment becomes not only reasonable, but is grounded as the only human way to live.

3. But that evil, we said, was structured into (worldwide) human society. In a world increasingly interdependent,[27] the selfish structures of one society on one continent can be contagious in others as well. In fact, if one society is culturally and economically dominant over others (e.g., United States' technological culture), then one may have one worldwide socioeconomic structure of selfishness. In order for the prophet's faith to work its solution, it too must be structured into a worldwide organization capable of combating an international contagion of sin by an international contagion of selfless love.

In the view of the philosopher Bernard Lonergan, the problem of human culture is that it necessarily divides humankind into classes and states, which will have their own short-term goals for their own self-interest. Each class will inevitably structure reality by its group biases and a general bias so that its system of interlocking self-interests is conceived of as reality.[28]

What is needed to solve this fragmentation of society into self-interest groups is

> a cosmopolis[29] that is neither class nor state, that stands above all their claims, that cuts them down to size, that is founded on the native detachment and disinterestedness of every intelligence, that commands man's first allegiance, that implements itself primarily through that allegiance, that is too universal to be bribed, too impalpable to be forced, too effective to be ignored.[30]

The cosmopolis that is the solution to the structures of evil in society is not a police force. Force is part of the particularist and short-term solutions of present structures. Cosmopolis must be above force and politics in freeing people from particularist and pragmatic solutions.[31] Cosmopolis deals with the larger intents of the human heart and mind, to transcend particular solutions and strive for worldwide community constituted by conversion of mind and heart. Cosmopolis must be above the tricks by which one group invents myths that denigrate the opponents; it must take the long view of history and purify human intelligence to cut through pain and suffering in its own members.

Lonergan the philosopher never identified cosmopolis with any present human reality, nor did Lonergan the theologian, nor, to the best of my knowledge, have any of his disciples. But I suspect that for him the church as mediator of Christian life and theology is cosmopolis. Whether he would propose that or not, that is the thesis on which this book will end. For it is a catholic community, a contagion of self-giving love, analyzing all the data of the sciences into a theological synthesis that orchestrates the dynamic of love into the scientific, socio-economic, and political structures of the whole world that is the solution to the universal structures of its malevolent self-interest. This church, made up of members already affected by the original sin of our world and incorporating in itself as institution the dynamics seeking its own self-preservation, is far from the leaven that cosmopolis must be. Yet, as locating at the center of human thought, loving, and action the mystery of Christ's self-giving love as the *logos* of humanity and world, it *is* the emerging proclamation of the kingdom coming. As it cries out to its Lord for healing, it not only proclaims, but also models the process of salvation. And while it cooperates in the grace of Christ, it also awaits it. While it waits, it celebrates the death and resurrection of the Lord as a thanksgiving for what is already at work and a dynamic of hope in the symbols of bread and wine handed over as human person for men and women.

This church touches the thinking and acting of our world, through its teaching power, and through socio-political action as a body in our world. In this sense it is what J. Metz calls an institution of the second level[32]—not totally enmeshed in the processes of this world, and yet incarnate in it, acting on it and being acted upon by it. Apart from its transnational action as a whole body, it acts also in its national constituencies, and through the local diocese. At a third level the communities themselves interact with the world. And at a fourth level there is the individual Christian acting out the charism of the prophet in singular freedom from institutional dynamics.

While one would hope that the church in its larger structures might affect through teaching and political action the larger socio-economic and political structures of our world, it remains that governments will move slowly and encumbered by self-interest groups. Thus, in many ways, the soul of this conversion of the world will take place at the level of individual conversion and especially at the level of the small community, such as the Catholic Worker community, *l'Arche,* etc. These communities exemplify and proclaim the dynamics of self-giving love effective in themselves and in their care for one another. Salvation, then, is operative in our world. But they also dedicate themselves to a special work of justice that governments are not doing for people, and so incarnate in the larger world a structural dynamic of salvation—salvation acting structurally in our world. And at a third stage they influence the larger institutions—the church itself as second-level institution, and the local, state, and national governments—to mediate justice at the highest structural levels. Thus salvation emerges for people out of individual converted Christians, cooperating in communities and changing structures as institutions so that the *logos* of self-giving love manifested in Jesus the Christ will triumph over people's shortsighted cycles of self-interest and bring in the kingdom that Yahweh has promised.

Epilogue:
Toward a Liberation Theology

The purpose of our survey of the Bible was to determine the scriptural bases of a liberation theology. In this epilogue we now want to pull together into one synthetic view the results of our study and then see how it correlates with some of the findings of a developed theology of liberation.

A. CONCLUSIONS OF OUR SCRIPTURAL SURVEY

1. Old Testament

We saw that God is not the detached and remote Absolute Being of the deists, but rather one involved with the solution of the human problem of evil in the world. After the fall, where sin was revealed to be simultaneously a rupture between God, humankind, and the world and a contagious accumulation of sin inevitably followed, Yahweh entered human history to save men and women from sin. Abraham's faith let God in as covenant partner of the Jews in salvation history.

It is when his people were most oppressed in slavery to the Egyptians that Yahweh most strikingly intervened, for he is always on the side of the oppressed. His deliverance took two forms. In a great act of unmerited mother love he delivered Israel from Egypt through plagues, the crossing of the Reed Sea, the gift of water in the desert, and the manna and the quail, and so led them into the battle for the conquest of the promised land. The accent in the Exodus and conquest narratives is on Yahweh's initiative and action, even though he chose to act by inspiring and energizing human agents of the deliverance. However, it is the second form of deliverance that really underlines human responsibility for liberation. For in his father love, Yahweh first brought individual Hebrews to assume leadership in their own government, by judges during the tribal times, and by kings in the nation-state. Second, he made all Hebrews responsible for establishing justice and peace by giving a law code, which all were to obey as service simultaneously of both God and other people.

146

However, these deliverances, as past events, were not enough, for human freedom was still influenced by an ambience of selfishness from the time of the fall, and each generation had to ratify that deliverance in its own life. Prophets had to swim against the tide of the prevailing disobedience and sin and frequently had to give their lives in fidelity to God's saving Word. Eventually the Jews realized that the just one would always have to swim against the tide of evil in the world and that this service of God was necessary to counteract the selfishness of the world and bring healing to humankind.

2. New Testament

When at last God's intervention in history from *outside* had reached its fullness, his mother love for us caused him to send his only Son to be *inside* human history as the human subject of that love: the Word became flesh and pitched his tent among us. By now Israel's own autonomy as a nation-state had vanished, and so Jesus came into the world in which we Christians must live—on the outside of political power, influencing it mainly by teaching and example.

He taught that our responsibility to God and our fellows in liberation was not exercised by strict (and fearful) observance of laws built on legitimate[1] self-interest, but on being so seized by love of the Father that we love the neighbor even more than our self—enough to send our child for the neighbor, or to lay down our life for him or her.

This teaching challenged the radical insecurity of the Pharisees (and indeed of all men and women), and so they did to Jesus what people do to prophets upon whom the Word of the Lord has descended: they killed him. Thus out of his own mother love for our liberation from sin and law, Jesus died for us—for all of us who do not believe his message and who exploit or persecute those who live it. He loved us. Yet God vindicated that message in human history by raising Jesus from the dead (and so promised life to all who so live), and by sending his Spirit among people to enable them to participate by faith and love in that divine Life that enables us to live radically, to stop clinging to life, and to give it for our neighbors.

Thus the father love of God can ask us to live up to the realizable ideals of the Sermon on the Mount. And when we do, we touch others and give them a sense of their own personal worth as subjects of our love. We too may go to death in that loving or because of it, but we have hope that we will not only (like Jesus) rise to a fuller life, but that the love we communicate to others will bring justice and peace to our world as a whole (as Jesus' love has been a leaven in two thousand years of human history).

3. Beyond the New Testament Data

We can theologize that our own leavening in the Spirit takes place on three levels: (1) our own individual life is a leavening of the lives of those around us, touching them and leading them to freedom in community; (2) the community is a leaven in society as a whole (both the church and the state), by holding up a more visible example of the dynamics of the gospel actually realizable in a group, and by undertaking the work of the Sermon on the Mount among and for humankind; and (3) the church as an institution of the second level teaches and uses political influence to form laws and governmental structures that will produce justice and peace. At the same time that the church influences the state, it must make some compromises in its principles to affect a body that does not share its faith commitment. But the church as a whole is kept on the track by the various church communities within it functioning as sects and leavening it, as well as by the charismatic living and teaching of individual prophets within it who live freely without institutional inhibitions. The church is, therefore, both the presence of the kingdom and the proclamation of the kingdom coming, whose painful birth the church celebrates in hope under the symbol of death and resurrection in a eucharistic meal, there each gives to one's fellow under the symbols of bread and wine.

B. TOWARD A LIBERATION THEOLOGY

Those who have even a passing acquaintance with recent books and articles on liberation theology will find these conclusions far short of the content and specificity of liberation theology. We must now say why this is so and where we must go from the foregoing scriptural base in building up a full theology of liberation.

1. Theology of Hope

The present-day theology of liberation springs from the theology of hope of the 1960s.[2] In its main outlines, this theology stressed the following:

a. The God of the Bible is the God of hope, not the God above us, but the God in front of us, pulling us into his future. The resurrection of Jesus Christ is the sign and presence of that future already among us.

b. Christian hope is grounded in the death and resurrection of Jesus Christ. Through his death, humankind remains faithful to God; through his resurrection, God remains faithful to humankind. Because Jesus is faithful unto death, God does not give up on humanity; because God raised Jesus, humanity does not give up on God. In other words, God not only ratifies the process by which his kingdom can come only through the suffering and death of human agents, but he enters into that process. Because he is in the process, it is sure, and so the basis of our firm hope.

c. Because God is in the process, all reality is human history, in process to the kingdom of God becoming ever more realizable until the Parousia. Thus the *pro-missio* (promise) of the kingdom is the ground of the *missio* (mission) of Christian love to our world. The exodus church exists *from* the eschatological kingdom of God and *for* the world. Church members, then, must be at work in the political process, bringing justice into the structures of this world. Christian theology must be political theology, dealing with the power options operative in our world.

When it comes to the content of this analysis of the power options and how they are to be used, the theologians of hope remain speculative and abstract.

2. Theology of Liberation

Those more closely immersed in the dynamics of oppression and liberation worked out more specifically the content and method of political theology. In particular Latin American theologians have developed a liberation theology that grows out of the internal and external forces of economic exploitation everywhere in their continent.[3]

a. Background: In general, liberation theology has three motivating forces.

First, Paulo Freire's notion of *praxis.* Freire is a Brazilian educator who worked out literacy programs for the uneducated in Brazil from 1959 to 1964. Since the method he used helped the underprivileged look critically at their world and so rise to a revolutionary consciousness, the military dictatorship banished him immediately after its coup in 1964. In 1968 he published his book, which provides the model for Latin American liberation method.[4]

Briefly, Freire discovered the essence of oppression to be that the oppressed classes have internalized as part of their own consciousness an image of themselves planted in them by their oppressors: they are poor or disadvantaged because they themselves are lazy, ignorant, etc. This causes them to acquiesce fatalistically and to submit passively to the oppression, and so not to participate actively in the creation of their own future. From this the oppressors cannot liberate them; the oppressed must liberate themselves, and in so doing they liberate the oppressors from their own oppression.[5] Thus the oppressed must assume the risk of freedom, losing what psychological and economic security the system affords them, to examine critically the world in which they live. They do this through a humanistic, liberating style of education. In contrast to the "banking concept" of education, where the teacher deposits in passive students the concepts of the system designed to maintain the status quo, Freire proposes education based on *praxis,* [6] where *praxis* is composed of action and reflection on that action. By getting adult learners to reflect on their own lives and action and draw their own concepts from that experience, *praxis* education produces learners who are active and ready for subsequent action based on their own knowledge.

Second, failure of the Decade of Development. The United Nations designated the 1960s a decade of development, in which the underdeveloped countries, with aid and technology from the developed countries, would increase their Gross National Product (GNP) by a minimum annual rate of 5 percent. While that aim was in some measure achieved, the underdeveloped countries considered the decade a failure. For one thing, almost all of a country's growth in GNP went into the pockets of the already rich. For another, most of the aid and technology from the United States was in the form of government loans, programs that were often a subsidy of U.S. industries, and private investments from U.S. companies which, by the end of the decade, were returning more money to the United States than was going out in aid. [7] Thus the United States' share of the world's wealth continued to grow during a decade that was supposed to reverse that trend. Latin Americans came to see development schemes as simply the most elaborate and subtle program of economic oppression from which they must be liberated. In a critical reflection on their own experience they concluded they had to liberate themselves.

Third, Christians for Socialism. In August 1968 about a quarter of the Latin Ameican bishops met at Medellín and issued statements denouncing the situation of injustice in Latin America as one of institutionalized violence. They attacked the neocolonialism of the national oligarchies, the neocolonialism of international monopolies, and the distortion of international economics. In the end, they denounced not only Marxism, but also liberal capitalism. In 1971 eighty Chilean priests celebrated the democratic election of Salvador Allende's socialist party by stating that there was no conflict between Christianity and socialism and that socialism ought to be the basis of a liberating economy for Chile. In April 1972 over four hundred Christians from all Latin American countries met in Santiago and issued a final document on Christians for socialism. This commitment to a socialist economy is a part of the methodology of liberation for most Latin American liberation theologians. [8]

b. The Method and Content of Liberation Theology: Wherever there is a movement to attain justice for oppressed people, some Christian within the movement writes its theology of liberation—black liberation, women's liberation, men's liberation, etc.—and all begin from their individual action and reflect on the God who moves them to liberty and justice.[9] However, the Latin American theologians have been most explicit about the method and content of their discipline, and we can summarize these as illustrative of all liberation theology.

1. The starting point of theology is the Christian experience of *commitment* to the poor and their struggle for liberation. This commitment grows out of Christian faith working through charity. In this way, the *orthopraxy* of actually following Christ in his liberating mission of preaching the Good News to the poor is prior to *orthodoxy*.

2. In this experience of solidarity with the poor comes the *insight* that God does not will this poverty in our world. God's salvation is not only liberation from sin in a world to come, but is achieved in the historical process of liberation from oppression in this world. If individual Christians are to be in union with God, they must be involved in the historical process of liberation here and now. Further, the church as institution must eschew any otherworldly salvation that tolerates or condones injustice in this world. This means that it must also eschew the specious political neutrality that implicitly lines up on the side of oppressive structures of the status quo. The church must commit itself to political movements in the struggle for justice.

3. From this commitment and insight grows a *praxis* method of theologizing. The liberation movement must begin from the oppressed people themselves and their reflection on their actions. The theologian aids the movement with analyses of the causes of the oppression (drawn from social sciences using class analysis) and by a rereading of the Bible and tradition through the eyes of the poor. Solutions of the problems will not be accomplished by the liberals, but by the radicals who have become poor with Christ poor, persecuted with Christ persecuted, etc. This theology will be critical and prophetic, and not so much oriented to the clarification of dogmatic statements.

4. With this foundational experience, insight, and method, liberation theology is not one branch of theology, but a transcendental dimension of all theology. Therefore all divisions of theology will be conceived anew: God, Christ, church, world are all seen in a new focus.[10] Among these, the Latin American theologians are specific about the following:

Anthropology will be prior to ecclesiology. If God has become human in Jesus Christ as the implementation of our world's having been created in him and finally tending to him (Jn 1:1–18; Col 1:15–20), then theology itself has become anthropology. It is in the man Jesus Christ that we study God and the world. The created realities of our world are now surging by their very nature toward the fullness of the cosmic Christ. Even the secularized world, then, tends toward Christ, and the Christian revelation makes humankind aware of what it is about, and, through God's grace in Christ, makes humankind hasten toward its completion. In some mysterious way, human political dynamics are the incarnation of God's salvation for humankind. This grounds our realization that the church is the servant of the kingdom of God coming in the world.

Christian salvation is not, then, an individualized relationship to Christ. Relating to Christ is relating to the cosmos and the social human reality that guides the cosmos. The kingdom of God is a community growing in our world, and Christian *moral theology* indicates that we must struggle to build the kingdom, especially in those social strucures that institutionalize justice or injustice, peace or war.

This process of growth of the kingdom means that *eschatology* is central in Christian efforts. The future is open to the development of the kingdom. There is a priority of utopian perspectives over factual ones as the new humankind in a new world opens up to those who work in hope.

Ecclesiology now looks at the church not as the whole of the kingdom, but as the servant of the kingdom coming to birth in the world. The church itself is an embodiment of the kingdom and its sacrament. It is the already present force of liberation in the world through the self-giving dynamics of Christians filled with faith, hope, and love.

Sacramentology studies the celebrations of this future-oriented faith, hope, and love as memorial and union with Christ's actions in our world. In the sacrament is the denunciation of our world's selfishness and the annunciation of our triumph over it. Especially in the Eucharist we effect our deepening embodiment with the cosmic Christ and our fellowship with one another in bringing all reality to him.

Spirituality, then, is that of the contemplative in liberating action.[11]

C. THE CORRELATION OF SCRIPTURE
WITH LIBERATION THEOLOGY

We began this chapter by indicating that our scriptural sketch fell short of the specificity of the current liberation theologies, because the liberation theologians have many tools of analysis and a development of the creative world that the scriptural theologians do not have. However, it appears that much of what is in the Bible is at the root of these perspectives of liberation theology.

1. Our study of the Bible pointed out that we must in life identify ourselves with the poor and oppressed. Exodus 2:23f. indicated that Israel's first historical remembrance of God was as the deliverer of an

enslaved band. Psalm 103:6 found God always on the side of the oppressed. The historical deliverances of Israel, conceived after the model of the Exodus, confirmed this in Israelite history. Further, the later prophets, from Zephaniah on, indicated that the poor had a special relationship of trust in Yahweh, so as to understand him better than others.[12] Jesus picked up this line of thought in the beatitudes, and the Jesus of Luke's Gospel has a special relationship to the poor (see pp. 126–27). Therefore the Bible presumes it is the poor and oppressed who will have a special relationship to God, which will generate special insight into his nature and his work in history.

However, it is true that the Bible could not see that both life and theology must begin from solidarity with oppressed classes.[13] Only after industrial capitalism in colonized countries had produced a continent in which 80 percent of the population is poor and economic analysis had identified the cause as class struggle could Christians place such a strong emphasis on identification with the struggles of a whole class of poor as the starting point of Christian action and thought. Nevertheless, the biblical emphasis on God's work with the poor and oppressed does seem to ground the liberation theologians' "option for the poor."

2. Our approach to Scripture has stressed the historicity of God's salvation. The Old Testament liberation took place in physical deliverance from Egypt, and the historical development of a government and law was the Hebrews' responsible liberation of themselves in history. The prophets made clear that a person's relationship to God is determined not so much by worship as by adherence to precepts of a law that establishes justice and peace on this earth. Wisdom literature confirmed that men and women must commit themselves to such action even if they die in the process.

The New Testament represents both an intensification of the historical process of salvation and a "stepping back" from it. On the one hand, by the incarnation of the Son (Jn 1:1–18), God entered into the historical process as a person in a climactic and final way. Henceforth the whole material cosmos is growing into the fullness of his body—personally the Son's to be handed over to the Father (see chap. VIII). God's personal immersion in history intensified every historical process, and especially the political, as a means of bringing the justice of Christ's presently growing kingdom to completion. On the other hand, the New Testament's relinquishing of the Old Testament theocratic governmental structure represents a certain refinement of direct political intervention by the people of God in the historical process, which we can best take up in relationship to the liberation theologians' points on anthropology (see pp. 151–52).

3. There is an autonomous dynamic of the world by which secularized processes themselves have a finality that moves the world toward God.

This perspective is present in the New Testament, although it did not form part of our limited sketch. Again, the prologue of John's Gospel holds the key: the world is created in God's *logos*:[14]

> In the beginning was the Word:
> the Word was with God,
> and the Word was God.
> He was with God in the beginning.
> Through him all things came to be,
> not one thing had its being but through him.
> All that came to be had life in him,
> and that life was the light of men,
> a light that shines in the dark,
> a light that darkness could not overpower (Jn 1:1–5).

We are speaking of the work of creation, and we say that the Word that became flesh in Jesus of Nazareth (Jn 1:14f.) is the intelligibility according to which the world was created. Therefore, apart from the grace that comes from explicitly believing that Jesus is the Son come to reveal the Father (1:18) in his death and resurrection, there is still an energy in the created world that moves to the consummation of all things in God, according to his *logos*. This is a deeper dimension of the words of Genesis, which saw all creation as coming from God, as good (Gen 1:3,10,12,18,21,25,31).

The *logos* in the world is the same as the *logos* made flesh as Jesus of Nazareth, and so both messages—in creation and in the grace of Christ—are the same:

> unless a wheat grain falls on the ground and dies,
> it remains only a single grain;
> but if it dies, it yields a rich harvest.
> Anyone who loves his life loses it;
> anyone who hates his life in this world
> will keep it for the eternal life (Jn 12:24–25).

There is a self-transcending power in all creation, which is intensified in the religious experience of one who is, through faith and love, in Christ.

The implications for liberation theology are that the church does not have to *control* the political power as if its message were inaccessible to the world by any means other than its control. In other words, that same world encumbered by the self-seeking structures of sin has deep within its being a drive for self-transcending love. The church does not have to destroy the state, but only help to purify the state's autonomous search for God if the church is to bring in the justice and peace that can be mediated politically in our world.[15]

The beginnings of such a movement to the autonomy of the secular order can be seen in the attitude to government in the Bible. We saw that both government and law were theocratic in ancient Israel, where the king ruled as the vicegerent of Yahweh, and law was both religious and civil law (see chaps. II–III). At the time of the Babylonian exile (586 B.C.) Judah/Israel lost forever this political autonomy. From then on, political power was in the hands of foreign nations who owed allegiance to other gods. Therefore law for the Jews became religious law, separate from the civil law of their rulers. Secularization of the state had begun.

Although Jesus must have been aware of the political messianism of the Zealots, there is no indication in (or behind) the Gospel tradition that he considered capturing the state as a means for bringing in his kingdom.[16] Nor did the earliest Christians see themselves as called to assume political power to bring in that justice and peace that is the object of Christianity. Such independence of the state manifests a kind of recognition of what we are calling "secularization." But on the other hand, we must not push this consciousness too far. It is simply true that Christians up until Constantine's Edict of Milan in A.D. 313 were disfranchised Jews in the eyes of the Roman state and had no chance to exercise political power. When this edict declared Christianity a legitimate religion, Christians immediately began to push toward using the political order as a way of creating justice and peace, until eventually they resacralized the state and political order during the Middle Ages. In other words, Christians knew somehow that the dynamics of their religion were distinct from those of the state, and yet they knew also, as historically oriented, that politics was a privileged way of bringing in justice and peace, one that they must use. Their confusion of the relation between these two orders of reality sets the problem that contemporary theologians must resolve if they are to develop a theology really liberating in our day.[17]

4. What we said in chapter VII (sections B and C) will manifest the correlation of the Bible with the perspectives of the liberation theologians on eschatology and ecclesiology. However, after the emphasis on political action just made, we might point out that the proper work of the church is still the inspiriting of the community for the work of liberation. The church baptizes its members into the rhythm of Christ's death and resurrection as God's unconditional love for us and our world. In celebrating this triumphant love Christians receive both the Spirit and the stomach to struggle even to death for justice and peace. The celebration of this love is done in a sacramental system, which generates an integrating spirituality. A sacrament unites spirit and matter, and so taps the depths of our senses, pas-

sions, and imaginations, where so much of our energy and power reside. This union of spirit and matter is the incarnation of the body of Christ growing in our world to the omega point articulated by Teilhard de Chardin. The Eucharist, where bread and wine are transformed into human body and Divine Person given over for our nourishment, effects our liberation from selfishness. The victory over the institutionalized violence of our world derives from our giving over our own bodies not only for the community of the oppressed, but also for the alienated oppressors, since love of the enemy is distinctively Christian.

There are some liberation theologians who consider violence an appropriate response to the violence of the oppressors. But it seems to me that everything Jesus said in the Sermon on the Mount, and exemplified in his life, identifies the way to justice and peace not through force and violence but through the persuasion of a love that genuinely conceives of the enemy as a person with a *logos* for justice and self-transcending love deep within. Clearly such love will have to be mediated through various strategies and structures of the world that have less than the full Christian faith-inspired ethic. But such strategies, if they are to lead to peace, must be coherent, and not in opposition to the love-filled ethic of Christ. That this conversion of our world can be achieved on a large scale by a community that is neither doormat nor violent is a matter of faith, and so can be maintained over time and space only by a community of believers who in hope sacramentally celebrate Christ's victory over the powers of darkness. In that sense his death is the life of the world.

e la sua voluntate è nostra pace

His will is our peace.

—Dante, *Divina Commedia,* Paradiso, III, 85

Notes

I. EXODUS AS GENESIS

1. "Modern" scholarship begins with Richard Simon, who, in 1678, subjected the Bible to a literary and historical analysis and concluded that Moses was not the author of the Pentateuch (the first five books of the Old Testament), and that unwritten (oral) traditions lay behind the Old Testament's literary history. In 1753 Jean Astruc separated two such strands of oral tradition on the basis of different names given to God in Genesis and thus laid the foundation of modern criticism's documentary hypothesis (see below, n. 2).

2. Scholars now generally agree that the first five books of the Old Testament were made up from four great strands of oral tradition:

J: The tradition that calls God *Yahweh* (German, *Jahweh)* in Genesis. This was first written in the tenth century in the southern kingdom. (This date precludes neither earlier collections of this tradition nor later editorial additions to it.)

E: The tradition that calls God *'Elohîm* (God) in the pre-Sinai material, probably written by members of the northern kingdom sometime after 900 B.C. It is not as anthropomorphic in describing God's dealings with humankind as is J, and so is less colorful. It stresses the Sinai covenant more than does J. *JE* were probably merged in one account sometime after the fall of the northern kingdom in 721 B.C.

D: Contains laws and customs deriving from the northern kingdom and collected mostly in Deuteronomy. It urges fidelity to the covenant and pure worship of God at the one sanctuary of Jerusalem. Its core was probably written in the seventh century and found in the Temple by Josiah in 621 B.C. (2 Kings 22:8–10). Later it would have been fleshed out by other materials to form the preface to the Deuteronomic history (Joshua–2 Kings).

P: Contains most of the cultic material of the Pentateuch, and was probably collected by the Priestly caste during the exile (540 B.C.). It is fond of genealogies, chronological precision, and cultic details. It urges Israel to be holy with ritual cleanliness. Probably the whole composition of the Pentateuch (Genesis, Exodus, Leviticus, Numbers, Deuteronomy) occurred no earlier than 450 B.C.

Of course, different kinds of material within each tradition are to be dated from different periods, but to do that would be beyond the scope of this book, where we will have to be content with the generally accepted datings of larger blocks of material.

3. For an example of how God works in human history to produce an inspired record of revelation, see my "Rahner and McKenzie on the Social Theory of Inspiration," *Scripture* 16 (1964): 33–44.

4. This process is explained at the beginning of chapter IV of this book.

5. Even the Bible, which conceives of the Hebrews as a united nation, refers to the group that came out in the Exodus as a crowd of mixed ancestry (Ex 12:38; cf. Num 11:4).

6. It is probable that the Hebrews migrated to Egypt at a time when other Semites (the Hyksos) were ruling there (1720–1550?) and so found favor with them.

7. Compare the techniques of any society that employs slaves. In Brazil and Cuba, for example, this technique of lengthening hours of work was used to control the slave population. On American slave plantations, genocide was not used, since an expanding agricultural economy needed more workers. Restricted conjugal or sexual practices were a feature of the Brazilian and Cuban slave economies, however. The same genocidal practices were used against the Jews in Hitler's Germany.

8. A modern variant might be the iron law of wages during the eighteenth-century industrial revolution.

9. What did they call their God if "Yahweh" was not yet revealed as his name (cf. Ex 6:3)? Old Testament scholars now think God was called *'El shaddai,* "almighty," which seems to have been in use in primitive Semitic societies: cf. the P tradition, and outside P, Num 24:4, 16; Gen 49:25.

10. Cf. M. Bourke, "Yahweh, the Divine Name," in *The Bridge* (New York: Pantheon Books, 1958), 3:271–84; cf. *Theology Digest* 7 (1959): 174–76.

11. J. P. Miranda, *Marx and the Bible,* trans. John Eagleson (Maryknoll: Orbis Books, 1974), p. 295.

12. See Miranda, *Marx,* p. 79, for the translation "therefore." This indicates a relation between Yahweh's nature and his action in liberation that we will more fully develop in chap. II.

13. The plague accounts occur in all the Exodus traditions. It may be that they describe normal (or even abnormal) changes in the Nile between July and April, but to the Hebrew mind, which did not recognize the western concept of laws of nature, even natural phenomena that saved them were a special revelation that God was saving them: his sign or wonder.

14. The actual route of the Exodus is much in doubt. Some think the Hebrews went straight east across the northern part of the Sinai peninsula to Kadesh Barnea, where, they think, Mount Sinai/Horeb is located. Others prefer a southern route involving a detour to the tip of the peninsula, where they locate Mount Sinai.

15. Again, this miracle could be explained by natural phenomena. The Hebrews, lightly dressed, could wade through the shallow Reed sea. The Egyptian chariots would have sunk in the water and their heavy armor would have caused the men to drown.

16. In fact Israel's history closely parallels the stages of human developmental psychology set out by E. Erickson in *Childhood and Society,* 2nd ed. (New York:

W. W. Norton, 1963), pp. 247–74. In the Exodus Israel is totally dependent on Yahweh as a child on its mother and must simply trust. In the desert, Israel develops a kind of autonomy in making choices for and against Yahweh, and a kind of initiative and industry similar to the developmental tasks of the two-to-twelve-year-old child.

17. Again the event could be explained by a natural cause: a landslide temporarily damming the Jordan was recorded as early as A.D. 1267 by an Arab historian and as recently as 1927.

18. The ark was the chest that contained the tablets of the law. Further, just as the adults of the Exodus were circumcised, so now their children must be (Josh 5:2f.). The manna that had served Israel in the desert now ceases, and the Passover meal is celebrated at Gilgal after the crossing (5:10).

19. In Israel, as generally in the ancient Near East, war was *holy war.* Near Eastern ideology saw its ceaseless war as the battleground of the competing deities of the various peoples. Marduk fought for Babylon, Asshur for Assyria, and Yahweh for Israel (Ex 17:16; Num 21:14). In this way Yahweh glorified his name by victory and extended his kingdom by conquest. In joining his fight, the Hebrews fought for Yahweh; the wars of conquest were wars of Yahweh, and so holy wars. For the Hebrews to initiate a war was to "sanctify" a war and its warriors (Jer 6:4; Joel 4:9). The warriors consecrated themselves for battle by sexual abstinence (1 Sam 21:6; 2 Sam 11:4). Yahweh was present in the camp (Deut 23:15) through the symbolic presence of the ark (1 Sam 4:7; 2 Sam 11:11). Yahweh himself is called a warrior (Ex 15:3; Ps 24:8), who fights for Israel (Ex 14:14, etc.) and leads its armies to battle (Judg 4:14; Deut 20:4). The enemies of Israel are the enemies of Yahweh (Judg 5:23, 31), and so they are to be exterminated under the ban, a practice common in the Near East, where the people, livestock, and possessions of a hostile city were dedicated to the god and completely (or partially) destroyed after the conquest. However, it must be pointed out that although there is a primitive mentality according to which the Hebrews bully Yahweh by telling him that his glory will suffer if they are defeated (see Num 14:13ff.), there is later a more purified notion according to which Yahweh does not depend on Israel (Ps 50:7–15). In the end, Israel does not fight for Yahweh, but Yahweh fights for Israel. They need liberation; Yahweh does not.

20. This may have been a prolonged storm covering the sky for a day, so that the sun reappeared where it had disappeared the day before. Or the "Book of the Just" may have recorded a rhetorical appeal for time to secure victory which in epic manner the Deuteronomist has turned into an event. In any case, Yahweh grants time and victory.

21. Miranda says that Deut 9:4–5 indicates it was because of the injustice of the Canaanite nations that Yahweh drove them out. He argues that *resha'* there, as elsewhere in the Old Testament, refers to injustice, which is opposed to the justice (*sᵉdāqâh*) of the people of the flood (Gen 6:11, 13) or the Sodomites. Yet I am not entirely convinced. Deut 18:12 seems to conceive of the detestable practices (*tô'ēbōth*) for which Yahweh was driving out the nations in terms of magical and idolatrous practices. See Miranda, *Marx,* p. 121.

22. See Num 14:35; Ezek 5:13; 6:12–14; 7:9; 15:7, etc., where "I am Yahweh" is an intervention of outraged justice chastising Israel. See Miranda, *Marx,* pp. 80f.

23. The exposition above is a theological understanding of the facts as Israel itself related the conquest. However, a recent hypothesis (advanced by George Mendenhall and Norman Gottwald in separate forms) argues from sociological analysis of tribal societies that early Israel was a slowly converging cluster of rebellious Canaanite peoples who revolted against the Canaanite city-states' centralized government, and so devolved into a tribal form of government with no special political functions over and above the minimal social ones for a tribe. Thus it was not nomads from the desert who invaded Canaan, but native proletarian rebels against political oppression. (For further information on this theory, see chap. III, n.6.) Obviously this answers the foregoing question about whether God was on the side of the oppressed: since the Israelites were not despoiling someone else's land, but merely liberating themselves from oppression in their own land, God was on their side. However, the question remains, "Why do the Israelites come to speak of themselves as invaders, reconquering the land given to their ancestors?" And so we would have to explain, in this hypothesis, Israel's subsequent assessment of the data.

24. During the period of the settlement in Canaan Yahweh's relationship to Israel also comes to be expressed as a contracted, agreed-on relationship in a covenantal form: He will be their God, and they will be his people (see Ex 6:6f.; 2 Sam 7:23).

25. See Ps 89 for a marvelous conception of Yahweh as the one who chastises Israel but is always faithful to redeem it.

26. The Babylonians captured Jerusalem definitively in 586, sacked the Temple, and took the leaders of the people into exile in Babylon. There they remained until Cyrus conquered Babylon in 538 and released the Jews. That emphasis on the law which is the beginning of Judaism grew up at this time.

27. For more Exodus water imagery, see Is 43:20; 44:3; 48:21. Yahweh will be Israel's guide back to Palestine (the guidance of pillars of fire and cloud) in Is 52:12; Zeph 3:20.

28. Whether for maintaining the patrimony (Lev 25:23ff.), or freeing the brother fallen into slavery (Lev 25:23ff.), or protecting the widow (Ruth 4:5), or avenging an assassinated kinsman (Num 35:19ff.). Blood vengeance is a feature of tribal society, which has no other methods of obtaining justice.

29. The same concept of Yahweh as redeemer is in Is 44:6, 24; 47:4; Jer 50:34; Ps 19:15; 9:12; 49:7, 15, etc.

30. As a later development; see chaps. II and V.

II. LIBERATION THROUGH GOVERNMENT

1. A therapist can manifest all the love and care and even reverence in the world for the patient, but this will not be *healing* unless it leads to responsibility on the part of the patient. On the other hand, the commands or advice of others to patients to assert themselves or to take prudent action have had no effect unless some kind of

loving rapport was previously (and carefully) set up between those giving the advice and the counselees.

2. Fromm, *The Art of Loving* (New York: Bantam Books, 1956), p. 35. It is important to note that mother love is not confined to the mother; father ought to have some of it, too, and mother ought to have some father love. Abstracting them this way, Fromm calls them "ideal types."

3. Fromm, *Art of Loving*, pp. 35–36.

4. The book of Judges gives a view of the conquest entirely different from that in the book of Joshua, which gives a synthetic theological view of God's majestic presence in the people, dominating the land immediately and effortlessly. Judges shows the conquests to be in diverse places, by diverse methods, a long, sporadic process, and begins by showing diverse leadership arising among the people.

5. This is congruent with Judah's ascendancy in the blessing of Jacob (Gen 49:8–12), which probably reflected the historical ascendancy of Judah during the united monarchy.

6. Yahweh had manifested himself as the God of nomads. When the Hebrews settled into an agricultural life (Judg 6:3f.), they adopted the culture and religion of the agricultural Canaanites. In particular, they entered into the Canaanite fertility rites to ensure the proper amounts of rain and sun needed for an abundant harvest. Between the pure Yahwistic ritual and the complete worship of the Canaanite gods were the syncretistic forms of Yahweh worship, from the sanctuary of Micah (Judg 17–18), dedicated to Yahweh with a Levite priest (but also with a carved image of Yahweh), all the way down to worship of Yahweh as a bull (the Baal symbol), practically indistinguishable from worship of Baal.

7. For the full vindication of this interpretation, see chap. IV.

8. The judge is not one who forensically decides lawsuits, but one who delivers the people from invading oppressors and restores righteousness by delivering the people to Yahweh's law. Thus Miranda finds the root meaning of *shāphat* (from which we get *shōphēt*, judge) as "to save from oppression," and not "to judge" (*Marx*, pp. 112f.).

9. It is difficult to know how a woman got such authority in the dominant patriarchal society of Israel. Judges indicates that the deliverance of an army as great as Jabin's into the hands of a (weak) woman would manifest that this was not the Hebrews' victory but Yahweh's (4:9). Note also the fact that it was Jael, the wife of Heber, who killed Sisera, Jabin's general. This same theology is also at work in the human weakness of Gideon. (The primitive notion of women as the weaker sex has been pretty well discredited by contemporary biologists and psychologists; it would be anachronistic to expect the Hebrews and early church to know their data!)

10. Some scholars have maintained that there was a center of worship, centered on the ark as a cultic shrine, at Shiloh (Josh 18–22), and perhaps even moved to other towns (Gilgal, Bethel, etc.) mentioned as places of meeting of the Israelites. However, the ark does not seem to have been a cultic shrine, nor was there a center of worship.

11. The Philistines were a coastal people of Aegean/Asiatic origin who invaded Palestine about fifty years after the Hebrews did. They had a superior iron culture, which gave them ascendancy over the natives in arms and military organization.

12. The concept of Yahweh as king is lacking in unity; there is no function of Yahweh as king that is the core from which other aspects of the royal function were developed: see Num 23:21; Ps 22:29; 74:12; 145:11ff.; Is 24:23; Zech 14:16. Therefore it is difficult to know exactly when the concept of Yahweh as king began in Israel, but it probably was implied before the monarchy was instituted.

13. The satire in 1 Sam 8:10–18 comes from the harsh experience of the oppressive tactics of the historical kings of Israel: conscription of their children into armies, use of sons as serfs of royal farmlands, use of daughters as domestics, the expropriation of private lands for the king, excessive taxation into slavery, etc.

14. The anointing of kings was a rite to confer the spirit of Yahweh on the king (see 1 Sam 16:13). In the time of the judges the Spirit came to a person in the time of crisis and remained only until it was solved. With the king, the Spirit was to be present for the duration of his reign, through all crises.

15. Note here again the theme of human weakness being exalted by Yahweh's power. Saul's family is the smallest family of the smallest tribe (the Benjaminites).

16. The Old Testament here indicates that the Lord's guidance of David leads him to fight for the Philistines but not, providentially, in the crucial battle against Israel in which Saul was slain (1 Sam 29:1–11).

17. Judah, Simeon, and the Calebites and Kenites were the principal southerners who were to make up the future kingdom of Judah. The ten Northern tribes and the two Southern tribes were never really one, but were just stitched together at the time of the united kingdom of David and Solomon; they would later break into two kingdoms.

18. It appears that v. 13 is a later addition, written in by those who saw that Solomon, the offspring mentioned in the text, did in fact build a temple to Yahweh, and so it *was* somehow in the providence of God for Yahweh to have a house in Jerusalem.

19. Cf. Jn 4:21–24.

20. Insofar as there is a special revealed covenant for kingship in Israel, it will issue in the final royal son of David, Jesus of Nazareth, whose kingship was not acknowledged in his historical life.

21. The story of Naboth (1 Kings 21) seems to indicate that the land of condemned criminals also passed into the royal estate, and undoubtedly there were many other ways for a petty despot to enrich the "state's" holdings.

22. Supposedly such lands were to be bought by a relative, the family's *gô'ēl* (a complicated instance of this may be found in Ruth 4), but increasingly they were bought up by the state and by larger landholders, who thereby acquired huge estates.

23. The 'process can still be seen in the agricultural communities of Arabia: ". . . The most small landed men in this country . . . and their portions of the dust

of this world are devoured . . . by rich moneylenders: that is, by the long rising over their heads of an insoluble usury. . . . The rate is fifteen to the hundred for twelve months, paid in money; but if yielded in kind,—the payment of the poor man! for every real they are to receive a real and a half's worth, in dates or corn, at the harvest rates. This fruit they lay up till they may sell it, later in the year, at an enhanced price. . . . The villagers are undone thereby; and most Bedouins fall every year behind, thus losing a third in the use of their little money. . . . The soil is fallen thus into servitude: and when the mostly honest (Moslem) husbandmen-landowners have at last mortgaged all of their debts, and are become tenants at will to those extortioners [of that which with a religious voice, condemning the unstable condition of this world, they call 'the dust'—which was theirs], they begin to forsake the villages" (Charles M. Doughty, *Travels in Arabia Deserta,* 3rd ed., London: Jonathan Cape, 1921, 2:355, 387, cited in Bruce Vawter, *The Conscience of Israel,* New York: Sheed and Ward, 1961), p. 179). Although such money-lending at interest was forbidden between Jews (Deut 23:20f.), the Pharisees and the rabbinic tradition after them found many ways of casuistically permitting it. An earlier age probably simply ignored the law, for there is evidence in the prophetic condemnations that usury was abundantly practiced.

24. Immediately after Solomon's death, the "natural" division between the northern and southern tribes broke into the open. The occasion was excessive taxation of the northern tribes by Solomon's son, Rehoboam (1 Kings 12), and the Bible finds the cause of the split in Solomon's idolatry (1 Kings 11:33), but at a human level it is simply true that there never was one kingdom under David and Solomon. At any rate, Jeroboam was proclaimed king by the ten northern tribes, and, to divert the Temple tax from the South, he set up shrines to Yahweh under the form of golden calves (symbol of Baal-Hadad) at Dan in the North and Bethel in the South of his kingdom, both previously shrines to Yahweh. This breach in pure Yahwism, however, soon led to complete syncretism and even idolatry, and this dividing of the people from pure cult in Jerusalem, which the Deuteronomic editor considers the "original sin" of Israel, eventually led to its downfall (2 Kings 17). At any rate, Israel had its own separate succession of kings from Jeroboam to the time when the Assyrians captured Samaria, its capital, in 722/721. Judah continued the succession of Davidic kings until 586, when city and Temple were sacked by the Babylonians and the leaders of the people taken to Babylon in captivity.

25. First there is the inevitable intrigue and double-dealing endemic to any human government. Second, and more important for the Bible, all of this sin is rooted in a refusal to worship Yahweh and live the distinctive way of life Yahweh had given them.

26. For more on the Messiah, see chaps. V and VI.

III. LAW AND SOCIETY

1. The interplay of God's grace and human freedom will be alluded to in our discussion of the New Testament, but it is one of the most difficult problems in theology and one we will not attempt to solve in this book.

2. A contract. Since we are at a time before written contracts in Israel, we are probably speaking here of a ritual agreement with solemn sanctions for its transgression. There is more on the covenant below.

3. Von Rad especially argued this point of view. Others have found the distinction unconvincing or too sharp; see E. W. Nicholson, *Exodus and Sinai in History and Tradition* (Richmond: John Knox Press, 1973) for a readable survey of the whole research.

4. A. Alt maintained in 1934 that the apodictic law was distinctively Israelite and derived from contact with Yahweh in the cult of the Israelite tribal league. Case law would have been taken from Israel's neighbors and adapted to Israel's needs.

5. For a convincing demonstration that law in Israel is inextricably bound up with Exodus liberation (and not Sinai), see Miranda, *Marx,* pp. 142–60. For Yahweh to reveal himself in any way is to reveal a thirst for justice expressed in laws. The Israelites could not have come out of the desert with a knowledge of Yahweh without a general orientation to justice expressed in at least a fundamental law leading to justice (which I assume is the Decalogue, at least in its kernel).

6. This hypothesis about the development of law in Israel seems valid whether one accepts as historical the biblical account of the descent into and exodus from Egypt, or one takes the sociologically based reconstructions of Mendenhall and Gottwald. See chap. I, n. 23, and G. Mendenhall, "The Hebrew Conquest of Palestine," *Biblical Archaeologist* 25 (1962): 66–87; *The Tenth Generation* (Baltimore: Johns Hopkins Press, 1973); N. Gottwald, "Biblical Theology or Biblical Sociology," *Radical Religion* 2 (1975): 42–57; *Tribes of Yahweh: A Sociology of the Religion of Liberated Israel 1250–1000 B.C.* (Maryknoll: Orbis, 1979). In either case, the law develops over time.

However, there are some differences. I have maintained that the Old Testament sees kingship as a part of the development of God's providence for Israel: government is one of the (God-given) ways by which liberation is achieved in a human manner. For Mendenhall and Gottwald, the kingship is a corruption of pure Yahwism. For them, the Hebrews were *'apiru,* fugitives without political or legal status, disfranchised members of the land of Canaan, who refused to be amalgamated into the decaying power structures of the city-states whose regal political structures were supported by religious ideology. These proletarians withdrew from such religio-political obligation to give allegiance to a nonpolitical overlord. Their submission to the rule of Yahweh, not mediated by a king-figure, was the only thing that brought them together and held them together as the twelve tribes of Israel. When, then, the king appears in Israel, supported by religious ideology of a special covenant with the royal family, this they interpret as a return to a politico-religious amalgam akin to the idolatry from which the religion of Yahweh was supposed to be liberation. The socio-economic injustices described in chap. II, then, are the inevitable result of a turning from the pure religion of Yahweh. For my part, I can reconcile this view neither with the Old Testament theology of kingship, nor with my understanding of the way in which God enters into human history, including human institutions such as government and law. I believe that God is present in human strivings for institutional rule, which mediates justice to society.

What, then, of the law? Is it also a political institution that is a corruption of the pure obedience of Yahweh's covenant of justice? In the first place, as we have mentioned above, the law we are studying was not an institution of the monarchy, and so it would escape Mendenhall's taint of inevitable corruption. In the second place, however, it does seem to be a part of the civil law of the people in a theocracy. It is not the whole of the civil law: if the monarchy did have its own courts and its systems of taxation, as the Deuteronomic historian attests, then there must have been civil laws governing these, and they do not show up in the ancient laws of the Book of the Covenant and the Deuteronomic Code. However, it is clear that even in New Testament times the Jewish nation was expected to live by these laws not only as part of religious practice but as part of its civil/ethnic life (e.g., the laws of stoning as punishment for offenses). Indeed, wherever the people got some measure of autonomy, the law tended to become the way of life of the people, civil and religious. The pharisaic tradition, which issued in the Mishnah, seems to me to point to legal observances in the direction of social control.

In the matter of the law as social control, Mendenhall has made himself clear (see "The Conflict between Value Systems and Social Control," H. Goedicke and J. J. M. Roberts, eds., *Unity and Diversity,* Baltimore: Johns Hopkins Press, 1975, pp. 169–80). For him, the law codes function as a covenanted value system to create a community by religious response of gratitude to God and not by the dynamic of social control, which is mostly concerned with maintaining a social order already (naturally) generated. Given the dichotomy that Mendenhall sets up, I would agree with him that the Old Testament law is more covenanted value system than social control, but it seems to me that the dichotomy is too rigid. I would see the law codes as being fundamentally a covenanted value system, but cast in legal terms and practiced as a way of forming and educating the community in the mode of social control. Perhaps this will become clearer as we proceed through this book, especially in chap. IX.

The implications of all of this for this chapter are that the Old Testament law codes are to be seen as fundamentally God's gracious invitation for the people to enter into covenant with him by incorporating his values. At the same time, the form of the invitation is that of *law,* which the individual Israelite is bound to observe as part of making the whole people a *locus* of liberation for themselves and for their world, and in this sense law partakes of the notion of institutionalized social control. As such, it is still part of God's gracious liberation by which the Hebrews cooperate in their own human liberation.

7. In 1954 George Mendenhall proposed that the Israelite law codes were structured according to a pattern found in fifteenth- to thirteenth-century B.C. treaties between the Hittite suzerain and other vassal states. He found the following elements in those treaties consistently (and so in the codes): (1) a preamble introducing the sovereign, (2) the historical prologue describing previous relations between the contracting states, (3) the stipulations outlining the nature of the contract (mutual rights and duties), (4) naming of witnesses to the treaty, (5) the curses-and-blessings formula, conditioned upon observance of the stipulations. All of these elements have been challenged and debated in the past twenty years, and much of this treaty form was discovered to be missing in the Exodus legal materials.

Nevertheless, it remains helpful to refer to this pattern in attempting to discover the nature of Old Testament covenant and law. A useful summary of this material is found in Dennis J. McCarthy, *Old Testament Covenant* (Richmond: John Knox Press, 1972).

8. It appears likely that there was a collection of material of an apodictic nature, probably from the time before and during the settlement, probably preserved by cultic use (which is related to apodictic style), which now appears as a block in Ex 22:18–23:19. There is a slightly later collection, of case laws (Ex 21:1–22:17), called in Ex 21:1 *mishpatîm,* which contains ancient material perhaps even from the time of the wilderness, but which was probably added to the block of apodictic material to form a primitive form of the Book of the Covenant sometime in the period 850–722 B.C. Cf. B. Childs, *The Book of Exodus* (Philadelphia: Westminster Press, 1974), pp. 453–58.

9. Since the commandments are not numbered in the Bible, the Jews, the Orthodox, Lutherans, and Catholics divide them differently. We are using the division of Philo, Josephus, and the Orthodox and Reformed churches, which seems best conformed to the Hebrew text.

10. Technically this used to be called "henotheism," or practical monotheism, as opposed to a belief that there can be only one God, which comes only later, as in Deutero-Isaiah.

11. Was this originally a prohibition against the idols of the Canaanite gods? Or an insight that even conceiving of Yahweh in images would inevitably lead to choosing god images of the neighbors and so water down pure Yahwism (see 1 Kings 12:28)? Or was there a deeper insight (expressed in Deut 4:15ff.): since Yahweh had revealed himself not in a visible image, but solely as a voice, the Hebrews were not to make an image of him. But what would this mean? Certainly not that images were of no use to express a spiritual and transcendent God, for a voice is just as material as an image. See the discussion in Childs, *Exodus,* pp. 404–9, and Miranda, *Marx,* pp. 36–44.

12. As the Book of the Covenant will make clear, this does not mean that there is no worship in Israel or any authentic religion. It means there is an indispensable link between worship and ethics.

13. Misuse could be in using the name in magical formulae, or curses, or especially, as here, in swearing falsely. Perhaps it was partly because of this fear of misuse, as well as a motion to transcendentalize Yahweh, that the Hebrews stopped pronouncing the name "Yahweh" and pronounced instead "the Lord" (*'adōnai),* and later, even more remotely, "the Name" (*shem).*

14. The command to observe the Sabbath was the core of the tradition, to which a variety of different reasons for observance was added, none of which ever became fully normative: imitation of God in creation, who rested on the seventh day (Gen 2:2f.), the rest as a sign of the covenant (Ex 31:12f.), simply because it was commanded (Deut 5:12ff.). The chief motivation clause is in Deut 5:15—to give rest to one's animals and slaves because the Hebrews in Egypt had needed such rest, too.

15. Originally it prohibited all these kinds of killing which called forth the retaliation of the *gó'ēl* (blood avenger); see Num 35:16–21. Later the verb *rāsah* (Num 35:20) came to mean killing out of enmity or deceit, and this meaning became predominant in the later prophetic and Wisdom literature. That meaning is already incorporated in this sixth commandment. See Childs, *Exodus,* pp. 419–21.

16. In this sense it overlaps the third commandment on the abuse of the Lord's name. That commandment looked at the matter from the sanctity of the name, this one explicitly from the standpoint of the injustice done the neighbor.

17. This verb, as opposed to the verb *hith'awweh,* indicates the kind of desire that necessarily flows into subsequent action.

18. Is this a confirmation of what we said earlier, that the prohibition of images really means that obedience to law is the proper worship of Yahweh? It will be impossible to follow the discussion of the rest of this chapter unless you have your Bible open to the Book of the Covenant and read the passages being discussed.

19. The Deuteronomic Code and the Law of Holiness take up slave laws much later in their codices (Deut 15:12–18; Lev 25:39–46).

20. It is not stated whether this is because of some inevitable damage to the woman, or whether there is a concern for prenatal life. It appears that the child was worth something as a productive element in the family, part of the parents' social security, as children are even now considered in the underdeveloped countries of the Third World.

21. Literally, "the law of the (finger)nail." It requires that in compensation for a lost member, the one who inflicted the injury must lose the same member. While this is primitive law, nevertheless it marks two distinct advances on more primitive law: (1) it prohibits the avenger from exacting more punishment than the earlier offense justifies (one cannot kill a person for putting out a relative's eye), and (2) historically (as in the Code of Hammurabi) it extended to the members of inferior social standing the protection that full-fledged members of that society enjoyed. The wealthy can no longer escape punishment for a maiming crime against the poor and oppressed simply by paying a fine.

22. A phrase unfortunately used in a fundamentalist interpretation by American slave owners in the middle of the nineteenth century. The fact that laws on slaves do not cohere with one another may show that Israel itself found some inconsistency with the notion of slavery.

23. The ransom imposed by the family was not the legal sanction but an act of mercy on their part.

24. Seducing an engaged woman is adultery and punishable by death.

25. Nevertheless, violation of a virgin is "cheaper" in Israel than in Assyria, where the seducer had to pay up to three times the *mōhar,* or bride price.

26. Charging of interest to a poor Israelite is explicitly forbidden—he must be allowed surcease simply because he has nothing. The Deuteronomic Code allows interest only on a loan to a foreigner.

27. These would be classified, in their original sense, as "Good Samaritan Laws," whereby a passerby must help out.

28. These feasts are, of course, social occasions for Israel, celebrations of its national identity. While they are directed explicitly at Israel's relationship to Yahweh, they also reflect the relationships of Israelite to Israelite.

29. All of these agricultural feasts were taken over from the Canaanites, directed away from fertility deities to Yahweh, and then historicized by some event of Israel's past. They dedicated the harvest and the whole agricultural year to Yahweh and tied God's action in the cycle of nature to his action in history.

30. A territory controlled only in the kingdom of David and briefly by John Hyrcanus at the turn of the first century B.C.

31. And, indeed, of Yahwism in general: "What made Israel unique in the ancient world was that its profoundest thinkers found themselves compelled to the belief that it was the object of the active loving concern of a God who would not allow Himself to be worshipped in isolation from the relations which men ought to have to one another" (Norman Porteous, *Living the Mystery: Collected Essays,* Oxford: Blackwell, 1967, p. 144).

32. This is confirmed by the conclusion of the covenant-making ceremony in Ex 24:11, where Yahweh was present to the elders of Israel when they ate and drank at the covenant sacrificial meal. In their binding themselves to the covenant they become his sons in communion with him.

IV. HUMAN ORIGINS OF LIBERATION

1. B. Lonergan, *Method in Theology* (New York: Herder and Herder, 1972), pp. 178f.

2. This was practiced by Old Testament exegetes such as A. M. Dubarle and H. Renckens, theorized about by K. Rahner, and developed into a coherent theory of Old Testament interpretation by L. Alonso-Schökel and N. Lohfink; see *Theology Digest* 13 (1965): 3–17.

3. *Theology Digest* 13 (1965):9.

4. A peculiar phenomenon of J's salvation history is the way in which the younger son supplants the older son as the vessel of God's election; so Isaac is preferred to Ishmael, Jacob to Esau, Judah to older brothers, perhaps here Abel to Cain.

5. Parenthetically, we must deal here with the question that has vexed the western analytic mind for centuries (at least from Augustine to Pius XII's *Humani generis* in 1950): is the man mentioned here a single historical individual who is father of the whole human race ("Adam"), or simply man in general ("humankind")? The eastern mind would not so dichotomize reality. With their notion of corporate personality the Hebrews could conceive of "Adam" as at one and the same time a single historical man with his wife, and the representative of the human race as a whole ("humankind"). Note that the proper name in Hebrew would have to be *'ādām,* without the article, as in Gen 4:25, whereas throughout Gen 2–3 the Hebrew text uses the article, writing *ha'ādām,* "the man," meaning humankind. Thus the modern translations use "the man" for Gen 2–3.

6. "Living" in a sense more than animals live; this is why Eve will be named the mother of the living, for she shares that divine breath imparted to Adam.

7. The Hebrew verb *yāda‘*, is a much more experimental and even determinative sort of verb than the English verb "to know."

8. Note also a child's spontaneous delight in naming things, and so attaining a mastery over them. Further, it is a mature person's act of ordering the world through language, by classifying and assembling.

9. Hebrew *'ēzer* means a helper (not in the subservient sense indicated by Calvin, but in the sense of a powerful one to be trusted—the way God is called man's help in Ps 33:20); *kᵉnegdó* means "like in front of him," someone to front him as a counterpart. It appears we are talking about a kind of communication in language.

10. V. 23 in Hebrew, man is *'îsh;* woman is *'ishshâh.*

11. Here, as always, Hebrew *bāśār,* meaning body, means not the body separable from the soul (western thought), but body-person. There is a profound theology here, which grounds the fidelity of the partners in a Hebrew marriage. It is possible that the story as here told (Eve taken from Adam's body, bone of bone) is an etiological story to explain the intensity of the sexual drive in man as an attempt of separated bodies to arrive at a primeval union. That kind of story can be seen in Aristophanes' charming myth in Plato's *Symposium* (189–192).

12. Indeed, in Abraham's story "leaving" will become a theme of Hebrew theology.

13. Of course the serpent was one of the phallic symbols long before Rabelais catalogued them. Does this mean that the sin was a sexual one (especially since Gen 3:1 follows immediately on 2:25)? Not necessarily. The Canaanites worshiped the snake as a fertility god. Therefore the sexual motif probably was taken up into the larger theme of Israel's obedience to Yahweh as its God. It appears from the narration itself that we are speaking of disobedience more than of any sexual sin; in terms of our etiological history, we are dealing with a paradigm of Israel's refusal to live by the covenant commands.

14. 1 Jn 2:16 reflects on this same order in human temptation and sin: "the lust of the flesh, the lust of the eyes, and the pride of life (RSV)." Note also the order of temptations Jesus undergoes in Mt 4:1–10.

15. Thus the woman, as in so many ancient myths, is conceived of as the source of man's miseries. Note Pandora's box in Hesiod, *Theogony,* 570ff.

16. Von Rad thus considers the story to have etiological motifs, explaining why serpents crawl and also the instinctive revulsion humans feel for snakes. It might also be a theological rejection of the Canaanite snake god. Some have found in v. 15 a *protoevangelium,* an intimation of a promise of a messiah in the seed of the woman who would crush Satan (represented by the snake and its seed), or at least an optimistic hope that humankind would emerge triumphant, because crushing the serpent's head is more definitive than the bite on the heel.

17. Of course, there would always have been sexual desire, intercourse, and

powerful strain at childbearing in any state of the woman. What the Yahwist is affirming is that the disorder, fears, and tensions in these are due to sin.

18. If he considered this evil, and not part of the ideal picture of Gen 2, then, of course, there is an implicit call for men and women to reject and counteract the effects of sin and re-establish harmony between the sexes by returning to God's plan.

19. Miranda points out the parallelism of structure: judicial question (Gen 3:9; 4:9) leading to curse (of earth, Gen 3:17; 4:11; cf. Gen 12:3), and of death (2:17; 4:8, see below). It appears that the prehistoric story of the fall is continued in historical terms in Gen 4.

20. Thus they represent two of the principal ancient ways of life. There are anachronisms in the tale: civilization is well developed (v. 2b), sacrifice has been instituted, other peoples already exist (vv. 15ff.). However, we are not dealing with strict history, but with theological history.

21. This is in parallel with the question to Adam (Gen 3:9), "Where are you?"

22. Probably this nomadic tribe in history is infamous for exacting enormous vengeance for a wrong done its members (see Gen 4:24); J makes this into a *theologoumenon* stressing Yahweh's protection of all life, even the murderer's; note his protection of the thief in Ex 22:3.

23. As Miranda points out, the first man cursed by God was Cain, not Adam.

24. The genealogy of Adam (Gen 5:1–32) links the Adam story to the flood, just as the genealogy of Noah (Gen 10–11) links the flood with Abraham. The decrease in the ages of men in the genealogies symbolizes the increase of sin, for sin is the opponent of life. There is one history of sin, describing humanity's "solidarity" in sin.

25. There are evidences of vast floods in the ancient Near East, which have been recorded in the myths of all the Mesopotamian peoples, most notably in the Babylonian Gilgamesh Epic.

26. With Lamech we have the introduction of polygamy (4:19) and the increase of revenge (v. 24). (At the same time, civilization is also growing: occupations diversify [vv. 20–22], and people call on the name of God, v. 25.)

27. The story probably originally explained the origin of the vine and wine, and was taken over to explain the dominance of the Semites (descendants of Shem) over the Canaanites, descendants of Ham (Gen 9:25–27). The celebrated justification of slavery in America by this text has absolutely no basis in the Bible.

28. Who were the patriarchs? Israel's own view is that they were Semites (see the genealogy from Shem, Gen 11:10–16), and Arameans (Haran is in Aram-Naharim, and see Deut 26:5). An amazing amount of the detail in these patriarchal sagas has been discovered through archeology to have the ring of genuine historical reminiscences; see R. de Vaux, "The Hebrew Patriarchs and History," *Theology Digest* 12 (1964): 227–40. The patriarchs probably were a tribe of half-nomadic Amorites who moved out of the Syrian desert between 2000 and 1700 B.C. Perhaps the change of name from Abram to Abraham in Gen 17:5 represents a change from eastern to northwestern Semitic language, a change explained in our text by a later popular

etymology. Their relation with the *'apiru* (note almost the same consonants as *'br* in Hebrew) is disputed. These are a people mentioned by cuneiform texts throughout the second millennium, from southern Mesopotamia to Egypt, with different social conditions. We now think them nomads who invaded the regions of sedentary civilizations and remained there without acquiring ownership of house or land (Noth). Therefore, they are called invaders (in the texts), people without a country (De Koning), who sell themselves into service as mercenaries or slaves (Alt; von Rad). Over a period of time they could become the proletariat of a country, in Mendenhall's terms.

29. Indeed, there is no healing relationship between persons or between societies without such acts of trust.

30. It is important to see that the covenant is not for eternal life. The Hebrews did not have a real concept of eternal life. What was important to Abraham was *this* life and prosperity *here.* Nor can there ever be a heavenly bliss detached from a modicum of prosperity in this life.

31. This translation (see John Sheehan, *The Threshing Floor,* New York: Paulist Press, 1972, p. 42), which may jar readers familiar with "In the beginning God created the heavens and the earth," is as old as medieval Jewish commentators. The translation scholars choose depends on which vowels they wish to supply under the Hebrew consonants. In our translation chaos is present at creation, and God puts order into formless matter. In the more traditional translation, God creates the world in its first stage as a formless mass and then in subsequent stages articulates it into our cosmos. In either translation, God creates easily, with supreme power, whatever is. (Chaos is, but it isn't too!) There is, perhaps, a chaotic power that he subdues, but it counts for nothing.

32. With all their wisdom about God and the world, the Greeks never came to a conception that God created the world (in time) with sovereign power.

33. The Hebrew verb *bārā',* "to create," has the connotations of effortless creation without any material needed. The author knew the Mesopotamian creation myths of the great conflicts between the gods and the divine/mythical forces of Chaos (Tiamat, Baau, etc.), but he stripped any mythical element of all power to resist Yahweh.

34. For a while a style of Old Testament interpretation ("concordism") attempted to show that this Hebrew development paralleled the scientific concept of evolution. Yet there is nothing of evolution here: different beings are created on different days, and they do not evolve one into another. P knew of a hierarchy in created beings, but he knew nothing of evolution.

35. Semitic cosmogony was like this: The earth was flat, with mountains here and there, and some big ones at the ends. The sky was a firmament, a solid blue bowl over the earth to keep back the waters above it, which occasionally rained through its floodgates. Underneath the earth were more waters, which pushed through the earth to become springs, rivers, and seas. The stars were attached to the firmament, across which they glided.

36. Especially the stars of v. 14, and the sea serpent of v. 21, which had been deities in Near Eastern myths; see Ps 74; 89.

37. In this sense, women's liberation theology is certainly correct in referring to God as she. (In fact, if the human necessity of seeing God as mother and mother love is denied, human piety will exalt some female principle to fill that need, as Roman Catholic popular piety has at times overstressed the power of the Blessed Virgin as Mother of God.) On the other hand, what is one in God is twofold in humankind, and must be so considered. Any idealization of unisex misses the fact that it is necessarily in mutual complementarity of two different personal sets of qualities that man and woman together return to the kind of integrity found in God himself.

38. In this sense, too, God is a God of the future, who will set things right in the course of time.

39. If God is to work in human history it must be in a particular place and time and with a particular individual. This is a limitation of history, not of God. It implies, however, a decreasing extension of God's covenants with people. The covenant with Adam in creation was universal, extending to all. The covenant with Noah was in fact extended to the descendants of Shem, the Semites. And among the Semites a narrower covenant was made in Abraham with the Jews. The covenant with David was even narrowed to one family among the Jews. Only with Jesus Christ does the covenant extend once again to all humankind.

V. THE PROPHETIC RECALL TO JUSTICE

1. I prefer to think that prophetic schools from the northern kingdom, who came to Judah after the fall of the North in 721, composed Deuteronomy. But the reasoning above is valid if Deuteronomy were composed by Levitical circles from the North or the South, or southern prophets—all of which have their champions as authors of Deuteronomy in scholarly circles.

2. "Listen, Israel; Yahweh our God is the one Yahweh. You shall love Yahweh your God with all your heart, with all your soul, with all your strength. Let these words I urge on you today be written on your heart. You shall repeat them to your children. . . . " This prayer, the *Sh^ema'*, was recited each morning; it was central to Hebrew piety.

3. This scheme of obedience→prosperity is not "merely" a theological view. Some have said that Yahweh's covenant placed Israel outside the cycles of history. Rather, Israel, by observing Yahweh's revealed law, used the cycles of history. Israel saw that internal and external injustice made the people weak and liable to be conquered by others. On the other hand, when the people were observing their laws of social justice, they were strong and invincible to foreign powers.

4. Hosea, Amos' younger contemporary, confirms this vision of Israel: ". . . There is no fidelity, no tenderness, no knowledge of God in the country, only perjury and lies, slaughter, theft, adultery, and violence, murder after murder" (Hos 4:2).

5. Later law, Lev 25:39–46, forbade slavery of Israelites, but we know that as late as the fifth century B.C. the Jews had to sell sons and daughters as slaves (Neh 5:1–13).

6. Intercourse of closely related people with a same third person is prohibited sharply throughout Israel's laws (Deut 27:20; Lev 18:8,15,17, etc.).

7. Remember that in Ex 22:25f. (cf. Deut 24:12f.) the poor man's garment taken from him as a pledge had to be restored to him at dusk, for it was all he had to sleep in. Now this law is violated in the Temple itself! It may be that the sacrifices mentioned here were at the shrines of Canaanite gods (note *"their* god"), who had no particular concern for the justice done to the poor. Or these may be the shrines of the North syncretizing Yahweh and the Canaanite gods. However, the present editing of the text makes vv. 9–11 a direct refutation of their action and therefore the God of v. 8 must be Yahweh himself.

8. Note Amaziah's attempt to muzzle Amos in the same words, "Do not prophesy!" (7:16).

9. There is no enumeration in the oracle of the specific laws broken: rather, everything is a violation of that cardinal rule of the law, "You must not cheat any of your poor of his rights at law" (Ex 23:6); see J. L. Mays, *Amos* (Philadelphia: Westminster Press, 1968), p. 48.

10. There is in Amos a profound theology of Yahweh as God of the nations. He fills the cosmos, and he is concerned with justice throughout the world. If Israel is elected, it is to be the revelation of Yahweh's justice for all the world. See Mays, *Amos,* pp. 8f.

11. The fact that Amos can introduce the term so simply presumes that the concept was already known to his listeners. The Israelites expected a great day when Yahweh, as Lord of history, would finally and completely vindicate his people from the harassment of the surrounding nations. It would bring judgment on the nations, but victory and peace for Israel. Amos, however, indicates that, because of its sins, that great day in history will bring judgment on Israel itself. Later theology will transfer the imagery and the concept of the day to a final judgment at the end of time.

12. This, of course, is an instance of the kind of prophecy that is a foretelling of the future.

13. Like the concept of the Day of Yahweh, the remnant is introduced without any explanation; it presumably was something that the Israelites already looked forward to in the midst of their awareness of punishment for sin.

14. The text is obscure. Some, (e.g., Mays) say v. 13c is an interpolation of a later editor charging Israel with the worship of Assyrian gods introduced into northern shrines at the time of the Assyrian captivity. References to the god of Dan, etc., could then be a reference to Mesopotamian gods such as those (obscurely) referred to in 5:26. On the other hand, Amos in v. 14 could be simply referring to the regular shrines (even if syncretistic) of Yahweh at Dan and Beersheba, indicating that no idle recourse to Yahweh can save.

15. The text, however, does not simply say " I want cult and justice." Given an option between the two, this text says, "I do not want cultus, but rather, interhuman justice!" See Miranda, *Marx,* p. 55. Hosea says roughly the same thing in Hos 6:6.

16. Amos saw Israel's luxury as the result of oppression. He may not have been interested in the question of whether there can be honestly acquired luxury. It appears to me, however, that all luxury, superfluous wealth, can arise only because the system has defrauded someone somewhere; see Miranda, *Marx,* pp. 1–33. At least, luxury becomes unjust when it refuses to share with the poor, whom we always have with us.

17. The women of leading Israelite families. Bashan is northern Transjordan, famous for its pasture lands and cattle.

18. In those days, as in our own, beef consumed an enormous amount of grain (it takes twenty-one grams of grain protein to produce one gram of beef protein), thus taking needed food out of the mouths of the poor.

19. The practice of having different sets of weights and measures was explicitly forbidden in Deut 25:13–16; Lev 19:35f. Yet in the excavations at Tirzah, eighth-century shops were uncovered which had two sets of weights—for buying and for selling. Remember that universal weights and measures did not come into international usage until the nineteenth century. In Rothenburg, Germany, you can still see nailed up on the storehouse the different measures that were standard for trade in that town.

20. An American is reminded of our dry cereals for breakfast; they are almost devoid of the original nutritional value of the wheat.

21. In this survey of the prophets we cannot cover Micah adequately. His message is that although Yahweh has chosen Israel and Judah, they cannot so rely on the election (2:6–7) as to become unjust to their fellow human beings (as they are, 2:1–3; 3:1–4; 6:9–14; 7:2–4). Yahweh will punish them for that injustice, and bring back a remnant (2:12f.; 4:6–7; 5:6–8) under a Davidic leader (5:1–5) and make Judah the source of blessing for all nations (4:1–4). Thus his message is very similar to that of Amos.

22. Compare Jordan's reliance on the tourist trade in Jerusalem as a major source of income prior to 1967.

23. Otto, *The Idea of the Holy* (London: Oxford University Press, 1923). By this phrase Otto indicates that God is (1) a mystery, that which is "wholly other," separate from people; (2) therefore "tremendous," "awesome," inspiring a fear which repels people; (3) and yet "fascinating," attracting people to the sweet depths of profoundest reality.

24. *Mishpāt* means law, judicial act, right, justice, etc. Miranda establishes convincingly that its central meaning is the elimination of oppression and the realization of justice among people, especially as this is made definitive by the Last Judgment (a *mishpāt);* see *Marx,* pp. 109–37.

25. As a consequence of the covenant, one of the partners of a broken contract could take the other to a court of law and plead his case. This led to the development of the *rîb* (lawsuit) form in Israel's prophetic writings, where Yahweh summons his creation to hear his arraignment of his people who have broken his covenant. Note the form in Mic 6:1–4ff.:

Now listen to what Yahweh is saying:
Stand up and let the case begin in the hearing of the mountains
and let the hills hear what you say.
Listen, you mountains, to Yahweh's accusation,
give ear, you foundations of the earth,
for Yahweh is accusing his people,
pleading against Israel:
My people, what have I done to you,
how have I been a burden to you? Answer me.
I brought you out of the land of Egypt. . . .

Yahweh goes on to describe the benefits he has conferred on his covenanted people. And what is his complaint? That they have not kept his covenant for the good: "What is good has been explained to you, man; this is what Yahweh asks of you: only this, to act justly, to love tenderly, and to walk humbly with your God" (Mic 6:8).

26. In this sense, Yahweh Sabaoth and the Holy One of Israel are in synonymous parallelism in v. 24, but each of them has slightly different emphases. Yahweh Sabaoth may indicate the creator God who marshals the heavenly hosts, but more likely it means the leader of Israel's armies, the God of the conquest. On the other hand, the Holy One is the creator God who sets the laws by which people reflect his holiness on earth. See the Lord "our judge, law-giver, king," as our savior in Is 33:22; also 29:19-21. For another view that the Holy One means the one devoted to justice, see Hab 1:12f., where "Your eyes are too pure to rest on wickedness, you cannot look on tyranny." That Yahweh, by whatever title, is a spirit of justice, see Is 28:5-6; 30:18.

27. For a marvelous satire of the magical view of religion, see Ps 50:12-23, especially vv. 12f., "If I were hungry, I should not tell you. . . . Do I eat the flesh of bulls, or drink goats' blood?"

28. Another statement of it is found in Is 29:13f., where we get the word "mouth-worship"; it is a part of the theology of the Isaian school in Is 48:1.

29. *Môt* is the Hebrew word for "death," but as a proper name it signifies a Phoenician god of death and rising, and hence the fertility god of the agricultural cycle, the god of the underworld (Sheol). The Egyptian equivalent would be Osiris.

30. And so Ahaz had to change the Jerusalem altar and introduce Assyrian cult practices.

31. This had been indicated also by Amos 9:11-12.

32. Jer 44:15-19 shows us that this reform was not just "on top," but actually affected the ordinary people. The exiles in Egypt complained that as long as they had offered sacrifice to Astarte they had prospered in Judah. When the Josian reform had made them stop, the country collapsed. Therefore, they were returning to their idolatrous cult, the old magical religion, which would guarantee them prosperity.

33. Ezekiel, writing during the exile, described this new phenomenon, not in terms of covenant, but in terms of the spirit: "I shall give you a new heart, and put a new spirit in you; I shall remove the heart of stone from your bodies and give you a heart of flesh instead. I shall put my spirit in you, and make you keep my laws and sincerely respect my observance" (36:26f.).

34. Obviously such a theology clashes with our experience of good and humble people who have not prospered in this world; it also gives rise to the book of Job, as well as some of the reflections of our next chapter.

35. We might add that conditions of economic privation and oppression tend to force people into lives of lawbreaking as the only way to survive in an evil system.

36. Even in the New Testament the disciples were astonished when Jesus said how difficult it is for a rich man to enter the kingdom of God (Mk 10:23).

VI. WISDOM AND THE KINGDOM OF GOD

1. Prov 11:1 is a rare example: "A false balance is abhorrent to Yahweh, a just weight is pleasing to Him," as a corroboration of Amos 8:5–6. Otherwise there is an occasional general statement equating generosity with service of the Lord: "The man who is kind to the poor lends to Yahweh" (Prov 19:17; cf. 14:13).

2. Sheehan, *Threshing Floor*, p. 186.

3. It is possible, too, that the psalmist is an individual who simply associates his deliverance with the great deliverances of his people. However, the imagery speaking of Yahweh's enthronement seems to refer to a cultic ritual of Yahweh's kingship in which the Israelite king would have taken a central part.

4. Again here is the word *sa'aq*, which ties the psalm to all the occurrences of Yahweh's hearing the cry of the oppressed that we mentioned in the preceding chapter.

5. The Septuagint (probably correctly) considers Pss 9–10 to be one psalm in a double acrostic form. From Ps 9 to Ps 146, then, the numbering in the Septuagint, and in the Vulgate, which is based on it (and so in most Catholic Bibles), lags one behind the numbering in the Hebrew text (on which the numbering in Protestant Bibles is based).

6. This is the theme of our book. How far this is from the philosopher's view of God as pure act, thought thinking itself, even the wholly other! The Hebrew Bible affirms that God is not only the one who acts, but the one who acts out of compassion for the poor—that is his nature.

7. This is made clear even in those psalms celebrating Yahweh as the warrior God who leads his troops into the Holy War. In almost every case, Yahweh is seen as performing all his feats of war and subjugation in order to vindicate the rights of the oppressed and deliver them from violence. Thus the war imagery of Ps 147:10–11 is for the needy, in v. 6; war imagery in Ps 33:16–18 is for justice, in v. 5; the imagery of 18:14–16 finds its justification in v. 28, and so on. Miranda treats this at some length in *Marx*, pp. 118–23.

8. For intimations of a glorious life beyond the grave, one might consult Ps 16:9–11; 49:15; 73:23–24, all of which can be interpreted as Yahweh's postponement of physical death for the just person on this earth.

9. Since the eighteenth century critics have, on historical, literary, and theological grounds, ascribed the present book of Isaiah to a whole Isaian school, comprising the work of Isaiah himself (chaps. 1–39), that of a disciple who wrote during the exile, called "second Isaiah," or Deutero-Isaiah (chaps. 40–55), and that of a "third Isaiah," or Trito-Isaiah, who wrote during the troubled times of the rebuilding of the Temple after the exile (chaps. 56–66).

10. But Israel's repentance is not the cause of their return; rather, Yahweh's forgiveness and restoration is a free gift, beyond their deserts (43:25).

11. For God's nature is justice; see Trito-Isaiah's formulation of this in 61:8; "For I, Yahweh, love justice, I hate robbery and all that is wrong."

12. Deutero-Isaiah, in parts of his work other than the four songs, refers to Israel (Jacob), the whole tribe, as the Servant (41:8; 4:1; etc.). Often when the names are not given it is still clear that it is Israel who is addressed as the servant (43:10). Within the songs themselves, 49:3 explicitly calls Israel the Servant. However, this conflicts with vv. 5–6 where the Servant is said to have the mission of bringing Jacob and Israel back to Yahweh. Thus many have said the Servant must be an individual, and this accords best with the fourth song. It would appear that the solution here is the same as that for Adam (see chap. IV): the notion of corporate personality in Israel made it possible for an individual to embody the whole people, and thus both are meant; there is no dichotomy.

13. It might be that "*light*" indicates that the Gentiles are to learn something or understand something, perhaps Yahweh's law of justice, which will bring them to salvation. It is not likely that it would be a revelation of Yahweh himself apart from his action in history to bring justice to Israel.

14. Whether these be Jews who do not want to hear his message of salvation for the Gentiles, or the Gentiles themselves who do not like his message. Jeremiah had suffered the same treatment (see 11:19, 21; 18:18; 20:8–10), and he too rose to confidence in Yahweh's ultimate vindication of himself (11:20; 18:23; 20:11).

15. We experience even today horror of aversion toward those with birth defects, crippling childhood diseases, etc. (We even go so far as to eliminate them from society under the guise of mercy to *them*!) It is possible, too, that the Servant's very early physical pain or pain of rejection caused so much interior anguish or neurosis that it distorted his face into an aspect of suffering too awful to look upon.

16. It is clear that the long life of v.10 does not refer to prolongation of physical life, as in the Psalms (see n.8, above), since the Servant has already died.

17. They would have been allured by the physical science or philosophical systems (skepticism or Platonism) as an alternative to the Jewish revealed wisdom, and by the mystery religions' easy salvation as opposed to Yahweh's insistence on justice among people.

18. The Jerusalem Bible, in the book of Wisdom, has poorly translated *dikaiosynē*

(which stands for the Hebrew *sedeq*, "justice") by "virtue." For the Hebrew mentality it is "justice," not "virtue," which is the generic term, to be divided into temperance, prudence, fortitude, and just exchange.

19. The seer is not a prophet. It is said that apocalyptic replaces the prophetic genre of literature in late Israel (from about 200 B.C. to A.D. 200).

20. The four beasts represent the last four great world kingdoms, just as Nebuchadnezzar's dream (Dan 2:31–45) had represented four kingdoms as metals. The kingdoms are in code, as is so often the case in apocalyptic; here they probably represent those of Babylon, Media, Persia, and Alexander's reign carried on by the Seleucids (the horns).

21. Some think that the title "Son of man" represents a Jewish borrowing from an Iranian *Urmensch* (primitive man) or the *anthrōpos* of Hermetic and Gnostic literature. However, it is more likely that "Son of man" means "a human" as it is used in parallel with "man" in Hebrew poetic parallelism (cf. Ps 8:4). In this case, the humane aspect of the final end and eternal kingdom is contrasted with the beastly aspects of the pagan kingdoms.

22. It seems inconceivable that any Jew who had been raised on the Mount Zion Temple/Davidic king covenant tradition could locate an everlasting kingdom in anyone other than the ideal Davidic king (messiah) of 2 Sam 7. This is why the title "Son of man" becomes a messianic title.

VII. THE KINGDOM COME

1. These statements are rare, and were collected mostly at the very end of Jesus' ministry; see Jn 14:25f.; Mk 16:15; Mt 28:18–20; Acts 1:8.

2. The Greek word *kerygma* means "proclamation." In time this became a word to describe a brief summary of the good news about Jesus' death, resurrection, and exaltation, aimed at evoking belief in unbelievers. Examples are in Acts 2:14–40; 3:12–26; 4:8–12; 5:29–32; 10:34–43; 13:17–41.

3. The first three Gospels (Matthew, Mark, Luke) have many of the same oral and written sources, and so recount many of the same stories in parallel accounts. Sometimes, however, changes of details made by one or the other author indicate special theological emphases the evangelist wants to make in *his* Gospel to *his* community.

4. The German form-critics used the phrase *Sitz im Leben* ("situation in one's life") to designate the concerns of the community that preserve, shape, and generate the stories in particular forms in the oral tradition. One may distinguish three life-situations in the transmission of the gospel tradition: (1) the *Sitz im Leben Jesu*, the circumstances impelling Jesus to a particular act or utterance and shaping the style of his response; (2) the *Sitz im Leben* of the early community, whose liturgical needs, for example, dictated what words would be recalled, and the rhythmic and solemn way in which they would be phrased; (3) the *Sitz im Leben* of the evangelist himself, who was responding to the needs of the community for which he was writing his Gospel.

5. J. Moltmann, *Religion, Revolution, and the Future* (New York: Scribner's, 1969), p. 4; see also M. Eliade's myth of the eternal return in *Cosmos and History* (New York: Harper & Row, 1959).

6. The Greek verb *ēngiken*, in the perfect tense, indicates that the kingdom has already arrived as a present fact; see the discussion in C. H. Dodd, *The Parables of the Kingdom* (London: James Nisbet, 1961), pp. 37f.

7. In late Judaism the Old Testament belief that sin and human misery came from the devil (Gen 3:1–5,13; Wis 2:24) was concretized in a conception of Satan as the prince of this (evil) world. In the popular mind, the demons who took possession of a person were responsible for human misery as the devil's agent. Thus there was a reign of Satan. When Jesus cast out demons, then, he was overturning the reign of Satan and replacing it with the kingdom of God, whether this was by casting out actual devils who possess human beings or by physical healing in a culture where physical evil was ascribed to the devil.

8. Other texts indicating that the kingdom of God has come in Jesus' own lifetime are Mk 4:11, 26; Lk 4:43; 8:1; 9:11; 16:16.

9. See 1 Thess 5:15, which might indicate that Paul numbers himself in the ranks of those who will be alive when the Lord returns. At least his church at Thessalonica understood him to be saying that in A.D. 50, and by the time of his second letter to them they had begun to quit work and await the second coming (2 Thess 2:1–3). Even as late as A.D. 56 Paul thought the time was short before the end of the age (1 Cor 7:29–31).

10. See the same distinction between the kingdom of the Father and the kingdom of the Son of man in Mt 16:27f.; 20:21.

11. The four actions (taking bread, blessing, breaking, and distributing) are almost technical terms in the New Testament indicating the Eucharist. Note that only in this eucharistic act do the disciples recognize Jesus (Lk 24:31).

12. Perhaps this is most explicitly true of Jesus in Lk 1:32f., where the angel tells Mary that Jesus will receive the throne of his father David in an everlasting rule (cf. 2 Sam 7:12–16).

13. Serious exegetical study of the passages reveals different subtle grades of acknowledgement of the title. Thus Mk 14:61 has a positive answer to a formulation by Pilate, which looks like a Christian profession of faith and so demands a positive answer of Jesus. In this form, it is a part of Mark's own church's proclamation of faith. Yet even there, Jesus goes on to explain the title by the title "Son of man" (see below).

14. If so many considered him as messiah in his lifetime, and he was crucified as such, it would certainly be strange if the thought never occurred to Jesus!

15. One or two more occurrences are possible, depending on variations in the reading of the Greek text.

16. Jn 12:34 is not an exception, since here Jesus' opponents are merely echoing his own words.

17. Some think Jesus used the title in all three ways; others that only the uses

referring to his earthly condition are historical; others that only the apocalyptic ones are authentic; and some deny that Jesus used the term at all, but that the church developed the theology of the Son of man out of its own theological reflections on his exaltation. See N. Perrin, *Rediscovering the Teachings of Jesus* (New York: Harper & Row, 1967), and *A Modern Pilgrimage in New Testament Christology* (Philadelphia: Fortress Press, 1974).

18. Again I would ascribe to Jesus' own religious genius the identification of these two widely different roles (apocalyptic judge and vicarious redeemer through suffering) under the one title.

19. That this is central is proved by the fact that Jesus had spoken obscurely to the crowds up to this point in Mark. Now in 8:22–26 he cures a blind man by stages, symbolizing the opening of the blind disciples' eyes. Indeed, after the first prediction of the passion, the text says, "He said all this quite openly." Then after the third passion prediction and the climactic statement of 10:45, the unit closes with the other curing of a blind man in Mark (10:46–52), thus bracketing 8:22–10:52 as a unit on the real meaning of Jesus Messiah.

20. The prediction in Mk 10:32–34 even includes the details of mocking, scourging, and spitting explicitly foretold in Is 50:6. Again, whether the recounting of these details is due more to the early church's theological reflections or to Jesus' own prophetic consciousness is beside the point. What we are seeking is the New Testament theology of Jesus' liberating life. When, in the rest of this book, I say that "Jesus said," I am not making a statement arising from historical criticism. I am simply affirming that Matthew or Luke affirms that Jesus said, undoubtedly as a way of indicating what the early church, under the guidance of the Spirit, believed to be most central to its faith. Questions of historical criticism are simply much too subtle for us to deal with in this book.

21. It is true, as C. K. Barrett pointed out in "The Background of Mark 10:45," in A. J. B. Higgins, ed., *New Testament Essays* (Manchester: Manchester University Press, 1959), pp. 1–18, that the verbal correspondences between Mark and the words of the Servant songs are not exact, but the Servant theme still seems to me clearly expressed in Mark's formulation.

22. The early hymns of the church incorporated into Paul's letters follow this same pattern of lowliness and death according to God's will issuing in resurrection and exaltation; see Phil 2:5–11: "His state was divine, yet he did not cling to his equality with God, but emptied himself, to assume the condition of a slave, and became as men are; and being as all men are, he was humbler yet, even to accepting death, death on a cross. But God raised him high and gave him the name which is above all other names."

23. This might be one of the reasons for John the Baptist's introduction of Jesus as the Lamb of God (Jn 1:29).

24. It is possible that "Son" is substituted for "servant" because the Greek word used to translate *'ebed Yahweh* (the Servant of Yahweh) was *pais*, which can mean either servant/slave or child/son.

25. The words about healing the blind, freeing captives, etc., are a reflection of Is 42:6f., which many consider to be the second half of the first Servant song; this

direction of the Servant's work has a resonance in the first Isaiah (35:5), so the whole Isaian school has the aim of healing the physical ills of its society.

26. The possession of the physically sick by demons indicates that illness and physical pain have been connected with Satan's rule over people since the fall. Even in cases like Lk 8:48 where no demon is mentioned, it is faith that saves, indicating that physical sickness is healed by spiritual means. Further, Jesus gave this healing power to his disciples (Mt 10:1; Lk 9:1; 10:17ff.; Mk 16:17f.; Acts 3:6f.; 5:30; etc.). Contemporary faith-healing in the church and also healings from psychological ills achieved through spiritual conversion or through a spiritual existential therapy like Thomas Horah's or a Christotherapy like Bernard Tyrrell's indicate that God still delivers people from physical illness through faith in Jesus Christ; this is liberation.

VIII. INCORPORATION INTO CHRIST

1. God's intention in the beginning had been union with humankind in the Garden of Eden, and through humankind, union with all creation. Humankind ruptured that union and so necessitated the series of covenants by which it was to return to closer union with God.

2. The physical realism of this statement may strike us as gross; it so struck those who first heard it (Jn 6:60–66). Yet that a sacrificial meal was to effect a union between those who ate and God himself was a part of the Old Testament theology of the Communion sacrifice. This is the incarnational fulfillment of that Old Testament desire for union of God and humanity.

3. Note that in baptism, through the work of the Spirit, all Christians, Jews as well as Greeks, have entered into the one body of Christ. This will be a constant of Pauline thought.

4. Some stress the physicality of body in Pauline thought (note the whole personal union through sexual intercourse of the prostitute and the Christian as part of Christ's body in 1 Cor 6:15–17), while others interpret the body as a powerful image for a spiritual union of Christ and members. I am more inclined to see the former line, leading to a eucharistic theology (1 Cor 10:16f.) and the cosmic Christ, as dominant in Paul's thought.

5. W. Pannenberg has based his whole understanding of Jesus Christ as God-man on the theory that in the resurrection of Jesus human history has already come to its (future) completion and its effects reach retroactively into the life of Christ (and into the lives of all of us). See his *Jesus—God and Man* (Philadelphia: Westminster Press, 1968).

6. There is a division among New Testament scholars over whether the apostle himself wrote the epistles to the Colossians, to the Ephesians, and the Pastoral Epistles (1 and 2 Timothy, Titus). The arguments over vocabulary, style, copying, and the development of theology (see any introduction to the New Testament for the technical details) are ambivalent. I take the position that Paul indeed was the author of Colossians, but made use of a scribe who had considerable freedom in literary expression; this occurred to an even greater degree in the composition of

Ephesians. The Pastorals would be written by second-generation disciples of Paul who would, then, according to the first-century conventions of pseudonymity, be justified in ascribing the letters to Paul himself because of their discipleship.

7. Most New Testament scholars now consider Col 1:15–20 a Christian liturgical hymn. The provenance of the hymn is disputed, some finding it an adaptation of a Gnostic myth of primitive man. The popular theory now is that it comes from early Christian reflection on Christ as the personified Wisdom of God (see Prov 8:22–31; Sir 24; Wis 7:21–30; 9:1–4). J. M. Robinson has divided the poem into two strophes, originally simpler, corresponding to vv. 15–18b, 18c–20. The first strophe would have been a hymn to the Son, and strophe B a baptismal and ecclesial explication of strophe A.

8. Note the similarity with the kingdom's being accomplished in (past) history, present now, and yet to be fulfilled at the end of time. Thus the kingdom of the Son of Col 1:13 corresponds to the kingdom of the Son of man in Matthew (see chap. VII), which will be turned over to the kingdom of the Father, as in 1 Cor. 15:24.

9. Note the same notion of exaltation as a result of human humiliation in the early Christian hymn used in Phil 2:5–11.

10. See E. Lohse, *Colossians and Philemon* (Philadelphia: Fortress Press, 1971), p. 55.

11. The Valentinian Gnostics spoke of the *plērōma* as thirty spiritual emanations from God, yet separate from him, as the source from which the physical world eventually came into being. Thus the *plērōma* is for them a term indicating the whole of the world apart from the divine One. Paul, then, may be using his Gnostic adversaries' own term against them, indicating that in the physical body of Christ as united to its head resides the fullnesss of the whole world, physical as well as spiritual, united to the one God.

12. Lawrence Kohlberg, building on researches of Jean Piaget, has studied the growth of the child's moral reasoning from a preconventional to a conventional, and finally a postconventional stage. Louis Monden, in *Sin, Liberty and Law* (New York: Sheed and Ward, 1965), has developed these ideas of the psychologists in a moral theology, and so we will follow his *schema*, with brief elaborations from Kohlberg.

13. This is the preconventional level of Kohlberg, where moral values reside in some quasi-physical order of bad acts and physical needs, rather than in persons and standards.

14. At this level there is no conscience, but only what Freud called the superego. Here occurs that aberration called the scrupulous conscience, which prescinds entirely from personal freedom and intention and is harassed by always falling short of the perfect fulfillment of the physical act by which salvation is "won" or "grace preserved."

15. Kohlberg separates this theological division into (1) the conventional level, at which children between seven and twelve years of age begin to orient themselves to conforming to the expectations of persons (the beginnings of personal relationships), and need to know, therefore, the rightness or wrongness of things; and (2) the postconventional level, at which moral value resides in conformity to shared

and sharable standards, rights, and duties, as these are attained by one's own conscience.

16. One could even obey a law because, while it is not "right" for the person's development, it is subsumed into a larger web of society's laws, and being a member of society is "right" for the person's development.

17. Further, one must follow one's conscience, even if it is wrong, for only so can one eventually experience the evil as such, and so reform the conscience toward the objectively good, which produces subjectively the development of the person.

18. The developmental psychologists also point out that one cannot pass from one level of morality to another without passing through the tasks appropriate to each stage. Thus one cannot teach a religion of pure response to elementary school children. They will not understand it. They must go through a morality of law (in religious education, the Ten Commandments) at the instinctual level, then be brought to see gradually that this is inadequate to answer questions at the pre-pubescent level, and so move to the second level of morality. Religious education's main task is in helping the child/adolescent/adult focus their own difficulties in the stage they are in, and so help arouse the desire and possibility of moving to the personal stage of religious morality.

19. Supposedly this problem of the relation of Mosaic law to Christian faith and practice had already been solved by the Council of Jerusalem described in Acts 15. There the apostles had decided that pagans need observe only abstinence from meat sacrificed to idols, from fornication, and from nonkosher meat (Acts 15:20), and were free from other observances of the law. However, that "council" seems to be Luke's conflation of accounts of two separate meetings on the subject, and the decision was the result of a longer, drawn-out process than Luke's schematic history allows. Nevertheless, it is true that at the time Paul wrote Galatians he was not the only Christian leader who saw that the Christian as a "new creature" was free from the Mosaic law.

20. Paul has creatively reinterpreted the passage, which originally referred not to crucifixion, but to the impaling of an already dead criminal as a sign of horror and a deterrent to further crime.

21. The notion of a God sending his only-begotten Son to die for sinners (Jn 3:16) is a staggering one. Unfortunately, we have become so accustomed to it that it no longer overwhelms our cold hearts or changes us.

22. Joachim Jeremias has documented that the Aramaic expression *Abba* is so intimate an expression that it was simply not used for God as Father in the Jewish tradition. Jesus' own unique sonship was such that he used it, and evidently he and the Spirit taught Christians to use it as a sharing in his unique sonship, which would come only from an identification with Jesus' own person.

23. One can conceive theologically of this dogma in a number of ways. At one end of the spectrum one could conceive of original sin in an almost physical way, whereby it would be transmitted through the genes in sexual reproduction; or in an automatic way, where it results in even an infant's fixity of will in evil. At the other end of the spectrum, it could be seen as the accumulation of world sin, a miasma of selfishness influencing and afflicting everyone born into the world. The view

advocated here finds the "explanation" of the dogma much closer to the latter end of the spectrum, close to the explanation advanced by P. Schoonenberg in *Man and Sin* (New York: Sheed and Ward, 1965). See an earlier explanation of the social transmission of sin in W. Rauschenbusch, *A Theology for the Social Gospel* (Nashville: Abingdon, 1945), pp. 57–68.

24. This formulation can give the impression that Jesus has objectively accomplished all things and we are automatically saved. God has taken the initiative, and he has accomplished our redemption in Christ, but we must ratify that by our commitment of faith and our living out of his life of the Spirit in us, as Romans goes on to point out.

25. One thinks of the servant in the parable of the talents (Mt 25:14–30; Lk 19:11–27) who, out of fear of his harsh master, did not trade with his money, but hid it. He was "safe," but the master judged that a false response, not enough.

26. As a rule, Paul uses *justification* for the possession of the Spirit in this life that frees us from Adam's sin and helps us to perform the continuing works of Christ, which save the world. In this effectiveness we have a hope that *salvation* will come, for Paul generally reserves the word "salvation" for the final possession of complete happiness, which refers to the consummation of all things in the final kingdom.

IX. THE CHRISTIAN RESPONSE(ABILITY)

1. The New Testament is made up of widely diverse writings, which embody diverse theologies of the Christian life. Each author tended to perceive and emphasize different aspects of the Lord's teaching according to his own personal background and the traditions and needs of his own Christian community. But the church of the earliest centuries decided that all twenty-seven books of the New Testament as a whole were its Sacred Scriptures, and so canonized (regularized) these as its official Bible. Of course, readers of the New Testament will, because of their own personal and confessional backgrounds, tend to emphasize some readings more than others. The canon, however, forces us to attend also to aspects of the message that are not so naturally congenial to us. In other words, though it is difficult for us to get the diverse theologies of the New Testament into one unified view, nevertheless we must hold them in some dialectical tension with one another and so treat the New Testament canon as a whole calling us to life. One may spontaneously be a Pauline Christian, but the person who does not attend to Matthew also will finish by not being a Christian at all.

2. This is the investigation of the redaction-critics, who investigate the situation in the life of the evangelist to see what his message was for his community, and so for us; see our introduction on the writing of the Gospels, pp. 88–90, and especially p. 178, n. 4.

3. Obviously this motif of the new Moses, like any other, can be overdone. B. W. Bacon in 1918 picked up the ancient theory of Papias that the Gospel was divided into five books, made up of five major discourses, each ending with the formula "And it happened, when Jesus had finished (these words) . . ." plus, in the

next verses, a geographical movement to a new place (see Mt 7:28ff.; 11:1; 13:53; 19:1; 26:1). These five discourses, prepared for by the narrative sections preceding them, form five books comparable to the five books of the Pentateuch, made up of narrative and legal material. Thus, according to Bacon, Jesus was to be seen as the new Moses giving a new law on a new Mount Sinai.

Now it appears that Bacon has overstated his case. There are, indeed, five major discourses (although the number must not be stressed too much, for Mt 23 is really a sixth discourse, separate from Mt 24–25). But the correspondence to the Pentateuch breaks down in many ways: (1) The discourses are generally not made up of legal material, (2) the relationship of narrative to the following discourse breaks down by Mt 18, (3) the correspondences of the narrative sections with the "parallel" narratives of the Pentateuch are lacking. Further, there does not seem to be widespread typology of Jesus with *Moses as lawgiver* in Matthew. However, in the context of his Judeo-Christian concerns, Matthew does seem to be using this motif of Jesus as the new lawgiver on the mountain here in this one discourse (Mt 5:1–7:27). The passages on the fulfillment of the law (5:17–20), the antitheses (5:21–48), the passage on the kernel of the law (7:12), the final parenesis to do the law (7:24–27), as well as the setting on the mountain, seem to me conclusive for this motif.

4. Whatever it might mean, "poor in spirit" does *not* mean those who have wealth but are emotionally detached from it. Most likely, it means either the *'anāwîm* (the devout poor who are clients of the Lord because they have no other patrons), or the poor in the sense of the Qumran devotees who have chosen to be poor in anticipation of the kingdom.

5. The Greek word *dikaiosynē*, "justice," "righteousness," in Matthew is a translation of Hebrew *sedeq*, which originally meant "according to a (legal) measure." It then came to mean conduct "measured" by the law, just or right conduct. Thus the primary meaning here: seeking justice means to be holy. Only in the context of the biblical tradition as a whole does it come to signify the interhuman justice that is meant by our word "justice." Consequently, the word reinforces the legal context and resonances of the sermon for Matthew's readers.

6. This can be seen especially from the comparisons of Jesus with Moses throughout the first two chapters of Mt; see W. D. Davies, *The Sermon on the Mount* (Cambridge: Cambridge University Press, 1969), pp. 10–18.

7. This may be taken in two ways: (1) The old law is still in force and you must observe it. The Pharisees are hypocrites and preach the law, but do not practice it. If your observance is not better than theirs, you will not enter the kingdom (taken in this sense, v. 20 goes with vv. 17–19). (2) Completion of the law and prophets will ask for virtue far deeper than that of those who adhere strictly to legal observances of the old law. Yet only this deeper virture will admit you to the kingdom (in this sense, v. 20 goes with vv. 21–48). The latter is our view.

8. So called because Jesus first states as a *thesis* the traditional understanding of the old law ("You have heard it said . . ."), and then poses *against the thesis (anti-thesis)* his new command ("But *I* say to you . . .").

9. This claim by Jesus to issue law at a level superseding the God-given law and traditions of the elders is unprecedented in Jewish literature. (It approaches a claim to divinity.)

10. I owe this summary of the Lucan sermon, as well as the development of the Lucan ethical demands, to Quentin Quesnell.

11. Harvey McArthur, *Understanding the Sermon on the Mount* (New York: Harper & Row, 1960), gives twelve different types of interpretation of the Sermon. Our three categories, plus the "interim ethics" of Albert Schweitzer (see n. 13, below), are those judged most fundamental by Joachim Jeremias, *The Sermon on the Mount* (Philadelphia: Fortress, 1960).

12. Thus a society could judge that smoking marijuana was morally wrong, yet refuse to legislate against it because it was not a serious violation of the public order. In that case, the society might be judging that the violation of privacy by enforcement officers could be a greater disruption of the public order than tolerating the smoking. The powers of the state ought to be used to protect those moral values essential to the common good.

13. The third interpretation given by Jeremias is A. Schweitzer's "interim ethics." Schweitzer thought Jesus believed the apocalyptic end of the world was imminent, and so in the brief interim before the coming of the kingdom Christians could make an all-out effort to *do* the works of the Sermon. (The situation would be similar to that of a football coach asking for every last drop of energy in the waning moments of a game.) This type of ethics does seem present in Paul's call for celibacy (1 Cor 7). However, it would not explain Matthew's use of the Sermon fifty years after the death of Christ and after the (supposedly apocalyptic) destruction of the Temple, A.D. 70.

14. This is the dominant theme of John's Gospel, that we enter into Jesus' own relationship with the Father in some way. Note especially chaps. 14–17, and most especially, "But to as many as receive him, he gave the power to become children of God" (1:12).

15. It must be admitted that an obvious (but false) interpretation of this prohibition of anger, lust, etc., has caused a great deal of neurosis in our society. If one unjustly attacks me, I will naturally be angry. Repression of this anger as "unchristian" will be psychologically unhealthy. The anger is *not* immoral, it is simply a fact of human nature, amoral. If I go on to act out of the anger, that can be unjust, a sin in terms of the Decalogue. However, it seems to me that the Sermon promises that those who enter deeply enough into the love of God and people can have even that spontaneous (amoral) rush of anger healed—so that I would burn to do justice, but not feel retaliatory urges against the one who injured me. This is, however, a gift and not accessible to us through our human striving. This will be clearer as we move on to the third essential quality of the Sermon.

16. All great religions stress asceticism as a way of coming to God, and see simplicity of life as an essential part of asceticism.

17. There Luke surrounds the success of the preaching with repetitious accounts of the practice of sharing in the early church. This would seem to be a concrete

example of Jesus' words in Jn 13:35: "By this love you have for one another everyone will know that you are my disciples." This sharing of goods among Christians is the motive for Paul's collections in Gal 2:10; 1 Cor 16:1–4; 2 Cor 8–9; Rom 15:25–31. It is generally admitted by critics that this communism of goods is an idealized version of what life was really like in the early church. Luke never makes it a norm for the church. It is more an indication of the heights of self-giving to which some Christians were led by the Spirit in the days of its first fervor.

18. For a modern example of this, see the life and works of Dorothy Day of the Catholic Worker movement.

19. It is also possible to translate the *hina* in a purposive sense: "Just as I have loved you in order that you love one another." This would reinforce what we have been saying: that it is consciousness of God's love for us which floods our own hearts and makes us able to love one another with that same love.

20. Both the Gospel and the Epistles of John seem to have been the work of a disciple of the Johannine school. There is ample reason to think that the same disciple who finished the last stage of the Gospel also composed the first epistle shortly before the end of the first century.

21. A docetist believes that the Word merely *seems* (*dokein*) to take human flesh. Behind this general description may be a Gnostic tendency to view matter and flesh as evil, but we need not argue that point here. In any case, the first letter begins with a strong affirmation that the Word was flesh—seen, heard, and handled (1:1–4).

22. Authors differ as to whether the letter is substantively from James, the brother of Jesus, who died in A.D. 62, or from a later author conversant with both Jewish and Hellenistic parenetic traditions.

23. This seems to be a passage of Scripture overlooked by those churches that had a policy of renting pews, especially those in which the front pews went to persons making the highest contributions. Other examples abound.

24. Many areas of conduct are illuminated by the Sermon and by James and John. However, service of the poor through the sharing of worldly goods does seem to be a prior and privileged concern of the New Testament as a whole. This is a central concern of any ethic of any time, but it seems especially necessary for the salvation of a consumption-oriented society recently jolted with a revelation of the finiteness of the world's resources under the Spaceship Earth image and talk of "lifeboat ethics."

X. WILL IT WORK—UTOPIA OR EUTOPIA?

1. A contemporary example is the heroic commitment to the destitute dying in India by Mother Teresa, who ascribes her commitment totally to the love of Christ given her; see M. Muggeridge, *Something Beautiful for God* (New York: Harper & Row, 1971). For other contemporary examples, see *Time,* December 22, 1975, pp. 47–56.

2. This social magnitude of sin is expressed in Johannine theology by "the world"; see P. Kerans, *Sinful Social Structures* (New York: Paulist Press, 1974),

pp. 60f. Kerans's whole fourth chapter is an excellent summary of the work of P. Ricoeur, B. Lonergan, and P. Berger on the social character of sin, and is followed here.

3. This analysis of society derives from the sociology of knowledge as developed by Peter Berger and Thomas Luckmann. Again the development of their ideas follows the insightful summary in Kerans, pp. 73–76.

4. Thus a society could develop a mother god and a theory of the ontological superiority of women to legitimate a matriarchal social structure. (One should not think that a secularized society growing out of the Enlightenment does not have its own crypto-metaphysics and theology legitimating its structures!)

5. Kerans owes this analysis to Bernard Lonergan's *Insight* (New York: Philosophical Library, 1957).

6. Kerans gives the following example: ". . . A young man who has spent years developing the self-image of a gruff, brusque he-man ought to find this behavior inappropriate with his wife or his young children. It is possible for him to recognize this; it is also possible to overlook the newness of his present situation and the inappropriateness of the old patterns. This oversight can be unconscious, neurotic; but it can also be a choice to so read the situation that one's earlier self-understanding remains intact"(p. 70).

7. Kerans, *Sinful Social Structures,* p. 77.

8. A fuller survey of the various positions is found in John H. Yoder, *The Politics of Jesus* (Grand Rapids: Eerdmans, 1972), pp. 15–19. A more recent example of the same position is Jack Sanders, *Ethics in the New Testament* (Philadelphia: Fortress, 1975).

9. See Yoder, *Politics,* pp. 16f.

10. *Summa Theologica*, II-II, q. 40. Indeed, it *would* appear immoral to abandon the common good to defenselessness. Remember (chap. IX), the Sermon does not ask Christians to be doormats, but people actively challenging in a nonviolent way the aggression of others. The Sermon has its own defense: truth and love challenging and touching the aggressor.

11. For a sophisticated contemporary defense and elaboration of the just war theory, see the writings of John C. Murray. There is a masterful synthesis of the arguments for the just war in Richard A. McCormick's article, "War, the Morality of," in the *New Catholic Encyclopedia* (New York: McGraw-Hill, 1967), 14: 802–7.

12. Not "vindictive." "Vindictive" refers to my desires for personal revenge; "vindicative" refers to the redressing of a just balance in society. By so doing, it helps keep in check the individual's need for revenge, but it also aims at preserving the society's established relations.

13. I leave out of consideration the fact that the order we want restored is most often one already out of balance between rich and poor, so that one is often being asked to conform to structures of injustice. Thus "law and order" is an ambivalent phrase. When society's order is good (a just distribution of goods and services), then law is a good instrument for the common good. But when the order of society is

bad (so that crime is not illegal or not punished when the upper class exploits the lower class, e.g., in price fixing), then law is bad and its enforcement is but one more tool of the oppressors.

14. Published in Latin in 1516. The word comes from the Greek words *ou,* "no," and *topos,* "place," therefore "nowhere."

15. See the exposition of such "archeology" or "protology" in M. Eliade, *Cosmos and History* (New York: Harper & Row, 1959), and its critique in C. Braaten, *The Future of God* (New York: Harper & Row, 1969), pp. 42–46.

16. And so the problem is how to move from the real world to a world in which such ideal conduct is universally operative. I owe much of the following argument to Q. Quesnell, *This Good News* (Milwaukee: Bruce, 1964).

17. In the midst of the scandal of Lockheed's bribery of foreign officials I asked a businessman if there was a code of ethics among American businessmen that would govern such cases. He replied, "There is no such thing as a code of ethics in business." (Later, another businessman was terribly offended by the first one's position.)

18. For example, recall again the argument of Rom 1:16–4:25 that human striving according to law (Old Testament or natural law) is impotent to justify us.

19. As the popular-song-become-hymn so correctly has it, "Let there be peace on earth, and let it begin with me."

20. I know a middle-class woman who lives on the edge of the inner city, where every house in the block except hers has been burglarized. She knows her turn is coming soon, yet she is free from all anxiety over this—the goods do not mean that much to her. The further extreme of this freedom is expressed by the words of Janis Joplin, "Freedom's just another word for nothing left to lose."

21. In the 1960s the hippies rejected the consumer society and tried to enter countercultural communes. These seem to have foundered because they were not founded on that faith commitment to Christ that sustains true community.

22. If, as the prologue of John's Gospel has it, everything in the world was created through the Word, then all of it has as its deepest hunger and drive a desire to transcend itself in an order toward God. There is a necessity to move toward God in all human nature. Teilhard de Chardin makes this a part of the evolutionary hypothesis, and the basis of his firm hope for the phenomenon of man.

23. Further, a group tends to work for its own survival with more self-interest and effectiveness than the prophet, who can more easily be a martyr. It is of the nature of the group to want to stay alive to structure its vision permanently in the world, sometimes even to the detriment of the message of death-for-life that it proclaims. This becomes increasingly true as one moves into political structures, which are "effective" by compromising to stay alive.

24. This is expressed in the Old Testament as the tension between the prophet and the priest. I think it safe to say that no widespread reform came directly from the work of any prophet. The ordinary response of people to a prophet is to reject the message and kill the prophet (see Acts 7:52; Mt 23:29–39; Lk 11:47; etc.). It was the

priests, as ministers of the institution, who (sometimes through the *mediation* of the prophet's community of followers) caught the message and codified it in Old Testament laws, thus structuring justice into the lives of all members of the nation.

25. This brings up the dialectic between the perfect and the imperfect. Should the community set its standards high, so that only those with an extraordinary commitment and cohesiveness could be members, and so be a clear light to the world? Or should it expand its membership far and wide so that structural change is more universally present in more members? Ernst Troeltsch in *The Social Teaching of the Christian Churches* (New York: Harper, 1960), pp. 331–42, developed a useful distinction between the church and the sect. The church is large-scale and institutional, with ties to secular society; it involves obligatory membership and so practices membership from birth through infant baptism; it tolerates a failing membership, which it heals through a sacramental system. The sect, on the other hand, is small-scale, made up of those members who can measure up to a rigorous asceticism; thus its membership is voluntary, made up of adults who freely commit themselves to its practice; for those who cannot measure up there is no healing, but explusion from the sect. It is separated from secular society, with which it has no ties. Thus the sect serves as a leaven in the world by challenging the world almost from outside it. The church enters into the world, leavening it through mutual influences, which comprise it but nevertheless allow it to influence secular structures.

26. That is to say, we must know that it is reasonable for us to leap beyond reason to a faith-solution to the problem of evil. This insistence of the Catholic tradition on a symbiosis of faith and reason was magisterially stated by the First Vatican Council; see DB 1795–1800; 1816–1820. An older Catholic apologetic argued from the historicity of the Gospel accounts of the miracles and the miracle of the resurrection. A more adequate contemporary apologetic is to begin from the faith of the early church, as in C. F. D. Moule, *The Phenomenon of the New Testament* (London: SCM, 1967), and the evidences of the solution at work in one's world, as above.

27. Cf. Marshal McLuhan's provocative expression, "global village."

28. See the discussion on pp. 132–34.

29. Lonergan's writings are full of his own vocabulary. As will appear, cosmopolis is not an identifiable entity at this stage of discussion; it is an x, a cipher whose content is to be filled out by subsequent discovery.

30. Lonergan, *Insight*, p. 238. The whole discussion of bias as rooted in human common sense and culture, and its reversal through purification of human reason and will ranged over chaps. 6–7 of *Insight*, especially pp. 191–244.

31. This is not to say that national governments or even a world government with some coercive power is unnecessary. On the contrary, books like R. Pickus and R. Woito, *To End War* (New York: Harper & Row, 1970), and Gerald and Patricia Mische, *Toward a Human World Order* (New York: Paulist Press, 1977) argue that the basic Christian message must employ a strategy of legal, civil, and supranational structural dynamics in order to implement peace and justice in a world in need

of basic conversion. But such powers must take direction from the long-term solution that cosmopolis provides.

32. E.g., in *Theology of the World* (New York: Herder and Herder, 1968), pp. 120f. Indeed all of his fifth chapter deals with the church in this process in much more sophisticated detail than we can here.

EPILOGUE

1. "Legitimate" comes from the Latin root for law, *lex*, and so means "lawful."

2. See J. Moltmann, *A Theology of Hope* (New York: Harper & Row, 1967); *Religion, Revolution, and the Future* (New York: Scribner's, 1969); *Hope and Planning* (New York: Harper & Row, 1971); *The Crucified God* (New York: Harper & Row, 1974); W. Pannenberg, *Theology and the Kingdom of God* (Philadelphia: Westminster Press, 1969); J. Metz, *Theology of the World* (New York: Herder and Herder, 1969), among others. C. Braaten synthesizes the thought of diverse members of this school well and makes some stimulating contributions of his own in *The Future of God* (New York: Harper & Row, 1969). A critical overview of the school is that of W. Capps, *Time Invades the Cathedral* (Philadelphia: Fortress Press, 1972).

3. See R. Alves, *A Theology of Human Hope* (Washington, D.C.: Corpus Books, 1969); H. Assmann, *Theology for a Nomad Church* (Maryknoll, N.Y.: Orbis Books, 1976); E. Dussel, *Ethics and the Theology of Liberation* (Maryknoll, N.Y.: Orbis Books, 1977); G. Gutiérrez, *A Theology of Liberation* (Maryknoll, N.Y.: Orbis Books, 1973); J. P. Miranda, *Marx and the Bible* (Maryknoll: N.Y.: Orbis Books, 1974); among many others.

4. In English, *Pedagogy of the Oppressed* (New York: Seabury, 1970); it is certainly the key to understanding the central dynamics of liberation.

5. Freire finds that the oppressors themselves are oppressed by the dehumanizing system they lay on the oppressed. They thereby become alienated from human community and trapped in a frenzy of acquisition, which makes them slaves of working, getting, spending. This is a central insight, corroborating the New Testament vision that the enemy is in need of redemption through the act of love that summons one to conversion from misery and sin.

6. The Greek word *praxis* means "exercise," "transaction"; Freire uses it to mean both action and the reflection following upon the action.

7. A brief popular sketch of this section can be found in G. Dunne, *The Right to Development* (New York: Paulist Press, 1974).

8. The tragedy of the United States' intervention in the overthrow of Allende's government, through government agencies and the funding of counterrevolutionary forces, is that it proved what the doctrinaire Marxists have always said: a socialist government cannot be established and maintained through free elections because the reactionary countries will not permit it. What is left to Latin Americans, then, is violent revolution, wars of liberation aided by Cuban, Russian, or Chinese forces. The United States is largely to blame for this situation.

9. See, among others, J. Cone, *A Black Theology of Liberation* (Philadelphia: J. B. Lippincott, 1970), and L. Russell, *Human Liberation in a Feminist Perspective* (Philadelphia: Westminster Press, 1974).

10. This vision is what creates Juan Luis Segundo's series of theology books, *Theology for Artisans of a New Humanity*, 5 vols. (Maryknoll, N.Y.: Orbis Books, 1973–74).

11. The liberation theologians have not spoken of the doctrines of the Trinity, but they have worked out new approaches to Christology; see L. Boff, *Jesus Christ Liberator* (Maryknoll, N.Y.: Orbis Books, 1978); and J. Sobrino, *Christology at the Crossroads* (Maryknoll, N.Y.: Orbis Books, 1978).

12. See A. Gelin, *The Poor of Yahweh* (Collegeville, Minn.: The Liturgical Press, 1964).

13. Poverty in the Old Testament was identified as a scandalous condition that could have no status; see Gelin, *The Poor*, and Gutiérrez, *Theology*, pp. 291–96.

14. It may be that the use of *logos* came to John from Hellenistic culture, where it meant the eternal principle of order in the universe (as in Heraclitus), or the mind of the pantheistic god directing all things (Stoics), or the created intermediary between God and creatures who gave meaning and plan to the universe (Philo), or the expression of the mind of God helping to create, order, and save the universe (Gnostics). However, in all these notions the intellectual is stressed, as is common in Greek culture. But the prologue seems to speak of a Word that is more than the intelligibility of the cosmos. It is active, like the Hebrew word *dābār*, which means both word and deed. This Word creates the universe, is source not only of light but of life, is an active agent like the personified Wisdom of the Old Testament Wisdom literature. Thus a Semitic background seems more likely for John's conception. In any case, in Jn 1:1–18 this Word serves as something both alive and at work in the world before Jesus comes in the flesh. (Note the Rabbinic notion that the Torah pre-existed and ordered the world before it was given to Moses.) For a detailed discussion of the provenance of the *logos*, see R. E. Brown, *The Gospel According to John* (Garden City, N.Y.: Doubleday, 1966), in appendix II, 1: 519–24.

15. This is the insight operative in the theologians who see the growth of humankind as incorporating a process of secularization, whereby religion removes itself from control of processes (science, politics), which have their own autonomous relationship to God and humanity as a partner with religion. This purifies religion as well as science. Nevertheless, this means that such religion must be necessarily oriented to political action.

16. I say this with full realization that the opposite thesis has been advanced by some, especially by S. G. F. Brandon, *Jesus and the Zealots* (Manchester: Manchester University Press, 1967). Their arguments are more fanciful than substantial; see their refutation by M. Hengel, *Was Jesus a Revolutionist?* (Philadelphia: Fortress Press, 1971).

17. Gutiérrez calls the relation of church and state *the* problem in liberation

theology. Incidentally, the same evolution of consciousness also indicates the reason why socialism as a national economic program is not advocated in the Bible. It takes time for structures to be so articulated in a technological society that socialism could be the only viable, liberating economy. That stage of development was in no way possible in the New Testament world.

Scriptural Index